On The Monster's Back

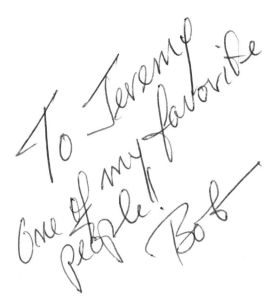

On The Monster's Back

—ɯ—

Heroism, Love, and Survival - One man's daring escape
from the Armenian Genocide of the Great War.

Robert D. Lamson

ISBN: 1503093204
ISBN 13: 9781503093201
Library of Congress Control Number: 2014919794
CreateSpace Independent Publishing Platform
North Charleston, South Carolina

If you can force your heart and nerve and sinew
To serve your turn long after they are gone,
And so hold on when there is nothing in you
Except the Will which says to them: "Hold on!"

—Rudyard Kipling, "If"

Introduction

—∿—

We were together on the patio of his beautiful home overlooking Puget Sound, enjoying the sunset just after what turned out to be our last Armenian dolma dinner together. He looked at me for a few moments and laid down his pipe. He reached into a weathered satchel and presented me with a dog-eared, taped cardboard box, its contents of loose pages yellowed over time. Souren Barkev Tashjian was over eighty years old, happily married for many years and still stout and vigorous, yet knowing his life was nearing its end.

He handed over what I could see was a rough-and-ready manuscript and said, "If you have the chance, I hope you can do something with this. The story is all there, but you know my English isn't very good, and I wrote it in many sittings over a long time. It is quite disjointed, I know. I hoped that I might somehow use it to help prevent for others what happened to me, but I haven't been able to."

I was a bit taken aback, as I knew his amazing personal history. Carefully, I thumbed through the pages, aware of the effort it had taken and the considerable stress he must have endured to type over 160 pages, many with handwritten notes in the margins. I felt honored that he was giving me this devotedly written record and entrusting that I would advance his intentions in sharing it with a wider world.

My first memories of Souren were from when I was about five years old. He was my great-uncle, my grandmother's brother. I learned later this made me one-quarter Armenian. At that age I didn't know what to make of this robust, friendly man with the strange accent, who talked about faraway lands called Armenia and Turkey. I loved his sense of humor, particularly the subtle practical jokes he would play on his older sisters—my grandmother and my great-aunt—at family gatherings. But as I grew older, I understood there was something even more deeply intriguing and compelling about him.

Over the years, as my own life experiences produced truths and gave me perspectives that could not be learned any other way than through time, I came more and more to appreciate Souren. I admired his seemingly boundless energy, his love of life, concern for others, and his wide circle of admirers. I loved his food—he was a master cook of Armenian dishes—and I came to welcome the sweet-smelling smoke of his pipe. I marveled at the blend of personal sophistication with his man-of-the-earth "let's go fishing" simplicity.

During many times together and at family gatherings, I drew Souren out as much as I could. Here was a man who had repeatedly dodged death in the midst of the Armenian Genocide in Turkey during World War I. This was often the subject of our conversations. He had terrifying experiences and personally witnessed the fatal progression of events by which Armenia had been savaged in what would become Hitler's philosophical underpinning for the Jewish Holocaust during World War II. The circumstances surrounding his own narrow escapes clearly drew the parallels between the Armenian Genocide and the Holocaust.

So by the time he handed me his manuscript on that late summer evening in Seattle, I understood its significance. The story begins when Souren was a boy of twelve living with his middle-aged mother in the port town of Smyrna. It was a period of revolutionary change in Anatolia that would lead to Turkey's involvement in the First World War, the "Great War," of 1914 to 1918. Souren and his mother found themselves in a swirling storm of sectarian rivalries, economic and social chaos, and signs portending worse to come. This soon culminated in government-ordered mass cruelty, now considered the first great genocide of the twentieth century. During World War I, the world's attention was concentrated on the Western Front. Events in Anatolia, though reported repeatedly by significant observers and also strenuously protested by several diplomats, were ignored or considered secondary.

A radical party known as the Young Turks had usurped control of the Turkish government. Its leadership, organized as the Committee of Union and Progress (CUP), was commanded by a trio of ruthless revolutionaries known as the "Three Pashas": Mehmed Talaat, Ismail Enver, and Ahmed Djemal. Shielded by the diversion of worldwide attention, they embarked on a mission to "re-Turkify," in essence to cleanse, what was left of the Ottoman Empire, eroded over the centuries. Their vision was to eliminate virtually all non-Turkish institutions and non-Islamic citizens—Jews, Greeks, Armenians, Assyrians. But the CUP's priority in all this centered on ridding—by whatever means necessary—Armenians from what had been their homeland since nearly 200 BC.

As this treacherous course of events intensified, Souren became an Armenian teenager. He was ordered to report for Turkish military slave-labor battalions, and found his personal safety dissolved rapidly. Fortunately, so did his naiveté. Gifted with an incredible knack for rapidly reading perilous situations and instantly crafting survival options, through episode after episode, he maneuvered escapes.

Finally arriving in the United States in 1920, Souren worked his way through the University of Virginia medical school and interned at the Mayo Clinic. Over a period of nearly forty years, he was gradually able to pen his experiences piece by piece, hand pecking on an old mechanical typewriter. Those typed pages, and the many intriguing hours I spent with Souren over the decades, yielded the record of events at the core of the epic tale that follows.

I have taken certain literary license in telling it in the third person. For the purpose of deepening readers' understanding of the story's contextual setting, I have also added detail to character descriptions, geographic locations, and historical events described more briefly in Souren's original manuscript. In addition, I have included references to other documented historical events and individuals that Souren did not mention in his manuscript but which had significant influence upon it. In a few particularly personal instances, names of family or friends may have been changed in respect of privacy. These storytelling enhancements do not alter the factual core of Souren Tashjian's manuscript tracing his death-defying journey. His story is so extraordinary as to seem fictionalized, but it is, unbelievably, all true.

Robert D. Lamson
February 2015

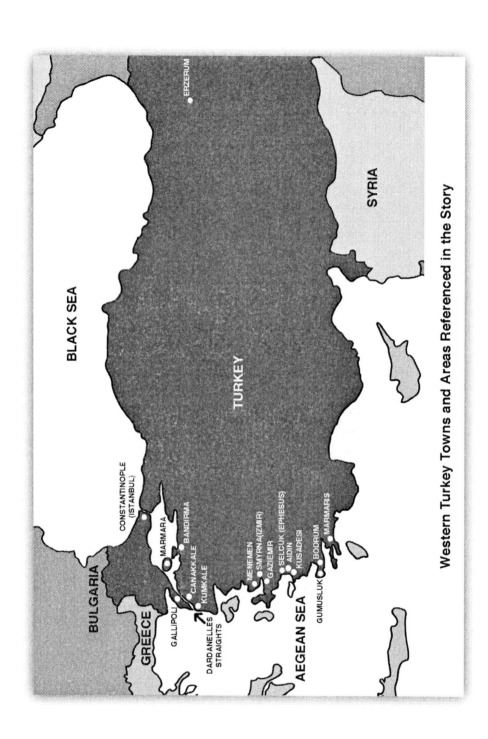

Western Turkey Towns and Areas Referenced in the Story

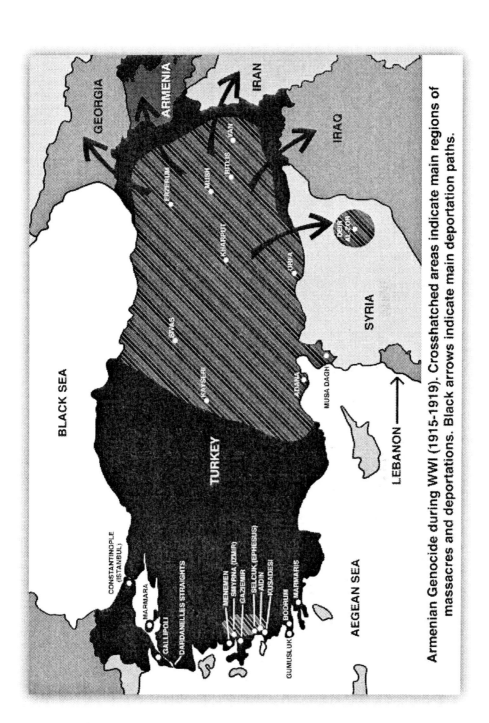

Armenian Genocide during WWI (1915-1919). Crosshatched areas indicate main regions of massacres and deportations. Black arrows indicate main deportation paths.

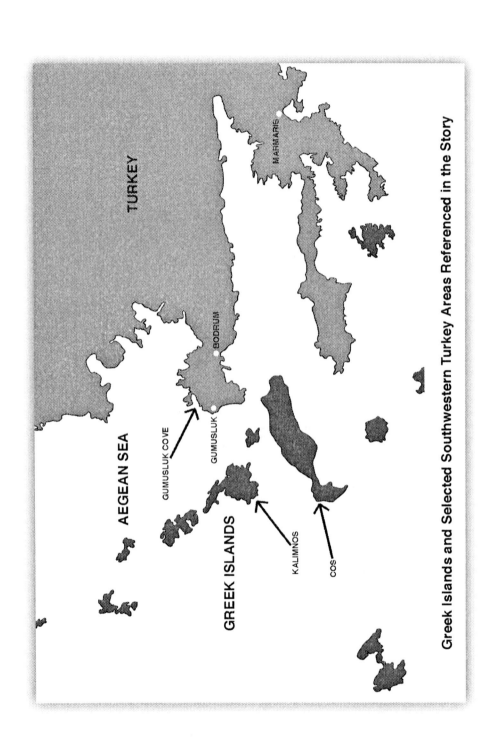

Greek Islands and Selected Southwestern Turkey Areas Referenced in the Story

Prologue

1873

Sophia Varjabedian had been staying for a while with her grandmother in Bitlis, Turkey. Grandma stared intently at the streaks of finely ground coffee that had dried out against the walls of the upturned cup. Sophia nervously chewed her biscuit, knowing that her grandmother was looking for patterns, patterns that would tell of truth and of the future. What would Grandma find? Would she discover that Sophia had taken some coins from her father's pocket? It wasn't as if she needed the money. She only wanted to seem important when she visited the slipper shop. Mrs. Azadian, though pleased to have made a large sale, looked with suspicion at young Sophia, who had never come alone to make such an expensive purchase. The gleaming slippers had tempted the child for weeks. She could see herself in this dazzling pair of lightweight slip-ons, delicately stitched in iridescent colors. Her friends would stare in envy and admiration when she debuted them at the upcoming church picnic. Emboldened by strong desire and the certainty of results, Sophia placed the shoes on the counter. She tried to meet Mrs.

Azadian's eyes, but she could bring her own no higher than the slipper maker's hairy chin.

Grandma cocked her head and clucked as if she'd made an unfortunate breakthrough. Sophia swallowed her biscuit, which went down like a handful of gravel. She leaned over to see what Grandma saw in the coffee grounds.

"What is it?" Sophia asked. Her grandmother's countenance had transformed into a look of anguish. Sophia was about to confess to the old woman what she had done, her guilt having finally become unbearable. Suddenly she didn't want those slippers, not if it meant bringing this sadness to her dear grandmother's face.

"*Anoushig*, my little cutie," the old lady said softly.

Sophia became instantly attentive, because her grandma used this term of endearment judiciously.

"I see you will marry well and have many children. That is clear. But I also see a perilous path for one of your sons' life's journey." She continued, "There is to come another tragic time for our people, when many will die and others will be dispersed. Your son will be caught up in this and encounter extreme dangers. In the midst of the turmoil and destruction, I see that he will be saved from the sword, but only barely, and by an unusual course." The old woman's voice trailed off. She closed her eyes, a tear ran down her cheek, and with her right hand, she crossed herself. Then, making a fist, she pounded her chest three times.

Sophia was frightened, unsure of what to do with this information.

Years later, she began to understand.

—≋—

In 1876, Sophia graduated as valedictorian of her class at Mount Holyoke School, and a few days after was introduced to a handsome, youthful minister visiting from Erzurum, Pastor Hagop Tashjian. Their love affair was swift, and they married within months.

Family tragedy soon followed the wedding, however. Sophia's father was a wealthy landowner and grain farmer, and in the fall of 1877, the contents of his granaries were confiscated for the sultan's army during the Russo-Turkish War. When the supplies were exhausted, Turkish soldiers brutally murdered Sophia's parents.

Returning to Erzurum, Badveli Hagop Tashjian, as called by his Armenian title, and Sophia lived under numerous government restrictions. They could not leave the city without a special passport. He could not own or carry a gun. Their small library was repeatedly invaded and scrutinized by Turkish officials who viewed almost any word they did not understand as a source of suspicion, perhaps even the seeds of a revolutionary plot.

In more personal ways, for over a decade, Sophia and Hagop were nevertheless happy in Erzurum, including the births of their first five children. But conditions gravely worsened in 1889, beginning with the massacre by Turkish soldiers of a courtyard gathering of Armenian youth. The event launched an ensuing series of mob attacks on Armenian businesses, homes, and places of worship—including the reverend's church. Life became one of unending anxiety. Two years later the reverend gladly accepted a pastorate in Bardizag, a small town near Constantinople. The family moved, and Hagop served this pastoral appointment for two years.

In 1893, Sophia and Hagop moved the family again when he was transferred to the Congregational church in Smyrna. In the eastern and central interior of Turkey, Armenian massacres continued off and on. Smyrna and Constantinople, however, being cities with sizable populations of European and American diplomats, businessmen, Christian missionaries, and educators, had—not as yet—endured similar events. Still, Sophia and Hagop saw a trail of refugees pouring into their city for years after their arrival. They decided the time was rapidly approaching when no Armenian would be safe, or have a life worth living, within the Ottoman realm. It was best to send their five children out of Turkey to America.

But then they had another child, one that quite surprised them. They worried, because he was much younger than the others. What if something happened before they had time to get him safely to America? Sophia prayed earnestly for wisdom, and the answer to her supplications was a name. Though the name registered with the government for her baby was Herant, his baptismal name—the one she believed God spoke to her—was Souren Barkev, which meant "saved from the sword."

Chapter One

—⚭—

1908

On a warm, sunny day in the bustling port city of Smyrna, Souren Tashjian walked through the bazaar. His mother had sent him for figs and olives, but he got distracted, as usual. The figs were to be purchased from Nikkos, the local Greek fig merchant. Nikkos was a favorite with most everyone in the neighborhood. Although middle-aged and with a slight limp, he was still robust, and his warm, broad smile twitched his mustache and complemented the twinkle in his eyes. Nikkos always allowed Mrs. Tashjian to buy on credit. Souren's father had been a reliable, respected pastor of the Armenian Protestant church, whose recent death was a loss to all. Nikkos's gesture of credit, though small, spoke volumes. Besides, his figs were plump and sweet. Whenever Souren came to pick up his mother's order, Nikkos would reach deep into the barrel for the finest selection, avoiding the dry, bruised fruit that he sold to indiscriminating customers.

Souren wandered through the narrow streets of the bazaar bordered on the east by the harbor, to the south by the Turkish quarter, to the north by the Frank and Greek quarters, and to the west by the Jewish and Armenian quarters. Vendors hawked their goods and caught up on the local news. In keeping with the Oriental custom, there was as much business as there was socializing.

The bazaar reflected the colorful complexion of the city of two hundred thousand denizens, half of whom were Greeks. Turks made up the second-largest group at about fifty thousand, twice the size of the Jewish population. The Armenian community consisted of about ten thousand members. Then there were the Levantines, inhabitants of Smyrna but citizens of European countries. They made up about 6 percent of the population. With the presence of over a dozen foreign consulates and missionary organizations, many other foreigners filled the flourishing streets of the rapidly developing ancient city.

Souren meandered for a good hour, people watching and eyeing all the goods available. He realized his mother would wonder what was taking him so long, and so turned at last in the direction of Nikkos's shop.

Before his father died, Souren's life had more order to it. He attended an American-sponsored missionary school, as his siblings had before him, and before they'd been sent away to America. Souren's academics included literature, mathematics, science, geography, French, English, Armenian, and music. Of course, Bible instruction was a required element, as was chapel attendance. But outside the school walls, Souren got himself another education—an education you could only learn on the streets, and from people like Nikkos.

"Souren," the Greek called to the boy making his way across the street toward him, "I have some tea. Come and sit down."

Souren was used to the ritual, and offered a small smile as he stepped into the fragrant, crowded shop. The bustle of the morning would ease right about now, so Nikkos had time for tea—and for stories. He loved to tell stories, especially about the folk hero Nasreddin. The legendary *hoja*, or teacher, was a Greek when his story was narrated by a Greek. When recited by an Armenian, he was Armenian. Even the Jews and Turks and Persians told his stories as if he were one of their own. So today, as Souren was sitting with Nikkos and listening to another wonderful tale, Nasreddin Hoja would be Greek.

The merchant sipped his tea, looking thoughtful. Young Souren took a drink of his tea and dutifully waited for Nikkos to begin. The boy had heard many of the hoja's adventures, but he never minded hearing them again, for often a detail would change, adding some suspense.

"Ah, yes," said Nikkos. "Here's one sure to make you smile, for you need to smile today," and he began like this:

"A neighbor came to the gate of Nasreddin's yard.

"'Would you mind, Hoja,' the neighbor asked, 'lending me your donkey today? I have some figs to take to the bazaar.'

"Hoja Nasreddin was reluctant to loan his donkey to this particular man, so he said to him, 'I'm sorry, but I've already lent it to Murad. He had to deliver tobacco to the British consul.'

"All of a sudden, the donkey brayed loudly behind the wall surrounding the yard.

"'But Hoja,' the neighbor exclaimed, 'I can hear it behind that wall!'

"'Who do you believe,' the hoja replied indignantly, 'an ass or a hoja?'"

Nikkos laughed uproariously, as if in telling the story, he, too, was hearing it for the first time and found it to be quite hilarious.

He glanced at the boy, hoping to see him laughing, but Souren's smile was merely a polite one.

Nikkos became instantly compassionate. "My son, everyone must die sometime. It is the way of all life. Your father was a good man. There is no one I know—Jew, Greek, Armenian, or even Turk–who has an ill word for Reverend Hagop Tashjian. You have much of which to be proud."

Souren stared down into his tea to avoid the eyes of his friend.

"But my mother cries," the boy said.

"So women cry." Nikkos made it sound like crying was the same as eating or sleeping. His answer was pragmatic. "Crying is part of dying. Your mother misses your father. Don't be afraid of it. Soon, she will laugh again. We all do. Armenians and Greeks have shed an ocean of tears here in Turkey, and we never drown. We swim."

Souren looked up from his cup and into the face of the merchant who had known his parents since they moved to Smyrna in 1893. Nikkos had been so important to all of them, and had been critical in smuggling Haig, Souren's half brother, onto a Greek merchant ship and to the safety of America. That year, 1894, the empire's Christian subjects had lived in fear. Rumors swirled in Smyrna of atrocities against Armenians in the eastern provinces. Reverend Tashjian knew his eldest son was in danger. At the age of seventeen, the government would consider him a threat. Haig attracted suspicion if for no other reason than his being a healthy, intelligent Armenian capable of any number of military tasks.

Souren knew the story well. Hagop Tashjian had visited Nikkos in his shop one day, and his grim countenance had moved the Greek. "What future does my son have in this country? The authorities look at him as if he were already guilty. And guilty of what? Of being born in the same town where the revolutionaries recruited their followers? Guilt by association," the reverend fretted aloud. "Nikkos," the minister said, pleading with his eyes as much as with his voice, "how can I save my son?"

Nikkos pondered the situation, knowing fully the realities the Armenian minister referred to. The Christian population sensed impending doom. They had learned to be on their guard.

"Badveli," Nikkos said, calling the minister by his Armenian title, "come back tomorrow afternoon, and bring the boy."

The Armenian obeyed the command, for Nikkos had delivered it with authority and confidence. When the reverend returned the following day with Haig, Nikkos motioned the two inside. He spoke loudly and gaily, mentioned the weather, the fig crop, and the good fortune of having rich Westerners spending their money in Smyrna. He poured tea as if readying for a relaxing visit with two friends. Instead, his antics signaled a bystander, who walked in and repeated that the weather was fine and the fig crop nearly ready to ship. The two Greeks exchanged glances. The man, who was never introduced, walked back to the street and disappeared into the crowd.

"That is your contact. He will smuggle Haig onto the ship for fifteen lira. Do you have fifteen lira, Badveli? Bring me the money next Thursday when you pick up your regular order of figs. That evening, you will return to my shop with Haig. I will give you further instructions then."

And so it happened that Haig was hidden in a shipment of figs before it was loaded onto a ship destined for a European port. After the box rested on the ship's deck, Haig waited till dark. A knock from the outside told him it was all clear to climb out. Without a word, he followed his guide to the captain's quarters and was told in the strongest of terms to remain out of sight during the day, but that he was free to move about the captain's cabin after dark.

It was still three days before the ship was scheduled to leave port, and Haig's father worried over his decision. What if the Turks searched the ship? What if Haig were discovered trying to escape? Surely, they would kill him! But what choice did Reverend Tashjian have? His wife, Sophia, felt strongly that her husband had made the right decision. Though Haig was not her biological son— his mother had died in Erzurum during a typhoid epidemic—she loved him in her own way and hated to see her husband eaten up with worry.

They had borrowed the money from a German missionary for whom the minister had worked. The Tashjians were not in the practice of borrowing anything, let alone money. The request for a loan struck the missionary as indicative of an emergency, and the advance was granted.

And so the Tashjians saved quietly and carefully over the next several years and smuggled five of the remaining six children via Germany to America. Only Souren was left in Turkey that spring in 1908, when the godly minister was laid to rest amid much sorrow on the part of the orphans and staff of the Kaiserswerth Deaconess Orphanage, where he worked, the American Board missionaries, his many neighbors and friends, and his widow and youngest son.

Mordecai the tailor walked in from his shop next door. Nikkos poured a third cup of tea. Mordecai, who was Jewish, was descended from those whom the Spanish king and queen expelled from their country in the fifteenth century, but he didn't hold a grudge against Christians in general. Like most Sephardic Jews, his complexion was swarthy, his hair dark, and his nose bulbous. He rested his deep-set brown eyes on the son of his late friend Hagop, for whom he'd made a suit some years back, the same suit in which the pastor had been buried in two weeks ago.

"He says his mother cries," Nikkos stated as the tailor took his seat at the small, now-crowded, octagonal walnut table, just twenty-one inches in diameter and less than two feet high. Souren absently traced the mother-of-pearl designs with his left index finger.

Mordecai spoke compassionately to the boy. "Yes, of course. They do that a lot, and even more so when death robs their home. But you know, Souren, at least your father died of illness and not massacre."

Nikkos nodded in agreement.

Mordecai continued, "It wasn't fifteen years ago when parts of this despotic empire ran with the blood of Armenians. Bloody Sultan, indeed! And your father and mother cared for the refugees who made their way here—penniless, traumatized, and frightened. We cannot escape death, my son. But to be a Jew or a Greek or an Armenian in this country and to die of cancer as your father did, why, it's a sort of blessing." The Jewish tailor finished with this adage, "There is no beginning without an end."

Suddenly Mordecai jumped to his feet. "Customers!" he announced, and took a few brisk steps toward the door, where he stopped and turned around. "My boy," he said to Souren, "you are now the man of the family. Come over anytime. I'll fit you with a suit." And with that generous gesture, he struck out and could be heard greeting a few Europeans and inviting them to come inside. "Bonjour, messieurs, entrez, s'il vous plait!"

"He's right, Souren. You are the man of the house."

Nikkos's words knocked Souren like a slap on the back of the head. He lifted his rich brown Armenian eyes to meet the gaze of the Greek's. Souren pulled his shoulders back and took a deep breath. A shout from outside drew their attention.

It was a nomad on a donkey announcing a caravan of camels. Pedestrians were to make room for the gangly creatures upon whose backs the Ottoman economy rested. Laden with five hundred pounds of grain and produce, as well as highly valued commodities—not just for the city folk in Smyrna but the undying appetites of Europe and America and the Middle East—these simple animals strode through the narrow streets all day long. Shoppers pressed up against shop walls and stood inside doorways until the odoriferous procession passed. Nikkos's threshold filled with passersby, and he took the opportunity to interest them in his produce.

"I've the best figs in all of Smyrna!" he shouted. "You won't find any better in taste or price."

Souren slipped through the crowded doorway and stood watching the camels. He never tired of the spectacle. The colorful kilims draped over the backs, the bags and boxes hanging off the sides defied logic, for surely they should come tumbling down. And yet, as if they understood their role, the bags and boxes rolled up and down with the camels' gait, patiently holding on as they made their way to the quay to be loaded by eager crews on waiting ships.

In the wake of the passing caravan, the street filled instantly with waylaid shoppers. Among the throng Souren noticed Ali, a peddler who specialized in a business with very low overhead: secondhand clothes. Ali dragged his rickety cart and called to passersby in broken English, some Greek and Italian, and even a little French. He offered a selection of whatever he'd happened to come by, literally. If a person were unlucky enough to be lying in a drunken stupor when Ali walked past, he'd likely awake to a cool breeze on his bare skin. Corpses were just as unlucky. Death was no reason to let a good pair of shoes go to waste. Ali's practical nature paid his bills and afforded others a selection and price they wouldn't see anywhere else in Smyrna.

"Souren," he called to the boy, "I have something to show you."

Ali got worked up over certain acquisitions. His excitement urged Souren forward, weaving in and out of the stream of humanity that flowed through the streets.

Souren greeted Ali in Turkish and asked, "What have you got today?"

The peddler grinned with as many teeth as he had eyes. His eyes were as good as his decayed incisors, for he suffered from trachoma and was half blind. Still, Ali's sight proved good enough to spot valuable garments.

"My boy, this morning I found a perfectly good uniform, insignias and all!"

Souren looked into the cart. He saw a tattered pair of pants dotted with brown, which he deduced to be blood, either of the man wearing it or the man he killed or the sheep he had slaughtered. None of the clothing was as clean as Souren's after his mother had done the laundry. In fact, the odor of Ali's merchandise made Souren cringe. But his curiosity kept him fixated on the goods. Ali's calloused and filthy hands dug through the contents. Exultantly, he held up his prize—a soldier's uniform in unusually good condition. No bloodstains, Souren noticed, and very little wear.

"Where did you find it, Ali?"

"I was passing a tavern on the quay," he said, "and I heard some arguing followed by loud laughter. I crept closer to the doorway. That's when I saw a naked man run past me with nothing but a pair of shoes and a fez! The next thing I know, his pants, his jacket, and then his shirt come flying out after him, but he didn't turn around. He just kept running. The laughter inside swelled, and no one came to claim the clothes. I snatched them up quickly and raced to my cart. I shoved the uniform under everything else in case someone recognized me and came to claim what will certainly be a week's worth of food! So, what do you think, Souren? Allah must have smiled on me today."

Just then three Turkish policemen, or *zaptiehs*, strolled toward the peddler. As a precaution, Ali quickly hid the treasure beneath the worn and soiled, but still usable, clothes.

"Ali, have you a dress today?" one of the policemen asked. "I have a girl I want to impress!"

Souren left the peddler with his customers and continued toward home. As he strolled through the gate of the Armenian quarter, he greeted the two Turkish soldiers stationed there to keep an eye on the foreign influence within. The Germans, Scottish, French, and Americans were among the many Western nations with churches, schools, and hospitals in this neighborhood. Their missionary endeavors extended to the Greek quarter as well. The soldiers liked the Armenian boy, for he'd often bring them olives or eggs as a snack, breaking up the monotony of spying on people who were pretty much just going about their business. The soldiers had little, if anything, to report to their superiors. But suspicions prevailed in the sultan's palace, and Western influence had to be monitored. The soldiers passed the monotony with songs, drink, sleep, and backgammon.

Once inside the Armenian quarter, Souren passed a group of young men, one of whom—Hagop Basmajian—gesticulated in an animated fashion. The subject of his monologue appeared to have to do with an article in the newspaper he was holding, a newspaper in the Armenian language. The men eyed the pastor's son as he walked by. Souren knew them all by name, but at his parents' insistence, he spoke little to them. They were openly political revolutionaries, called Tashnaks, and some in this quarter considered Hagop Basmajian and his gang to be a danger to all Armenians.

A couple of years ago, when Souren had asked his father why he could not talk to these fellows, his father sighed heavily.

"Souren, we must not even give the appearance of associating with those who espouse revolutionary ideals."

"But you've said they are brave. I've heard you say so."

"You heard that, did you? What else do you know?"

"I know that some people say we aren't real Armenians."

"Oh?" the pastor asked. "And why is that?"

"Because you work for the Germans at the orphanage, and the Americans at church."

"I don't serve foreign countries. I serve God and our people, and anyone else the Lord brings across my path."

"But why do they say those things then?" Souren had asked.

His father, a gentle man with a distinguished beard and slight build, folded his arms and stared straight into his youngest son's eyes and all the way down to his soul. In fact, that's how Souren knew he *had* a soul; when his father gazed so directly at him, the boy felt him plumb the very depths of his being. He tried to look away, but it never worked. It was as if he were in a trance, one that precluded all but his father's voice.

"It's all quite complicated," the minister began. "But let me try and explain a few important things to you. Whether we are Catholic or Orthodox or Protestant, whether we sing the old hymns or the new ones translated by missionaries, we are nevertheless one people—Armenians! And whether we make our home in Turkey or Russia or Persia or America, we are still one people. Whether we speak Turkish or Armenian, we are still one people. Unfortunately, we have disagreements among ourselves. Some Armenians feel strongly that, as Ottomans, we should show loyalty to the sultan. But Armenians in some parts of the empire suffer terrible outrages and injustices, and the sultan has not protected them."

"So they fight back!" Souren interjected. Souren thought the *fedayees,* as the freedom fighters were called, had exciting lives. He liked the idea of brave Armenians sneaking guns across the border from Russia and then giving them to other Armenians so they could protect themselves. The law forbade Armenians to own a weapon. If they were caught in possession of a gun, it would cost them their life.

"But God has called us to peace, so we must be very careful about taking up guns," the reverend said as he probed his son's soul. "We have to find some way to be good citizens of the empire and at the same time protect ourselves from injustice and violence."

Souren's disappointment registered in his expression.

His father laughed and said, "You want to be a hero. To grab a gun and solve the problems of the Armenians. I admire your thirst for justice. I do! But a mind loaded with wisdom should come before a gun loaded with bullets." He leaned back in his chair, cocked his head to the side, and asked, "Do you think your father is a coward?"

"No!" Souren countered loudly without a moment's hesitation. "But I wish Protestants could fight."

"Peace is the only way."

"But what about when someone kills an Armenian? I don't understand why God says we have to let people kill us."

"I am not saying for you to *let* someone kill you. I am not suggesting you not defend yourself, but you must be wise, and you must love peace, or you will choose violence to fix your problems. That's what some Armenians are doing. Their solution is to fight, but where is that getting us?"

Souren didn't know how to answer his father. What he did know was that the young men's talk in the neighborhood *did* make a sort of sense, when they cursed the sultan and swore allegiance to an independent Armenia. Souren assumed this meant moving to a different place where everyone was Armenian, where everyone would like each other, and where they could even carry guns if they wanted. And they wouldn't be killed by Turks or Kurds anymore, either. Why didn't his father want this, too?

Souren had loved his father. It was true he'd worked long hours and was away most days, even Sundays since he had to preach. When he was home, Hagop often seemed preoccupied or just plain exhausted. In previous years, the work had tired him, but this past year his fatigue had increased, and his body had withered. By the beginning of the New Year, Souren's father could no longer carry out his many responsibilities. He was confined to bed. For years Souren had longed to have his father to himself instead of sharing him with the rest of Smyrna, but he never dreamt of it turning out the way it had.

To Souren, his father had been bigger than life. Everyone knew Reverend Tashjian, and it seemed that most, if not all, people actually liked his father, which made the boy very proud. When he'd become sick, Souren reasoned to himself that, because his father was an important man, and since he worked hard doing good things, God would not let him die. In truth, Souren expected his father to climb out of bed, put on his suit, and charge out the door for his usual activities. After four months of intolerable suffering, the minister went on to "a higher plane of ministry," as one of the missionaries referred to it. Souren was told that he could rejoice that his father was now in heaven. If this was supposed to comfort him, it didn't. His father was gone, and he felt very alone.

Reverend Monchou of the Greek Protestant church came to visit Souren and his mother in the days and weeks after the funeral. He avoided the American platitudes, to Souren's great relief, platitudes declaring that his father was now in heaven and no longer suffering. Monchou concentrated on reminding Sophia of all her husband's admirable accomplishments for the Armenians throughout Turkey. Pastor Tashjian's ministry had stretched from Cappadocia to Erzurum in historic Western Armenia to Bardizag in Western Turkey.

Souren basked in the happy reveling. The stories enabled him to visit his father, at least in memory. Monchou's recollections removed the sting of death if for no longer than the length of his visit. And when he left, Souren's heart sank. Sophia recognized her son's grief, so she continued the reminiscing.

Souren and his mother recognized a greater bond than had existed before. They had only each other now. It was at once frightening and comforting. Sophia, in spite of her grief, would strive to be both father and mother; Souren would take care of his mother in a way that would make his father proud. No words were exchanged. The conversation was a silent one where mother and son acknowledged their new life together and their new responsibilities, promising tacitly to protect and encourage the other.

He was only twelve, but Souren felt suddenly grown, or almost anyway.

—⟶—

That summer, all of Turkey shook with tremors that intimated a great political quake. On July 24, Sultan Abdul Hamid II was forced by a group of progressive thinkers called Young Turks to reinstitute the constitution, which he had suspended in 1876. Though Souren wasn't exactly sure of the meaning of this news, he understood that life for Armenians in Turkey was changing. Nikkos said that now Greeks would have the right to vote, that all in the empire were equal. He and Mordecai had talked of it for days, as did everyone else at the market and in the neighborhood.

At school, the teachers celebrated the advances of the kingdom—not the Ottoman kingdom but God's kingdom—which did not include extolling the Armenian political parties. In fact, the missionaries urged less politics. Yes, Armenians had been massacred in the past, but under a new government, peace was possible. But only if forgiveness preceded it.

The Americans felt sure their efforts to convert the empire to Christianity were evidenced in this revolution. Despotism was to be replaced by democratic rule, the rule of Christian nations. Their hard work had paid off. At school, equality, liberty, and fraternity prevailed. Students of various nationalities and faiths competed with one another on the athletic field and in the classroom. And it seemed to Souren to work, at least when he was at school. But back home in the surroundings of his neighborhood, he could not ignore the differences he observed and the tensions that lurked beneath the surface.

"Hmph, history tells me not to trust these Young Turks," Sophia muttered when Souren came home and reported about the positivity going on at school. "Once they take power from the sultan, do you really think they will share their power with us? With the Greeks and the Jews?"

"Why not?" Souren asked.

"Why not? I'll tell you why not. Because we are not Muslim."

"But at school the Americans say everything has changed. It's different this time. They say the Turks have watched the missionaries and learned from them. And Hagop says Armenians get to vote and have representation in the government."

"Listen to you." Sophia shook her head. "When did you become interested in politics? It's dangerous to flaunt recent changes. I've told you over and over not to fraternize with revolutionaries like Hagop. The Americans are silly if they think this upheaval will lead to a Christian Turkey. 'A fool spoke. A wise man believed.'"

Despite her expressed doubts, Souren convinced his mother to join him in watching a parade to celebrate their ostensible freedom. A prominent Tashnak who lived in the mountains of eastern

Turkey, where he'd protected Armenians from lawless Kurds and Turks, had turned himself in to the Turkish authorities, and instead of being punished, he was celebrated! Surely that was proof that this time, it would be different for Armenians. With this thought in mind, Souren and his mother walked to Resadiay Boulevard, only a block from their house, to await the procession. They were joined by Miss Ely, a local teacher at a girls' school.

"There's trouble already at the boys' school," Miss Ely told them. "Fanaticism has engulfed the place. Two young men were expelled last week for singing nationalistic songs that called for revenge against Turks."

Sophia shook her head and clucked her tongue. "We are treading new ground, Miss Ely. This year will certainly prove an historic one."

The ladies suddenly jumped, startled by the sound of an explosion.

"Mama, it's fireworks!" Souren said excitedly.

His mother raised her eyes to the sky just as another round of sparks and smoke exploded over their heads.

Shouts rang out amid the blasts. Voices spontaneously joined in patriotic songs that wafted on the breeze. Armenians cast furtive glances when a group of young men belted out lyrics telling of revolutionaries' exploits and referring to Armenia as a "nation."

"This is what I mean," Miss Ely whispered. "Inflammatory lyrics to taunt the Turks."

The crowd braced itself for what might come next. But nothing did, except an ox-drawn cart that held the figure of a lovely young Armenian woman named Araxe who looked the very incarnation of the *République Statue* with her laurel crown, and a branch in her left hand. Robed in a heavy dress and capacious cloak, she resembled Marianne of France; she symbolized the Armenian nation, once fettered, now free.

"Can this be?" Sophia asked Miss Ely, who shook her head in disbelief.

Members of the Tashnak Party held sticks decorated with colorful ribbons and enormous crepe flowers mounted on the top. These men smiled broadly and stopped to mingle with spectators. They shouted slogans to the people, along with promises for tomorrow and decades to come. Their composure was not only one of glee but of smugness, for they had long defended the rights of all Armenians. Now they were guaranteed participation in the upcoming elections.

The crowd of Tashnak supporters was made up in large part of transients and refugees from past events like massacre, famine, and unemployment. These supporters had lived outside Smyrna and knew firsthand the injustices an Armenian faced in the more distant outposts of the empire, where local officials imprisoned Armenians for small offenses like neglecting to wear their fez at all times. Noticeably absent from the crowd were members of the wealthy class, *amiras*. They lived in their mansions outside the sweltering city during the summer months. Their allegiance was to the sultan, and they feared the consequences of this alliance between the Tashnaks and the Young Turks.

Mrs. Avakian, a widow friend who lived nearby, approached.

"Sophia! Is this really possibe?" she exclaimed.

"Maryam, God can only know. I certainly never thought I'd live to see the day."

"My Kevork says the Young Turks are educated and very progressive," said Mrs. Avakian.

"That's what I've heard, too," Sophia replied. "But I'm not sure what to think."

"My Kevork," she said, "says we should throw our support behind the Tashnaks. What do you think, Sophia? What would the *badveli* have said?"

Souren, too, had been wondering what his father would have said and done in the midst of this unprecedented change. He waited to hear what his mother would say.

Just then, Pastor Adanalian approached them. He greeted Sophia first and offered kind words about her husband. Pastor Adanalian, who had just returned from three years' study in America, had replaced Mr. Tashjian as pastor of the Armenian congregation.

"Badveli," Mrs. Avakian said, "what are we to make of this? My Kevork says the Young Turks are educated, that they have been living in exile in Paris and have embraced modern ways."

"Mrs. Avakian, as Christians we must be obedient to our government. I look forward to the changes a new regime will—"

"But what of the Tashnaks?" she interrupted him.

"That's another matter," the pastor said. "This talk of arming ourselves troubles me. We will be focusing on recent events and our response to them at our annual Week of Prayer."

Souren was getting tired of the adults' uncertainty and handwringing. So he followed the procession down the boulevard, intoxicated with joy and national pride. He was transfixed by the beautiful young Armenian woman with the laurel crown atop her head and the branch in her hand. Her body rocked gently as the oxen negotiated the stops and starts of the parade. Long, thick tresses fell past her shoulders. Her deep brown eyes of the same color explored the crowd, as if she were seeking someone in particular.

"She is Armenia," a man's voice whispered from behind, but he had gone by the time Souren could see who it was.

Chapter Two

—◊—

1909

A respectable-looking man and two women walked along at dusk. Souren's mother had met up with Souren's best friend, Armen's, parents and strolled with them to the weekly meeting at the church. The boys were not with them.

Armen had told Souren about the beautiful women who sang in a Greek tavern near the market, and persuaded Souren to accompany him to watch that evening while their parents were busy. As the boys waded through the narrow, noisy streets toward their destination, Souren caught sight of something and stopped to peek in one of the taverns.

"Not this one, Souren!" Armen tried to pull his friend away, but Souren, a little stronger than Armen, locked his knees and swiftly removed his arm from Armen's grasp. For Souren had glimpsed cleavage. He let his eyes travel down to a pair of silk-enrobed thighs, and became intoxicated by what he saw—as visibly intoxicated as the men drinking beer inside. Passersby congregated, pressing close to the boy who was mesmerized by the sounds of the pear-shaped oud—ancestor of the modern guitar—that the curvaceous Greek woman was plucking and stroking with obvious pleasure. She sang a simple melody about the man she loved rotting in prison for killing a prostitute. She wore bright lipstick, and rouge on her cheeks. But Souren couldn't decide if she was attractive.

"She's okay," Armen rendered judgment. "She's okay, but if you want to see more—and I mean more of everything—it's at Café Rosa's. C'mon! We're wasting precious time!"

Maybe hers wasn't the prettiest face he'd ever seen. Still, Souren felt an irresistible attraction to her lusty voice, her dancing breasts, and the mystery of those exquisite silk-and-lace-covered thighs.

He was startled out of his adolescent fantasy when Armen punched his shoulder. Turning around, ready to retaliate, he saw Armen had become panicked. With a quick tilt of his chin, Armen indicated a group of men who had gathered on the sidewalk just outside the tavern. Together, the boys stepped closer to hear. A business traveler had just left them and had told the group that thousands of Armenians had been massacred in the vilayet of Adana in Eastern Anatolia, five hundred miles southwest of Smyrna.

"Shooting, brutality, torture, fires, panicked screaming like I could not imagine possible!" he panted before moving on to tell others the news.

Souren backed away in shock. He left Armen there and began walking, mechanically. His feet took him to a familiar refuge.

Nikkos and Mordecai stood outside their shops in the midst of a half dozen other men, one of them the messenger himself. Mordecai eyed Souren approaching and tapped Nikkos.

"Souren, what are you doing out at night?" Nikkos asked. "What is it?"

"Um, I'm out with Armen," he said with a flash of guilt.

Mordecai hadn't looked up for several seconds. He stood engrossed in the messenger's report.

Nikkos motioned Souren to listen.

"Some of the Armenian radicals were planning an attack—" the messenger began.

An indignant Mr. Hagopian cut in. "An attack? Do you really believe that? If it were a group of Armenian revolutionaries attacking, all the authorities would have to do is to arrest them! This was a planned massacre! They never intended to let us be equal. Their mighty revolution will be our demise!" Mr. Hagopian's face contorted with fear and hatred. Souren knew Mr. Hagopian in a casual sort of way. He was always well dressed, had been educated in Europe, and was from a wealthy and respected family in Smyrna. He operated a fig store just a hundred yards away.

"My god! My god! How can this be?" someone groaned.

Three others began cursing the so-called promises of the Young Turks.

Souren slipped away. His mother would be home soon. She would know he'd been out on the streets and punish him with a guilt-inducing lecture about how his father had been a reputable man in the city and that Souren must never dishonor his name. He sprinted home, passing more animated clusters of people buzzing with what was sure to be tomorrow's headline: Slaughter of Armenians!

Sophia closed the door behind her and turned on the gaslight. Souren saw that her face was drawn and that she looked older than she had when she'd left for the meeting.

"Did you hear?" Souren asked in an even tone, knowing full well her answer.

"Yes." She eyed him. "Who came by with the news?" But before he could answer what he'd rehearsed, she continued, "I suppose everyone's talking about it?"

"Yes." The weight of the moment blinded his normally perceptive and inquisitive mother, who ignored her son's sitting in the dark waiting for her, something he had never done before.

"I'll be busy getting the orphanage ready for another deluge of orphans. I wish your father were here to help." She paused. "On the other hand, I'm relieved he did not live long enough to see another bloodletting. He was such a sensitive man." She sighed and added, "I'll go see Sister Henriette in the morning. We probably have a couple of weeks to prepare for the children."

"Should I go to school?"

"Yes, then come by the orphanage after school. I'll have some things for you to do."

She sounded exhausted. He watched her take heavy steps into the kitchen, where she turned on the stove to warm some water for tea. Souren followed after her and pulled out olives, cheese, and some lavash, a soft flatbread. She motioned toward the dried apricots, and he grabbed them, too. The kitchen filled with guests for the next three hours as American missionaries and members of the Armenian Protestant congregation stopped by to repeat what they'd heard and to prepare for how they'd handle the fallout. The teachers had to figure out how to maintain a peaceful atmosphere among their diverse student body, and to prevent possible retaliatory attacks between Armenian and Turkish boys the next day.

After the guests had gone, Souren went up to his bedroom. He looked out his window. His shutters had been latched over the locked windows, but he'd opened them enough to glimpse the Armenian quarter that had by now grown sleepy and dark. A little foot traffic punctuated the night. In a few hours, the sun would rise, and he would walk to school.

—◦◦◦—

After news of the events in Adana, several months passed in relative calm, and Souren and his friends passed much of that time playing marbles. As it happened, Souren was quite a master of the game. While the boys in the Turkish quarter could be seen playing their version with sheep's vertebrae, Souren and his friends owned marbles made of clay painted in solid colors of green, red, yellow, and blue.

The competition started by tracing a circle in the dirt. Competitors would choose a color. Then, each boy threw three marbles of the same color into the circle. About ten feet away, a line was drawn, from where players pitched their shooters. Whatever marbles a boy knocked out of the circle were his for keeps. His turn lasted as long as he succeeded in driving opponents' marbles beyond the perimeter.

That summer, Souren had amassed quite a collection. He'd won eighty-two new marbles since school let out, an average of about ten a week. He gazed at his collection from time to time, to admire its sheer quantity, and to bask in the lingering satisfaction of an elongated winning streak. He'd made it his goal to win one hundred, but he hadn't thought past what he would do after that. In fact, he won so many he had no more room in his pockets for them.

One day Souren rummaged through the kitchen cabinets searching for a bag he could use to hold all of his new marbles. He took down a sack of roasted chickpeas and emptied them into a jar. With great satisfaction, he filled the burlap sack with marbles.

"Where in the world did you get all those marbles?" his mother asked when she saw what he'd done.

Souren looked up and replied proudly, "I won them!" He held up the bag so she could marvel at it.

"You won them? That's a lot of marbles, Souren. Don't you feel sorry for all those other kids whose toys are now gone?"

"But I fairly won them," he said. He could feel his elation begin to wane. He hadn't stolen them or anything. He hadn't cheated. Why shouldn't he enjoy the spoils of his victories?

"If you win all the marbles, the children won't have any, and then you won't have anyone to play marbles with anymore."

"Oh," he said, trying very hard to grasp this concept.

"Why don't you return the marbles to the children?" his mother suggested.

But Souren just gripped the sack more tightly.

A few afternoons later, Souren, intent on adding to his growing bevvy of colorful clay spheres, stared hard at the circle in the dirt where one remaining marble rested. He took up his normal position at the line and made mental measurements as he cocked his head from side to side. He tossed the master marble upward and caught it, then deftly rolled it between his thumb and forefinger in search of the sweet spot. He was deaf to the world, which at that moment included the voice of his mother. With the greatest of calculations, he pitched his lucky shooter, and it lofted upward. On its way down, all the boys could see the aim was impeccable as the shooter headed straight for Armen's marble, the only spotted one in the quarter.

Smack! A sharp crack resonated as Souren's shooter hit the spotted globe and sent it sailing out of the circle. A roar went up from the boys, who were both cheering Souren's adroitness and mourning their own losses to the tune of three marbles each. No one was more glum than Armen.

"Souren!" His mother's voice interrupted his celebration. "I told you to pick up my order at Nikkos's before dinner. Now run along."

Souren collected his winnings and started off toward the market, holding his sack of marbles by the string he'd wound around the top. He knew the Greek would ask for him to retell the conquest in the greatest of detail, and he was already planning how he would begin.

As he approached Nikkos's store, he noticed a few of the other merchants had closed their businesses. When he entered the shop, Sophia's order was sitting on the counter, but no one was there. Voices came from behind a back wall, and just as Souren was going to investigate, Nikkos emerged and pointed toward Sophia's order on the counter. Then he disappeared again.

Souren crept across the floor and peeked around the corner, to where Nikkos had gone. It was the storeroom, and standing two deep in a half circle were the men who had closed their shops. They focused intently on a man at their center, a man who Souren recognized instantly to be an American.

The stranger, who Souren guessed was a journalist, wore a black tie around a stiff collar, a white dress shirt and waistcoat, black pants with a perfect crease on the front, and a pair of jet-black leather shoes. It was a hot night, so the visitor had draped his suit coat on the back of his chair.

His beard was typical of the time, a *pique-devant* as the French called it. Souren had heard others refer to the same style as a Vandyke beard. Mrs. Malikian, who knew all things regarding human nature, said that beards tell you a lot about a person. If she was right, then this man sitting before the collection of Smyrna's fig merchants was sure to be selfish, sinister, and as pompous as a peacock. Souren wondered how right Mrs. Malikian might be.

The American's mustache was thick, but not long, and curled up at the ends. His beard was well kept and much shorter than Souren remembered his father's. Mr. Tashjian had worn a more traditional look, something in keeping with his good character, according to Mrs. Malikian. But the sharp point at which this American's beard terminated made Souren wonder about his integrity, should a beard prove to be the expression of such a man.

The room was eerily silent. Souren's thoughts provided noise at first, but now he was ready to listen. Still, he heard not a word for what seemed a very long minute or two. He felt a tap at his elbow and turned to see Mordecai passing by. The Jew held his fingers to his lips to remind Souren to stay quiet. Souren nodded. Mordecai joined the others.

"The attack in Adana last spring was planned, of course," the journalist announced to his attentive audience.

Mordecai spoke up. "I beg your pardon, sir, but what proof can you offer?"

"The former sultan still has his spies and fanatical followers who look with suspicion on the Young Turks. In the midst of ruined Christian shops was a fully functioning, unmolested Muslim store with the word "ISLAM" scribbled in chalk on the shutters. Most definitely the owner was warned as to saving his establishment. Christ! The destruction of property was total. Damned if I've ever seen anything like it."

The journlist fiddled with the studs on first his right, then his left sleeve. After an awkward silence, he looked up, waiting for questions or perhaps a little admiration.

"Don't be downcast, not for long anyway," he said. "I have talked with the grand vizier, the head of the Turkish army, and the Sheikh-ul-Alam. I implore you to trust the Young Turks who stand against the despicable despot Abdul Hamid II. Yes, I am announcing in my article that Christians in the Ottoman Empire are finally safe. Devout Muslims are aghast at the rampage. It was the work of the ignorant peasant population manipulated by the deft and bloodstained hand of the former sultan."

One of the Armenian merchants spoke up. "Do you actually suppose the Turks and Kurds will sit back and let Christians enjoy equality?"

Another merchant broke in. "Tell us, sir, what did you see? We've heard so many rumors."

The journalist cleared his throat rather dramatically and began relating gory details to his attentive hearers.

"I talked to a young widow. She said a group of Armenians was led to a field and forced to lie down in a line. To save money on ammunition, swords were used to hack the people to death. She'd already thrown her infant into the stream and watched it drown.

"Now, she was to endure the mutilation of her three sons. A frenzied mob terrorized the helpless victims. After slaughtering most of the townspeople, the killers built a pyre and set fire to the bodies, some of whom were yet alive. The widow told me that she lay perfectly still with one of her sons tucked close to her, but her other sons were thrown with the corpses. She said, 'I think I heard one of them cry out.'"

The American shook his head and flicked the ash from his cigar as if it were the end of Act One in a performance he'd scripted. A weighty silence ensued.

"What I saw did not even compare to the massacre at Port Arthur, which I reported from China," he stated most authoritatively. "And the casualties I witnessed from the front lines of the Cuban-Spanish conflict pale in comparison to the victims of this massacre. The sheer scale of destruction of property and human life exceeded what I thought humanly impossible in the twentieth century."

"Monsters!" one of the Armenians murmured.

Most of the men present worked for British companies and were quite good, if not fluent, in English. As for Souren, English was the language of instruction at the American school. He followed the visitor's powerful narrative word for word.

"Monsters indeed." The journalist acknowledged the man by pointing his cigar at him and nodding in agreement. "I saw the corpse of a little girl whose lower jaw had been torn off. Her face was a gaping dark hole. An old Armenian man pointed to a pile of skeletons stripped of their flesh by dogs and told me their names, for they were his family members and his neighbors. I heard of a well ninety feet deep filled to the top with rotting corpses."

"You saw this?" someone asked.

"No. I had seen and smelled enough death to last me a lifetime. I couldn't bear the thought of another nauseating confirmation. I had my fill of half-eaten corpses, smashed skulls, and the spectacle of bloodied clubs that had done the ghastly work." He paused again. The men waited anxiously for him to tell more.

"I snapped a photograph of a seven-year-old boy stabbed and shot after his father was killed." The American held his thick cigar tight between his teeth and pulled out a picture. The men passed it around. "A bullet shattered his elbow. Then the Turks threw him out the window, on top of a pile of dead Christians. Only he wasn't dead. He cried out and was rescued by, of all people, a local Turk who knew his slain father. The Turk carried the pathetic child to the nearby missionary hospital, where he's making a remarkable recovery."

The journalist stopped abruptly, as if searching his memory for the next line. "Another poor Armenian widow recited her husband's murder. The man was offered his life if he would denounce his faith. When he refused, his torturers cut off his feet. Again, they offered him the chance to recant, and again he refused. This time, they cut off his hands, then his legs…his arms. Finally, they cut off his head."

There was another burdened silence as the American took a long draw on his cigar. He exhaled a thick curtain of smoke.

Souren shuddered. His body turned icy cold, and he reached up to cover his ears. He looked around at the other listeners and saw faces twisted with hatred, some lips pale and trembling, tears streaming down into beards. He fled the store, eyes wide with terror and his young body shaking. His knees were so weak he stumbled and fell facedown in the road. Passersby stepped around him. Several marbles rolled from the burlap bag he was still clutching. Shivering in fear, he got to his feet and ran straight for home.

"Where are my groceries?" Sophia asked. "Did you forget to pick up—oh, but you are pale, Souren." Sophia studied him closely. "Go on up to bed. I'll bring you some tea. We'll talk."

Souren explained to his mother all he had heard. She listened, shaking her head, sometimes wiping her eyes. She told him it wasn't news to her. She had known the most gruesome of details from the missionaries' reports being sent in from the affected towns and villages. She had tried to protect Souren from the specifics, but she knew her efforts might prove to be in vain, as they had been.

Smyrna may have been a bustling city in a Muslim empire, but the preponderance of Christian residents led to its being nicknamed by the Turks "Infidel Smyrna," or" Gavour Smyrna," which meant the same thing, a city of unbelievers. The Christians there—Levantines of European descent, Greeks, and Armenians—all celebrated their holidays and religious traditions with the greatest of freedom and unchecked enthusiasm, a description that couldn't be said of any other city in the Ottoman Empire besides its capital, Constantinople. Though the Armenian community had been sent reeling from the massacres of the previous April, Christmas preparations that winter did not reflect fear or a somber mood. Smyrna was as gay that holiday season as she'd ever been. In fact, massacres had become so commonplace, the Christian minority knew well how to recover quickly and move forward.

The special project this Christmas was to provide an uplifting celebration for the newest orphans. Mr. and Mrs. Tashjian had opened the girls' orphanage with the help of German missionary women, and Sophia remained very much involved in its daily affairs. She and Souren took delight in helping to plan events like the upcoming Christmas party at the Armenian Protestant church.

None of the orphans was without emotional scarring, but some also bore physical wounds. Deep divots in heads and limbs revealed places where a sword or maybe even a scythe had cut through skin and muscle. Missing fingers, diseased eyes, shattered bones, and open wounds had been nursed with the greatest of care. These girls, ages four through fifteen, were getting on with what was hoped would be normal life. They were learning a fair amount from books, but were also learning sewing, knitting, cleaning, and cooking, skills they'd need to fulfill their responsibilities as productive women in Armenian society.

Sophia and Sister Henriette, along with the rest of the deaconesses who ran the orphanage, busied themselves with making chocolate for the upcoming Christmas party. The German consul sent gifts of beautiful cakes and sacks of apples and nuts. Souren and Armen helped set up a large Christmas tree. At Sophia's command, the boys situated four large and two smaller tables for all the guests, which would include 112 orphans, the German consul, and the local Greek and Armenian Protestant pastors.

At five o'clock on December 24, the orphans arrived. Months of nurturing had replaced nightmarish memories. As the tree was lighted, every orphan face brightened with a smile. Cake and coffee were served, to the satisfaction of both grown-ups and children.

The young girls had come from villages where Turkish or regional Armenian dialects were spoken, but by now, all knew some German and the common Armenian language.

The German consul praised the kaiser and led a gregarious rendition, by the few who knew it, of "God Save the King." A few more speeches were made, and carols sung, before the girls received their eagerly awaited gift—a bag that contained an apple, two pieces of chocolate wrapped in green paper, a little German flag, and a handful of nuts.

Souren surreptitiously reached beneath his chair. He stood up, and, holding a bag of his own—a burlap bag with a string tied at the top—he went from orphan to orphan, handing each one a marble. The girls giggled because everyone knew marbles was a boys' game.

"Do you have a green one?" a little girl asked.

Souren rooted around his bag until he found the right color. When he held out the marble, a small mangled hand opened to receive it. Souren saw a thumb and four partial fingers. The scars were purple and raised. He willed himself not to recoil.

"Green is my favorite color," the little girl announced.

Souren reached into his bag again. "Here," he said triumphantly and placed two green marbles into her disfigured palm. She danced with infectious delight.

"Two green ones! Two green ones!" she shouted.

The rest of the girls began asking for their favorite colors, which Souren tried his best to satisfy, though sometimes he was forced to ask, "What is your *second* favorite color?" before reaching into his dwindling bag of marbles.

"Souren is playing Santa," one of the deaconesses said to Sophia. Sophia felt simultaneous pangs of love and pride as she watched her son parting with his beloved, hard-won marbles.

When the bag was empty, Souren walked over to Armen. He reached into his pocket and presented his friend with a blue speckled marble.

Chapter Three

─⚌─

1914

Once he had turned sixteen, Souren had stopped his regular visits to Nikkos's store. No longer did the sights and sounds of the infamous taverns amuse him. School took up so much more of his time these days. He would graduate in three months and looked forward to entering medical school. Becoming a doctor meant earning outstanding marks in school, and so far he had. Last year he'd excelled in all of his courses, which included American literature, rhetoric and composition, physics, chemistry, geography, and Bible classes from the Old and New Testaments. He energetically attacked current assignments in anatomy, physiology, and astronomy.

Substantial donations to the International College of Smyrna meant a brand-new facility for the boys' school on the outskirts of the city. There were funds to purchase state-of-the-art tools to measure earthquakes and to monitor meteorological conditions. American missionaries served as faculty, as did individuals who specialized in Armenian, Greek, and Turkish, reflecting the diversity of the student body. The overwhelming majority of students were Greek, but many Armenians, Turks, Arabs, and Jews also attended the school. Merchants and diplomats from Austria, the

Netherlands, Albania, and Poland also sent sons to this increasingly prestigious American school.

The red fezzes of the Muslim students dotted sight lines every morning when the young men gathered for chapel, where everyone's attendence was required daily. A respectable pipe organ accompanied the singing of hymns, followed by a scripture lesson, after which all would stand for prayer before being dismissed to their first class: compulsory Bible study. This—besides tuition—was the price one had to pay for an exemplary education, one that promised employment or further study in America or Europe. As a Protestant, with his deceased father's encouragement to use his mind even in religious matters, Souren enjoyed the spiritual part of the curriculum most of the time. But he often overheard grumblings from a few of the boys belonging to Armenian and Greek Orthodox churches. They resented any liberal religious interpretation, and now in these times also the political pacifism of many Protestants. The Muslim students did little complaining. Their fezzes reminded both students and faculty that they were there for an education, not conversion.

About eighty students were boarders, but the rest of the young men commuted to campus, including Souren.

His mornings were taken up with chores and the train ride to campus. Evenings excluded most leisure activities, as Souren studied hard, and even when he had no homework, he read books. The school library provided endless choices of classics, theology, and volume upon volume of science, which he devoured and redevoured.

The dress code at the school was strict. Each morning he donned his clean white dress shirt, attached his stiff collar, and brushed the lint from his black jacket. He carried his father's watch in his vest pocket. In another pocket was a small note-book and pencil. He knotted his tie and fastened the shirt studs. Souren had become tall for an Armenian, standing at exactly five feet nine. He was happy with himself as he gazed at his reflection in the mirror. He wasn't vain, not any more than other young men his age, but he was insecure enough to need reassuring. He often checked his chin and lip for hair, hoping to finally see a reason to start shaving.

He caught the 7:15 a.m. train, but always left about fifteen minutes of wiggle room in his morning schedule so that he could step out of his front door just as the girls arrived at the American Collegiate Institute, conveniently located across the street from his home. For this reason, Souren was the envy of Armen and his other best friend, Sarkis, who both lived on the other side of the station.

Souren had his eye on medicine and planned to go to America to study. Armen was a whiz at math and sciences and hoped to attend MIT in Boston. But Sarkis kept quiet about his future. When the boys shared dreams, his amounted to political monologues that Souren and Armen found dull and unimaginative, not to mention polarizing.

"Sarkis, what do you want to do? I mean, as a job? You can't make money talking about politics," Souren would say.

Sarkis would shrug. "We'll see," was all he'd say.

One day on the way to school, Armen asked Sarkis directly, "Are you going into politics?"

"He is not going into politics," Souren answered for Sarkis.

Sarkis eyed Armen. "Something like that." He stared out toward the campus as the train neared the station. "The world is changing. I can feel it." He surprised Souren with his seriousness.

"You bet it's changing, so I'm going to get out of here while I can," Armen retorted.

"You and so many other Armenians," Sarkis shot back. "What happens if we all leave?"

"We get jobs. We get married. We are free!" Souren broke in, thinking he had given the correct answers.

"I'm not leaving," Sarkis said.

"Well, Armen and I are. You'll wish you had."

The whistle blew. The train lurched forward before it came to a stop. The boys got off and walked the rest of the way to campus.

—⁓—

"It was the best of times. It was the worst of times."

Mr. White opened class that day the way he had the last two weeks. He was an American, but since Dickens was British, the English literature teacher affected an accent he thought clever as he recited the most famous line from *A Tale of Two Cities.*

"Cheerio!" Armen leaned forward and whispered in faux British to Souren, who sat immediately in front of him.

Sarkis sat two rows over and passed sarcastic messages to his friends. "Bloody good show, Mr. White. What a cheeky fellow that Dickens was!"

Souren enjoyed Dickens, and especially *A Tale of Two Cities*, but he could not overlook Mr. White's peculiarities whenever he quoted or read from the novel.

It wasn't only the mauling of the British accent. Mr. White was in every way an odd man. He didn't walk from here to there. He rushed, almost ran, from his desk to the back of the room to the hall. Wherever he went, he got there in a hurry. In the hallways at school, some of the boys would wait for Mr. White to pass by and then follow him with exaggerated motions. The thing was, Mr. White wore canvas-top rubber-soled shoes—a new fad in America—so that his racing around buildings was done noiselessly. The boys joked that Mr. White starred in his own silent movie.

Souren listened to Mr. White discuss the merits of Sydney Carton as a Christ type. "He was unlike Christ in that he was a sinful man, and Christ was sinless."

Before he could say more, Mr. Reed, the dean, appeared at the door. Mr. White hurried out. Thinking his return was a matter of seconds, the young men remained quiet and in their seats. After a few minutes, though, Sarkis tiptoed to the doorway.

"Nobody's out there. Souren, do your imitation of Mr. White."

The others chimed in. While he never trailed the literature professor in the halls as some of the braver boys had, Souren was known to rush onto the train and race to his seat with gait and bearing nearly identical to Mr. White's. The boys would laugh, and Souren, enjoying their hearty approval, might reward them with a quote from Dickens, perfectly imitating the horrid accent of their teacher.

"C'mon, Souren!" His fellow seniors enjoined him to entertain them.

Armen reached out and smacked him on the head. "Do it! I'll give you one American dollar. I promise."

Souren stood up quickly and rushed to the front of the classroom. The boys were snickering already. He picked up Mr. White's copy of *A Tale of Two Cities* and recited their professor's favorite lines. Much to his surprise, the boys laughed harder than they ever had done when Souren performed for them on the train. Sarkis, who had promised to stand guard at the door near the desk, walked back into the classroom so he could watch his friend. Pretty soon, Souren noticed Sarkis doubled over. He could hear him wheezing. Armen slapped his desk and buried his head in the crook of his left arm. The other boys roared with laughter. Souren was inspired to continue. He had an idea to write quickly and illegibly on the blackboard the way Mr. White did, but when he turned around, his teacher was leaning against the blackboard, arms folded and legs crossed at his ankles. He'd slipped in quietly behind Souren and had seen a fair amount of the performance. Souren's cheeks flushed red. Mr. White waited patiently for the ruckus to die down.

Mr. White took the book from Souren's hands and said, "I say, chap, jolly good show!"

The classroom erupted again. Souren returned to his seat, avoiding all eye contact, and waited an interminable fifteen minutes for the class to end. In the meantime, he pulled out his notebook and pencil. As he filed out after class, Souren dropped a note on his teacher's desk, apologizing.

Mr. White proved to be a good sport. He continued to rush about campus in his famous silent sneakers and to quote Dickens with his silly accent. He could have reported Souren to the dean, but he didn't, so Souren didn't get in trouble. He didn't get his American dollar, either.

—⚝—

Sarkis's family had come to Smyrna from Van—the bastion of Armenian heritage, the center of Armenian life, especially in the estimation of Vanites, the Armenians who lived there. The politically active Armenians, like the band of ardent patriots that Sarkis had joined, led by an Armenian named Yervant, celebrated the same pride in being Armenian that Sophia and Souren had, but they also believed in armed resistance. Souren and Sarkis came from families whose beliefs both intersected and diverged. Points of interest were nurtured. Points of disagreement sparked debate.

When Souren and Sarkis spoke of politics, Souren found himself speaking in defense of peaceful resolution. He advocated compliance with the current government and with the biblical standard of obeying those in authority, even to the extent of turning the other cheek. Sarkis always scoffed at what he considered to be Souren's naiveté. The day before graduation, Sarkis launched into one of his lectures against the current Turkish government as the two walked toward Souren's house. Souren was returning from a job interview at the train station, a result of Nikkos's having pulled some strings with his British friends.

"Souren, the Young Turks instigated a coup, for God's sake!" Sarkis threw up his arms and gestured impatiently. "They assassinated 'liberal' Turks! Now they've outlawed our clubs. No more Boys Scouts. No Armenian anything. How can you defend them?"

Souren had to agree that Sarkis had a point. He himself had been a part of a Scouting troop—he'd learned to play piccolo as a Scout—and had loved it. He and his friends had all joined, and it was a way they could express their pride in their Armenian heritage. But the Young Turks banned cultural organizations after its 1913 coup, fearing conspiracy and revolution.

Sarkis was still talking. "Do you think the so-called Committee of Union and Progress will stop there? Hell, Turkey is ready to join

Germany in this new war in Europe, and their officers are already arriving here to command our troops. The CUP is obviously preparing the country for war. When are you and other Armenians going to realize you have deluded youselves? Where's the equality promised six years ago that we supposedly celebrated with a grand parade? Was the blood of Armenians shed in the vilayet of Adana a gesture of equality?"

"That was Abdul Hamid the Second, not the Young Turks," Souren loudly corrected his friend.

"You actually believe that bullshit? It was the Young Turks' first assault! They want nothing more than for you and me to believe it wasn't them!"

"*Why* would they have done it, though? Armenians helped them take over. It was the deposed sultan who had reason to kill."

"That's just it!" Sarkis was exasperated. "Who would even think they were behind it? They're trying to hide it, but they're the ones who had the newspapers print that Armenians were collecting weapons in a plan to take over the region. They're the ones who started the whole damned rumor-milled thing."

"I don't believe your version," Souren retorted defensively.

"Well, we'll all know soon enough," Sarkis predicted.

Souren could not afford the European war come to engulf Anatolia. He had big plans to go to America, join his brothers and sisters, and become a doctor. In his heart, he knew he was mad at Sarkis because if he were right, Souren would be forced to enlist in the Turkish army and forgo his long-held dream of medical school.

"Sarkis, if there's war, what are you going to do? We'll all be drafted!"

Sarkis kicked a few stones around before speaking very quietly. In fact, Souren could barely make out the reply, but he thought he heard Sarkis whisper, "Fedayee."

Souren tossed a furtive glance. He saw no one within earshot.

"Sarkis," Souren pleaded as if his friend could stop a world spiraling out of control, "I want to go to college. I want to become a doctor."

Then Sarkis, who never appeared to give a wit for classic literature, quoted the Scottish poet Robert Burns in a silly Scottish brogue, reminiscent of Mr. White.

"The best-laid schemes of mice and men often go awry. And leave us nothing but grief and pain, for promised joy." He turned away and began walking in the direction of the train station.

That was the last time Souren ever saw him.

—⟋⟍—

Graduation finally came. The speeches were long and the auditorium packed with guests. There seemed to be as many people standing as were seated. Souren began to sweat in his suit. He craned his neck to look for Sarkis. He caught Armen's eyes and gave him a questioning look. The boys had known each other for so long that Armen knew exactly what Souren was thinking. Where was Sarkis?

After the ceremony, family and friends congregated for a picnic on the beautiful campus grounds in a neighborhood aptly named Paradise. Out of nowhere, a soccer ball appeared. The boys fell into two teams and began scrimmaging.

The mothers of the graduates laid out an exquisite array of appetizers and desserts. At least a couple of hundred *buregs*, delicate triangle-shaped pastries filled with cheese, were quickly devoured. Guests refreshed themselves on the warm day with a cool salad of tomatoes and cucumbers. There were endless trays of baklava, pistachio cookies, and *kataifi*, ropes of fragile pastry wrapped around a filling of nuts and soaked in a simple syrup. The boys and their proud families enjoyed a robust celebration, willfully forgetting the looming tension—at least for the afternoon.

"Did you hear about Sarkis?" Sophia asked Souren that evening. "He's gone, you know. His mother said he left Smyrna last night."

Souren scratched his head and looked bewildered. "Do you know where he went?"

"Probably left to join the fedayees."

"Yes, that sounds about right. But why couldn't he have stayed long enough to graduate?"

Sophia shrugged. "I think his father's relieved he escaped being drafted into the Turkish army."

Mother and son locked eyes.

"Souren, working for the railway will ensure you don't get drafted. I talked with someone from the American consulate. He feels certain that your being employed by the British will buy us the necessary time to find a way for you to leave Turkey."

"Sarkis left because he says war is inevitable. He doesn't think I'll get to America."

"Your brothers and sisters are all there. And you will be, too, but it's going to be a matter of timing." She wanted to change the conversation to something more positive. "Come now. Let me see the new railway uniform Mordecai sent over."

The graduation present had been delivered that morning as she was rushing around getting everything ready for the picnic.

Souren ran upstairs and donned his uniform for the first time. He strode into the kitchen with all the flair of a young man ready to make his way in the world. Because Souren's build was so much like his father's, sewing a proper uniform had proved a simple task for the talented and attentive tailor.

Sophia beamed.

"I'm so proud of you, Souren. And your father would be, too. I'm sure of it!"

—◆◆◆—

The excitement of graduation and Souren's new railway job was soon squelched by terrible news. A boycott of Greek merchants by local Muslims turned violent, and a swell of hatred against the Greeks rose in the South Marmara region. Pressure mounted for foreign companies to dismiss their Greek employees. It was their neighbor Mr. Terzian who brought bad news to Souren and Sophia.

Nikkos had traveled to a neighboring town where Greek fig merchants were being harassed. An important man within Smyrna, and an employee of the large British-owned Oriental Fig Company, Nikkos was sent to the troubled district at the behest of his employer. His mission was to convey his confidence in the ability of the British to protect the merchants, and in turn their customers, who, in some cases, had been driven off and even beaten by bands of ruffians enforcing an unofficial boycott of Greek commerce. Everyone knew the three-headed monster now in power had instigated the boycott. The Young Turks had many activists in Smyrna and plenty of willing Circassians and Kurds they could easily enlist to do the dirty work of intimidation. The country's leaders—Talaat, Enver, and Djemal—secretly sanctioned the extreme measures.

Gathering Greek business owners, all victims of recent acts of violence at their shops, was potentially dangerous. In order to prevent time for rumor to circulate, no one knew the exact location or time of the meeting until the hour before. The men assembled under the cover of darkness at the home of Nikkos's brother-in-law, who managed the packing of figs in a large warehouse near the quay.

After guards were posted around the perimeter of the property, Nikkos called the meeting to order. The tense exchanges reflected the fear of some and the determination of others. Already, tens of thousands of Greeks had fled the region. If Turkey entered the war on the side of Germany, who would protect the merchants whom the British employed? Nikkos expressed the concern of the Oriental Fig Company for the safety of its employees. He also pointed out that Greece, too, was pressuring Turkish authorities to stop the attacks and to punish those responsible for the lawless enforcement of the boycott. Nothing got settled, but the hour was late. The men left in pairs at fifteen-minute intervals to avoid detection by authorities or spies.

Nikkos shook his brother-in-law's hand, warned him to speak not a word of the night's events, and slid quietly out the back door, where his horse waited.

The following morning, Mordecai sat mending for a customer who expected his suit to be ready within the hour. As usual, Nikkos called out to his friend as he unlocked his shutters and propped open his shop door. Frantic to finish the delicate stitching, Mordecai did not answer. He did chance to glance up in time to see a group of four men enter Nikkos's shop. They weren't regulars. They certainly weren't Europeans or Americans. He recognized them as Circassians. These rugged-looking men wore large round caps called *kalpaks*, and soft leather boots into which their blousy trousers had been tucked.

Suspicious, Mordecai put down his work and walked outside. He heard a crash, and a voice that sounded like Nikkos's. Other shop owners appeared in their doorways. If they intervened, they could cause a riot. In the event these were men sent by the government, the shop owners could be arrested for interfering. If they didn't stand guard over their own establishments, perhaps those men inside Nikkos's store would ransack theirs. The shop owners' eyes met, tacitly agreeing on remaining where they were and hoping Nikkos would drive out the beasts inside. Everyone knew his legendary strength and his importance within Smyrna. Of the men on that street, Nikkos was the one with the most authority, physically and otherwise.

Mordecai crept around to the back door of his friend's shop. He heard the sounds of a man gasping. The Circassians taunted their victim.

"You goddamned Greek! We don't want your Christian money in Turkey! These are our figs that are making you filthy rich!"

Mordecai heard the sounds of boots thudding against Nikkos's body, one blow after another, until the Jew could bear it no longer. He stealthily approached the wall separating the back of the store from the front, the room where for so many years the men had gathered to talk business and politics.

"Get up, you filthy *gavour*! Take your cursed Greek money and go home to your infidel country!"

Mordecai heard Nikkos's body absorb another swift blow, but the Greek made no sound. He didn't cry out for help and apparently did not strike back with his own fists. Mordecai feared the worst. What should he do? What *could* he do? He had no weapon. His physique was slight compared to Nikkos's.

In a flash, his mind wandered back to the riots of 1872, when the Greeks, enraged by an accidental drowning death of a Greek boy that they believed had been his murder by a Jew, set upon the Jewish quarter. Mordecai was being badly beaten by a group of angry young Greeks when Nikkos—whom he had not yet met—stepped in, stopped the attack, and brought Mordecai to safety. It was the beginning of a long friendship. They were a pair of aging men now, and this time Nikkos needed Mordecai.

The Jew steeled himself. Before he knew exactly what he was doing, Mordecai stepped out from behind the wall. What he saw haunted him the rest of his life.

Nikkos's body lay smashed on the floor.

"Hey," one of the murderers called out. "It's a goddamn Jew! Are you here to steal from this Greek bastard?"

One of the thugs walked over to the trembling Mordecai. He grabbed him by the hair and pulled hard until Mordecai dropped to his knees. The Circassian continued to tug until Mordecai was face-to-face with Nikkos. His eyes were swollen shut, and his forehead was caved in above the right eye, where the force of a boot had crushed the skull. Blood ran freely from a multitude of wounds.

Mordecai panicked, but he couldn't escape the tight grip of the Circassian who held him down.

"Look at him! Look what we will do to anyone who works for the British or the French or the Russians!"

The man pulled Mordecai up to his feet. He could barely stand, for his knees shook with fear. Mordecai thought he was next. Instead, the men took their wages for the job they were sent to do by grabbing from Nikkos's store whatever they could carry. The four of them walked down the street with no fear of the police and as a grim warning to the other merchants whom they knew were watching from their windows.

Mr. Terzian stopped recounting the story for a moment. His shoulders slumped.

"Nikkos's brother-in-law who hosted the secret meeting was also found murdered. He'd been ruthlessly tortured. Someone in the room that night was an informant," he added despairingly.

Souren waited a couple of weeks before he paid a visit to Mordecai. He'd avoided doing so before now because he could not bring himself to pass by Nikkos's abandoned shop.

Mordecai smiled when he saw Souren, but his eyes were sad. Souren helped him carry a mirror to the cart out front. The boarded-up windows and door of Nikkos's shop weighed heavily on their spirits.

"His family left for Athens," Mordecai explained. "I have to leave, too."

"Why would you have to leave? You're not a Greek. They aren't going to come and get you."

"No, but this is—was—Nikkos's property. He leased it to me all these years. I'm the only tailor on this street of fig merchants. And I do a pretty good business!" He laughed bitterly. "He's gone. The family has left. I suppose the government will evict me soon."

Souren eyed the furnishings from the shop that were stacked on the cart. "Where are you going?"

"I'll move my shop to the Jewish quarter, where I belong. I don't feel safe here." He nodded toward Nikkos's old establishment. "I've lived too long, Souren. Too long, I'm afraid. But you are young. Go to America. Leave Turkey before it's too late!"

"We're trying, Mordecai. Mother says the timing isn't right."

"This is true, but I'll tell you something else that is equally true—time is running out for all of the Christians in this empire!"

—⚊⚊—

For years, Sophia received money from her children through the channel of the American missionaries. When hostilities broke out in the summer of 1914, the Ottoman financial system became a casualty of war, but through some back-channel maneuvering via an American company in Turkey, Sophia continued to receive the money.

By now, Sophia had saved enough to get Souren out of the country, but now that Nikkos was gone, she couldn't find a trustworthy man to smuggle her son. Sophia turned to the American missionaries for help. The best they could do was to continue to pass along money from her children and to lobby the Turkish authorities to allow their graduates to forgo military service since the young men were prepared to make an important contribution beyond that of being mere soldiers. As long as Turkey remained neutral, it was unlikely Souren would be drafted. Nevertheless, his mother grew more anxious by the day.

When Souren repeated Mordecai's warning to his mother, she replied, "Whatever happens, you must promise me you will not fight in the Ottoman army."

"But what if I'm drafted?"

"Your brother Edward intends to enlist in the army if America enters the war. You can't get drafted, Souren! You can't fight against your brother!"

Later that night, something woke Souren out of a deep sleep. He lay perfectly still wondering the source of the eerie feeling pulsing through his limbs. The objects in his room began to rattle. His bed felt like it was pitching forward. He jumped out and ran to the bedroom door. Flinging it open, he yelled, "Mom!" and ran down the hall to her room.

Sophia was sitting up in bed, too afraid to get out.

"It's an earthquake, Souren!" Her hoarse whisper frightened him.

"Mom." He took her by the arm and held her close as he guided her out of the room and down the stairs. They rushed outside to see their terrified neighbors huddling together. The chilly October air made the people shiver in their nightclothes. At first, some thought the British or Russians had bombed the city, which sent Mrs. Bayandarian two doors down into a fit of wailing despair. Soon, everyone agreed they had experienced an earthquake. The only comfort that realization brought was knowing that they did not have to fear bombs dropping from the sky.

The men discussed the prospect of damage to their homes. As unnerving as the strong quake had been, the situation would have proven far more dangerous had the upheaval occurred in the evening, when the gaslights were burning. As it was, their families suffered fright and their homes possible structural damage. They discussed the probability of destruction in other affected towns, especially those close to the epicenter of the quake, wherever that was.

"If it's Armenians who are victims," one man said, "we'll need to provide relief. We can't count on the government to rebuild Christian homes." The other men nodded in agreement.

The women stood together. They looked around tearfully, crossing themselves, lamenting to heaven for the disasters that had occurred of late and wondering if this was not a portentous precursor to a bigger catastrophe. Would there be war? More massacres? Perhaps the world was coming to an end!

Souren arrived at work on Monday to a scene of chaos. The earthquake, with its epicenter 250 miles southwest of Smyrna, had destroyed many miles of track and several train stations. Soldiers trying to return home on leave confiscated carriages and rode into Smyrna with tales of destruction in Burdur and Isparta.

"At Ketche-Bourlou, the entire roof of the station caved in. Windows were smashed. Everything torn to bits!" a soldier reported.

"And the stationmaster?" Souren inquired, for he knew the man and his wife lived above the station.

"Miraculously, he and his wife escaped without so much as a scratch!" the soldier said. He immediately launched into another sensational story.

"Seven trackmen lived in a house near the station. The quake demolished the building, but the roof came down in such a way as to shield them. They were pulled out alive and unharmed!"

"The streets are covered with debris and bodies," a very tired soldier recalled. "People ran out of their houses, but once outside, many were killed by falling stones or lumber."

"I saw one or two injured people. Everyone else was dead," another soldier added.

Souren learned that 70 percent of the stone houses had collapsed in the earthquake. Nearly all of the mud houses had been completely destroyed. Three or four thousand people were thought to have died.

The conditions at the train station in Smyrna that day were hectic. People who needed to get to Burdur and Isparta wanted tickets. Souren and the other employees would explain over and over that there weren't any stations standing between here and there. In many places, there weren't even tracks.

Around 2:00 p.m., well after his scheduled lunch, Souren finally received permission to take his break. He wanted to get away from the bickering, complaining, pushing, and shoving—all of which he was used to. Today, though, was beyond anything he'd experienced since taking this job three months before. He left the station to buy something to eat.

"Souren!"

Souren turned toward the familiar voice. It was Ali, the half-blind seller of secondhand goods. He rushed with his cart to where Souren stood.

"Oh, my son. It's isn't good." He was, of course, referring to the earthquake.

"I know," said Souren. "I heard at least three thousand thousand people died—"

"Alas, they're the lucky ones," Ali interjected.

"Why do you say that?" Souren asked.

"An earthquake by day is one thing, but an earthquake that comes in the night can only mean disaster!" He grimaced as if in pain. "So much war around us. Should we, too, be spared? Surely not. Turkey will enter the war on the side of Germany and be destroyed! The Young Turks are leading us to extinction!" Ali had lowered his voice. He feared the spies that he knew were enlisted to watch the quarters—Muslim and non-Muslim alike—and report suspicious people to the police.

"Did you hear about the mosques in Isparta? They were destroyed! The ground shook for nearly a minute. Then it rose up and with a great crash fell back to Earth. The mosques disintegrated. Only two minarets are standing in Isparta, and those are cracked from top to bottom!"

Souren instinctively looked over his shoulder. He didn't see anyone watching them. Ali must have sensed something, though, for he hurried off without saying good-bye.

Souren purchased food from a street vendor and made his way back to the station, which was as crowded and as raucous as it had been all morning. A few German soldiers approached. Souren watched them talk to a pair of Turkish soldiers, one of whom obviously understood German and translated for the other soldier. Souren wondered if Ali were right.

But why would a Christian country like Germany take a Muslim one as its ally, he wondered. Why would Muslims fight on the side of a Christian country? No, he decided, Ali was wrong. It simply couldn't be. It didn't make the least bit of sense.

Of course, Christians fighting Christians made even less sense, but it was a confusing mess that Souren had trouble keeping straight. Someone had assassinated the archduke in Sarajevo, and just like that, the world was at war. Austria-Hungary declared war against Serbia. Germany declared war against Russia, then France, then neutral Belgium for tactical purposes. Of course, this meant Austria-Hungary had to declare war on Russia. Montenegro jumped in. Japan, too. In Smyrna, British and French citizens were leaving amid fears of being treated as belligerents and, possibly, even arrested as spies.

It was, to Souren, the worst of times.

Chapter Four

—⚬—

1915

Sunrise brought the ubiquitous call to prayer: *"Allahu Akbar,"* (God is great). Souren remembered his father using the Muslim call to prayer for his own spiritual discipline as he uttered in Armenian, *"P'arrk' im Asttsun"* (glory to my God). So it was that the Christians had learned to live in the shadow of a religion not their own.

Souren inhaled the fall air deeply through a crack in his window and whispered, *"P'arrk' im Asttsun"*

This lovely spring morning had allowed Souren to forget for just a moment the current state of affairs in Turkey. From his bedroom window, he could see across the street to the American Collegiate Institute. The premises were quiet. Students wouldn't be arriving for another few hours. Down the hall was his mother's room. Her view included a wide swath of the Armenian neighborhood and a tiny patch of the harbor, with its cacophonous bustle of horse-drawn trams, camel traffic, donkeys, trains, and the continuous flow of exotically dressed pedestrians along the quay.

Tensions were rising as more Armenian men faced orders to appear at recruiting offices for compulsory service in the Ottoman army. So today, instead of throwing open the shutters and leaning out his open window to admire his eastern view of the city, Souren had merely cracked his window enough to allow him to unlock the shutters and push them slightly apart. From below, they appeared fastened. He knew he had to be careful, but he couldn't resist his morning ritual.

His promise not to join the army had left him and his mother vulnerable. In the past, Armenians paid a compensatory tax since, as infidels, they were considered unfit to defend the empire. All that tradition was said to have changed when the Young Turks took over.

In general, initially Greeks and Armenians were optimistically willing to participate in the new regime. Not only were they supposedly now allowed to have elected officials, but their men were considered to be rightful representatives of all Christian subjects of the empire and, therefore, worthy to defend it. But the flow of Christian trust and goodwill toward the empire and their Muslim neighbors had limits.

Since all of Souren's siblings had emigrated to the United States, he knew he would be considered an "enemy" of Turkey in the unlikely event that President Wilson declared war against it. That would make his life—and Sophia's—unbearably difficult. Sophia spoke daily with the American missionaries to discuss Souren's alternatives and to probe the possibility of America entering the war. This seemed quite unlikely, since Americans were stalwart isolationists and the conflict would hopefully end soon. That possibility offered some comfort.

"Souren will be fine," she was told. "We will petition the authorities on his behalf. In the meantime, you will continue to receive the money sent to us by your children. We should just bide our time and wait. Tell Souren not to do anything drastic."

Independent of potential "enemy" implications of his siblings being in America, Souren was already in a difficult and rapidly deteriorating spot. The authorities had announced they would arrest men like him as "deserters" should they fail to report. He had not yet been officially ordered to do so, though that slip of paper would inevitably come, probably in a matter of days. To calm his mother, Souren promised he would devise a way not to report.

Yet Souren's job at the British-owned railroad left him uncomfortably exposed. Since England and Turkey were now at war, railways were being confiscated by Turkey to be used for the war effort. Thus far, he had been safe and continued showing up at the station. Time was running out, though. He knew that.

Souren lay back on his bed and racked his brain for ways to escape what he felt certain lay in store. Because he no longer had studies to consume him—like Mr. White's literature class that opened up new worlds—he took to scripting his own situation and its near-term adventures. His life plans—to go to America, to become a doctor—would surely be thwarted by war. He was surrounded by enemies and viewed himself as his mother's only protector; he was trapped.

The shrill cry of a child suddenly stung his ears. He jumped from his bed, rushed to the window, and carefully peered through the shutters to make out the scene in the street below. To his horror, he recognized eight-year-old Vartanoosh, whose family had moved to Smyrna a few years before. Her mother had died shortly thereafter. Souren couldn't help himself and leaned out his window.

As he was about to call her name, he caught sight of the object of her fear.

"Souren!"

His mother appeared in her nightclothes behind him. Her voice pulled him back from the window. With a racing heart, he told her that Bedros was being dragged away and that his daughter Vartanoosh was running after him.

"Shhh." His mother held her trembling fingers to his lips. "You can't let them see you." Sophia, though a compassionate woman, thought only of her own son at that moment.

"I have to go down." Souren turned to walk out of the room. His mother caught him by the arm.

"You can't! They'll realize you haven't registered, Souren!"

Bedros was a kind man who cultivated roses, the flower after which he and his late wife had named their daughter. The Greeks had been targeted the last several months, but this arrest of Bedros, an Armenian, sent chills through Souren.

The two watched as the little girl, now hysterical with fear, flung herself on one of the Turks and begged to have her father back. Souren gasped when the tiny frame collapsed after being kicked to the side of the road. Vartanoosh got to her feet and ran toward her father. One of the soldiers thrust the butt of his gun against her back. She fell to the ground but scrambled to her feet in continued pursuit.

Souren turned away.

"Mother," he cried softly.

"If they beat a small child," Sophia argued, "what do you think they'd do to you? God help her," Sophia prayed aloud, then added, "And God help my boy."

"Mother!" Souren whispered, hearing the thunderous blow against their own street door. "Now it must be our turn...We're doomed!"

To his astonishment, Sophia's demeanor suddenly changed. She appeared calm and apparently unafraid. "Why? Be brave, my son. God will help."

Her calm bearing settled him down just enough to think clearly about their next steps. "Mother," he said, "run and put on some warm clothes They're breaking down our door—I'll go and hold them off until you're ready."

She didn't move, and Souren wondered if now again it was fear paralyzing her. In desperation he pushed her into her bedroom, begging that she dress herself in warm clothes. Then as hastily as he could, he dressed into the brass-buttoned uniform of a railroad conductor.

Souren always felt there was magic in uniforms and insignias. As soon as he felt its tightly buttoned neck and chest, he stopped being a youth. Fear made way for boldness; subordination gave way to independence. He reached for a small box of valuable papers and a few family heirlooms and charged downstairs to the door to meet the assailants.

As he opened the door, a husky voice yelled, "*Yassak!*" and he felt the point of a soldier's bayonet in the hollow of his ribs. "Halt. No one allowed to leave!" the voice repeated more resolutely.

Before he could make a decision or formulate an answer, Souren heard his mother's bare feet behind him. He turned to warn her. There she stood, turned to a white statue, garbed as he had left her in only her scanty nightgown. In her hands she held an empty hot-water bottle, her last Christmas gift from her oldest son in America.

"Mother, I meant clothes, warm clothes, not this," Souren moaned.

"Silence, you infidel," barked one of the soldiers.

Souren did not turn, but again felt the sharp point of a bayonet, this time in his back. He looked at Sophia, and his tearful eyes silently pleaded her to retreat. But she remained immobile.

Strangely, it was then that Souren felt his father's warm hand pressing on his shoulder. It felt just as it used to do when Sophia, in despair, would turn to Hagop to make Souren see the wisdom of her request or command when it was contrary to his desires. *Be brave!* a voice seemed to say. *You are not afraid! Conquer him with your mind.*

Unconsciously Souren stuck his right hand into his pocket and pulled out his railroad pass, with a picture of a locomotive. Holding it upside down, he said, "Hey! Can't you read? You will delay the train! I must go," and, pushing the soldier slightly aside, Souren left him to wonder who he was. Surprised that he was not further challenged, now somewhat assured of the magic of his conductor's uniform, and relieved by the success of his escape, he headed toward the American girls' school across the street to leave the box with its precious contents. Everyone at the school was alarmed and greatly astonished to see him pass the Turkish bayonet unmolested.

Slightly intoxicated by their praise, Souren decided to venture out further, leaving the school and walking toward the station as though normally to begin his daily task. He thought it best to continue to work that morning. If he were found missing, he'd draw attention to himself. But if he went to work, he might be ordered to go straight to the recruiting office. He had no idea what lay ahead that day, only that the arrest of his neighbor Bedros was a terrifying omen.

En route, he passed a cordon of soldiers who did not attempt to stop him. Upon arriving at the station, his confidence wavered—he couldn't see any of the British employees, just the faces of strangers, who watched him closely. Through sidelong glances, Souren noticed a red crescent on the left sleeves of the new employees. What he didn't realize, but soon would, was that with the forced departure of British executives, new railroad employees had replaced them. They were those lucky enough to have successfully bribed officials, and the red crescent they wore exempted them from military service.

Souren walked to his desk with an air of nonchalance. When he saw the dreaded letter stamped with official seals lying there, his throat tightened, and his chest constricted. Feeling the eyes of the others on him, he grabbed the notice and left, making sure he turned as if to go straight to the military recruitment office. He fought back tears and the sensation of wanting to vomit.

In other times, he would have run to Nikkos, who would have helped Souren just as he'd helped his brothers and sisters in the past. Souren turned a corner onto a crowded street. He slipped behind a couple of shops and unfolded the fearsome document. It read: "As an Armenian employee, you are discharged by military order and are to report promptly to the recruiting officer of your district." It was signed by the newly appointed Turkish director of the railway.

This he had expected. Still, the shock was great. How would he tell his mother? Souren wiped his eyes and shoved the letter into his pocket. He thought he had faced the worst tragedy of his life when his father had died. Then the death of Nikkos had plunged him into the same loneliness and unrelenting grief. Refusing to report for military duty might prove the greatest calamity yet.

He crouched low and hung his head. He felt himself a fool for daydreaming. He wished this to be a dream from which he would wake. As he pondered what to do next, Souren again sensed his father's presence in the form of a warm hand pressing on his shoulder. Again he thought he heard his father whisper, *Be brave! Conquer this with your mind!*

The notice gave him twenty-four hours to report for duty. Time was short. Risky as it would be to reencounter gendarmes, he had no choice but to find a way home and figure this out. His decision not to tell his mother proved futile because Mr. Terzian was at the house when Souren arrived at the back door. He had already told Sophia about the railroads, the Armenian employees, and the coveted red crescent badge. Sophia thanked Mr. Terzian as he slipped quietly out as Souren entered. Mother and son then each went to bed, too exhausted to think clearly.

The next morning, Souren stumbled down to the kitchen, his large brown eyes bloodshot. His face, once ruddy, was now a sickly, pasty white, and wet. Sophia studied her son carefully. He sat down and just stared, head bowed, at his coffee and bread.

Sophia passed her son an orange. "Please, Souren, eat something."

He sat transfixed.

"What is it?" his mother pressed him.

"I had a terrible dream," he began.

Sophia sat riveted, saying nothing as he recounted his violent nightmare.

"I was on the back of an enormous and vicious monster. Tusks grew out of either side of its warty snout. His hide was tough and smelled terrible. I was terrified of falling off and being killed and was clutching with all my might. It was crushing panicked people under its feet. They screamed and ran, but it always caught them. I was gripping so hard my nails were bleeding. A voice from somewhere behind me urged, 'Hold on.' I heard it loud and clear. It seemed like Father's voice. So I dug my fingers even more into its loathsome fur, but I was jerked violently back and forth. All the while, it kept lurching, lunging, and crushing people. It kept turning its head, trying to get at me with its fangs, and its breath smelled of rotting flesh.

"We lurched toward what seemed to be our Armenian quarter. There were fires everywhere. Mothers ran with babies held tightly in one arm and, with the other, dragging another child by the hand. The monster chased everyone all the way to the quay and then stomped and crushed them under its hooves. The looks in people's eyes, and the screams, were terrible, and I wanted to drown them out, but the voice again urged, 'Hold on!' So I continued gripping the disgusting beast.

"My hands became numb. I was sure I would fall off and be crushed and devoured like the others. My arms were burning. I was panicked because I knew I could not hold on much longer. Hard as I tried to hold on, I felt my grip loosen, and my arms and legs gave way, and screaming, I was sliding off its back—then suddenly I woke up. My heart was beating like mad. I felt sick to my stomach, and the pillow was soaked with my sweat.

"This was not just a nightmare, Mother; it felt deeper and much more severe. What does it mean? What can it mean?"

Souren rested his throbbing head in his hands and stared at the table. His mother sat in stunned reflection.

After a while she said, "I think you have experienced a premonition, as Armenians have been living alongside such a monster, now awakening. We will soon experience the full force of its ferocious nature, and for certain you are at great risk. But you, Souren, you are both smart and strategic. I believe this dream foretells that you will find a way to outsmart the monster and survive. You will use circumstances to manipulate it to save your life and scorn it at the same time. As you witness more devastation of our people, you will long to do battle. But the odds of killing the monster are overwhelmingly against us, so only with cunning will you escape with your own life. This whole picture terrifies me, but it is how I interpret your dream, my son. It is a warning, but it also serves notice that there is a way out. You have to figure out what that way is."

After being quiet and reflective for several long minutes, Souren finally looked up. "I think I know what I have to do."

His tone now seemed to her to be that of a man. Tears in her eyes, Sophia listened as he spoke almost breathlessly in short, choppy sentences. He outlined a bold but high-risk stratagem.

He noted that he was a consummate musician, having learned early in life to play the flute and piccolo, which were well adapted to both popular Turkish and symphonic music. He reminded her of his friendship with the Greek conductor of the military band at the nearby garrison who, whenever he needed a full band, would call on him to perform as a civilian extra. Through this connection, he would join the band. He explained that he knew this would not spare him from danger for long, but music did play an important part in Turkish military affairs. Traditionally, when moving toward an engagement with the enemy, each unit would be preceded by its band playing strongly rhythmic and vigorous patriotic tunes up to the point of encounter with the enemy troops. Then, the band would halt and disperse as action and the firing commenced. During the ensuing confusion, he intended to find his way to the enemy lines, surrender, tell his story, and find his way to the United States as a political refugee.

Sophia listened to her son's plan and, with both shaking hands silently grasping his, signaled her approval.

For some time, the authorities had stationed a guard near their home to keep an eye on foreigners, in this case the missionaries who ran the girls' school. Souren was grateful for all the times his mother thoughtfully had cultivated the guards' trust by sending him out to give them delicacies such as olives, bread with onions, and even sugar. Several had actually become friends who remembered the times he had eased their boredom.

Through a front window, Souren saw the familiar figure of Osman seated on a low three-legged stool outside the entrance of the school. He seemed to be enjoying the pleasant morning. The sun had just risen above the horizon and was draping the walls of the city in soft orange and yellow hues.

Souren went to the basement and rummaged through his mother's dowry trunk, which was filled with old-fashioned discarded clothes. He selected a few dresses and grabbed six pieces of silverware, which he wrapped in an old shirt. He shoved everything into a sack. Furtively, he crossed the street.

"What are you doing here?" Osman asked. "Do you want me to arrest you?"

The twenty-four hours were obviously up. He was offering Souren a friendly warning.

"Osman." Souren opened his bag and revealed the silk dresses. He could see this underpaid soldier wanted them.

"How much?" Osman inquired as he stroked the slippery fabric and admired the exquisite stitching of the lace.

"I want a uniform."

"You're joining the army?" Osman was surprised. He knew he was facing the elusive deserter the government wanted to find and march off to one of its hard-labor battalions.

"I want an army uniform and insignias."

"What kind?" Osman replied. "An officer's? That will be very hard to come by, Souren."

"No, not an officer. I'm joining the army band."

"Oh." Osman nodded. He remembered Souren played the piccolo.

"Go to Ali the peddler. His cart is over by the bazaar," Souren said.

"Sure, I know him. But when I get off, I have to stay at my post until I'm replaced."

"You don't get off for another two hours! Can you go the second you're finished?"

Souren reached deeper into the bag and whipped out the valuable silverware. The guard's eyes widened with desire.

"Get me that uniform, and you can have the dresses and the silver! But you have to hurry. I'll be waiting in the alley along the yogurt shop."

"Okay, okay," the Turk agreed. He hadn't been paid in three months. The fabric and silver would make him relatively rich for a short time. Even so, he fretted a minute or two before accepting with a slight slap of his right hand on his chest.

At the completion of his shift, Osman exited the quarter. He returned with a pack of clothes under his arm and met Souren in the designated alley. Souren inspected the garments. The coat was Turkish issue, the trousers German.

Osman moved his eyebrows quickly up and down, which could mean anything from "No" to "I tried my best."

"It was all he had," Osman pleaded with Souren's stern, silent gaze.

The boots were worn-out, but they would do. The belt looked almost new. The cap had tattered edges; nevertheless, it completed the uniform.

"What about the insignias? I need a musician's insignias," Souren said.

Osman answered quietly, "With this musician's coat, you don't need insignias—unless you are an officer, which you are not. Good-bye, and inshallah."

Back at his house, Souren stood before a mirror. He liked what he saw—a soldier. He stepped closer to investigate the tender mustache. It was sparse but, in time, would give him a certain degree of authority. Souren knew that a soldier without whiskers was useless. He would be considered a boy and elicit no respect. He opened an old wicker chest and dug out his piccolo. A rush of memories flooded him. This little tarnished piccolo he so proudly brandished for his Boy Scout marches would now be his ticket to safety if everything worked according to plan. He inserted it into his trouser pocket.

When Souren came down the stairs in uniform, Sophia could hardly believe what she saw. Souren was barely recognizable. The cap, which was gradually replacing the fez in the Turkish army, added years to his age. She even noticed the sparse mustache he'd just been grooming. She held his face gently in her hands and stared into his eyes. Then they hugged a farewell.

Souren walked to the barracks just a half mile from his home in the direction of the harbor. As he approached the military compound, he saw the band practicing vigorously. With a sidelong glance, the Greek band director looked at him inquisitively. After exchanging a few whispered words, the older man pointed at Souren's place in the band. Souren pulled out his piccolo and played as if he had always been a part of the group. Because of his uniform, his companions, mostly Greeks and Armenians, assumed that he had been officially assigned to this unit. His uniform also gave him access to lodging and ordinance in the barracks. Souren felt reassured by his current prospects.

After fifteen days at base camp, the order came for this unit to move to the front. At roll call, his subterfuge was discovered.

"Who are you?" the sergeant major, or *bascavus*, who administered the band inquired with raised eyebrows. "Where are your papers?"

Souren had anticipated such a situation. He reached into his pocket, withdrew two *medjidiyes*, and placed them in the official's hand.

The band administrator winked as he looked him in the eye and nodded slightly several times as if to say, "Okay, I won't expose you."

Souren retired to the dormitory and began to unbutton his uniform.

"Not so fast, piccolo man," a gruff voice behind him announced. "You are going to come with us."

Souren's heart raced as he turned around to face two Turkish guards. The bribed officer had reported him and probably even received a bonus for turning in an Armenian deserter.

The guards escorted Souren to a recently requisitioned Armenian ceramics and pottery factory that once produced plates, pitchers, and ornamental items. They took him twenty yards through a wide tunnel entrance between two shops, and under a bridge structure that housed an office. Souren stepped out of the corridor and into a dreary courtyard, where once merchants and manufacturers had located their shops. The shop doors still bore the names in Latin and English letters of former Armenian owners and artisans: Derderian, Kaloustian, Dadian, Kaprielian, Vartanian.

He noticed one wooden door on the opposite side of the courtyard. He did not have to go inside to know that behind it was a nauseating hole in the ground and a rusty pail for flushing. Soldiers stood guard along the walls, well armed and ready to fire on any man who might think of escaping.

Souren reckoned that he must be in the company of at least fifty deserters of all ages standing in small groups or sitting together on the ground. Many were in rags, some in mere vestiges of a uniform that they hadn't been able to shed before being captured as deserters.

We all share the same fate, Souren thought to himself. *We'll be marched to the most insecure and violent front or worked to death.*

"Souren!"

He recognized the voice and turned to see Ali the peddler, who was meticulously delousing his hair with a fine-tooth comb in the brightness of the sun.

"Ali? Why are you here?" Souren asked, incredulous.

"I'm a deserter like you, my son."

"You're too old to be a deserter! Besides that, you're half blind."

"That's exactly what I told them when they arrested me. They made me leave my cart right there in the street! I lost a fortune with those clothes, including some nice uniforms," he said as sadly as a rich man might who had lost his holdings in a bad investment. Actually, it was well-known that Ali had been collecting uniforms from army deserters.

Souren noticed that the old man had a black eye and bloodied lips.

"I fought them," Ali explained. Having no kerchief, he used his fingernail to scrape off the dried blood from the wounds. "What about you? What happened? That is a perfectly good uniform that I sold you and you now have on."

Souren just shrugged. He didn't feel like getting into it.

Ali didn't press him but pointed to the office over the entrance to the courtyard.

"You know what's going on up there?"

Souren looked up. "Let me guess, backgammon?"

Ali laughed. "You're close. It's a game, that's for sure. If you have fifty gold lira, you can purchase freedom for your male relatives. If you're rich, you don't have to fight the war."

"Fifty gold lira!" Souren exclaimed. "Shit! That amount would feed my mother and our neighbors on each side for nearly half a year!"

"Fifty for the government. But the officers get a percentage, too."

"That's Turkish patriotism for you," Souren scoffed.

Ali, now worked up, continued. "It's terrible. They raid homes and stores to get soldiers, while upstairs, the recruiting officer bargains for exemption fees with relatives."

Souren took a long look. He saw many important-looking men scurrying in and out of the office. In fact, there seemed to be more officials than *yorouks*, as common soldiers were called. These yorouks were normally fearless fighters, but months—years for some—of fighting with little food and no sanitation had ruined their morale and their health.

A seasoned warrior named Mehmet, a deserter, came and sat down next to Ali, his back against the cement wall. He told of his battles against what he called "the infidels," Christian soldiers from the likes of Bulgaria, Greece, and Italy.

"Let the cursed Young Turks fight their own battles! This makes fourteen times I've deserted the army. A few days of freedom are worth all the so-called victories in the world."

Souren noticed Mehmet's feet were bare. Neither his shirt nor his trousers looked like anything more than rags.

"Do you think they'll hang us?" Souren asked.

Mehmet laughed. "Can they hang us all? What of the army? More than half of the entire army is made of former deserters!"

Just then, an officer entered the courtyard and surveyed the pathetic group of men. He selected ten prisoners and marched them out.

"Where are they going?" Souren asked.

"If their families are rich and transfer everything to the government, they get to go home," Mehmet said. "If not, and the government wants to make examples of them, they'll be hanged. Otherwise, they'll go to the front to die of starvation, disease, or, more mercifully, from a bullet."

The dismal surroundings had not destroyed Souren's boyish appetite, and he was hungry as never before. He complained to Ali, and the peddler winked and pulled out a red kerchief. He opened it and displayed bread and olives. He presented it as if he were serving roast turkey on a silver platter. The food tasted good despite its musty odor. Olives certainly kept a lot better than bread did.

Seeing Souren and Ali eating, an envious prisoner started insulting them and threatened Souren, "Gorge your belly while you can, you filthy infidel! I'll wager that you'll soon be swinging from the gallows. You won't need any food there!"

Souren jumped up quickly, and, unable to swallow his last bite, he exclaimed, "Hanged? Wh-Wh-What do you mean? What have I done? I'm just sitting here!"

From the corner of the courtyard came a grunt. It was another prisoner—Bora, someone called him—who seemed to have been sleeping off a hangover. He wore the tattered and dirtied remnants of an imperial gendarme's brown uniform. The jacket was torn where a rank insignia once had been. Bora got up and ambled over to where Souren was standing. He stood much too close. His foul breath, yellow broken teeth, swarthy complexion, smallish black mustache, and watery wandering left eye made him grotesque.

"I'll tell you why you'll hang, you stupid infidel," he growled. "It's the design—the plan!" He smiled and paused to let his statement sink in. "I was the security aid to Mehmed Talaat Pasha. I've been everywhere with him."

"Then why are you here?" Souren asked, willing his voice to sound calm.

"I lifted a few lira from his desk and got caught. I was accused as a traitor and beaten." He showed Souren several bruises and scabs on his back and upper arms. "They sent me to a labor battalion, but I escaped. And now, I am about to hang—along with you." He chuckled again.

"You naive fool!" he continued. "Talaat and his Committee of Union and Progress have been arranging to purge the empire of all Christian dogs since the coup. Such will be better for Turkey's future." Bora widened his good eye and again smiled deviously at Souren, like a boy about to bite into a big piece of baklava.

Souren felt cold fear rise in his stomach and hot anger tighten his jaw. Oh, how he wanted to grab the filthy prisoner by his throat and kill him. With difficulty he controlled the urge and merely glared back at Bora, saying nothing.

As Souren was turning away, Bora chortled again.

"Wait, I have a something to show you."

The gloating prisoner reached inside his ragged coat and pulled out a crumpled, yellowed, and stained piece of paper. Handing it to Souren, he said, "If you can read, infidel, I am sure this will make your day."

Souren unfolded the paper and read as much as he could make out of the faded Turkish text. Across the top was "January 1915. Armenian Solution." Souren looked up. Bora was smiling at him like this was some sort of joke and Souren was about to come to the punch line. It read:

Close all Armenian Societies and arrest all who worked against the Government...Collect Arms...Excite Moslem opinion by suitable and special means in places where Armenians have already won the hatred of Moslems...provoke organized...Leave all execution to the people...and use Military...superficially to stop massacres, while on the contrary actively help the Moslems with military force...Apply measures to exterminate all males under 50, priests and teachers, leave girls and children to be Islamized...Carry away the families of all who succeed in escaping...On the ground that Armenian officials may be spies, expel and drive them out absolutely from every Government department or post...Kill off in an appropriate manner all Armenians in the Army...All action to begin everywhere simultaneously and thus leave no time for preparation of defensive measures...Pay attention to the strictly confidential nature of these instructions, which may not go beyond two or three persons.

On the one hand, Souren was incredulous, and on the other hand enlightened. It confirmed all the reports and rumors that the so-called Committee of Union and Progress was formally calling for the elimination of Armenians from the country and the confiscation of their possessions. He thought of his mother. He felt sick to his stomach, but he refused to give Bora the satisfaction he fiendishly awaited.

With a "you can't be serious" expression, Souren met Bora's smirk. He scrunched up the document and threw it at the feet of his would-be tormenter.

Bora adamantly insisted, "Oh no, no, no, this is no joke! My boyhood friend Ahmed Essad was the secretary at the meeting where it was agreed. It was a high-level secret session. Afterward, he asked me to make another copy of his notes. Only the top leaders were there—Talaat and Mehmed Nazim and Behaeddin Shakir, they presided."

He bared his jagged teeth again and said gleefully, "So, you wretched idiot, if not today, then tomorrow or the next day, you and I are destined to swing together!"

Souren sat down with a sigh. His heart raced as he contemplated this forecasted fate. He ached to pummel the disgusting prisoner, and he knew he was strong enough to do so. But once again his nightmare, desperately clinging to a monster's back, and his father's words intervened: *Use your mind!* Ever so slowly, panic gave way to courage and the mental pursuit of his options.

For his part, Bora became annoyed with Souren's unflappable demeanor, and seemed to give up. He picked up and unwrinkled the list of anti-Armenian policies. He folded it, shoved it into his coat, and went back to his corner.

Rumors began circulating among the prisoners to the effect that, since there were so many deserters, the officials were going to hang two of them in the city market as examples in order to improve the morale of the army. Naturally, the rest of the day was spent speculating who would be chosen.

"Allah be praised, it won't be me," whispered someone.

"Allah'a hamd", not me," sighed another.

As prisoners passed Souren, they looked at him with pity. But a glint in most of their eyes spoke of the satisfaction they felt at not being in his shoes.

"Why are they looking at me like that, Ali?" Souren asked in an anguished tone.

"Well, you're both a Christian and a deserter. You're the most likely victim, until they run out of Christians to hang. Then, the rest of us will do."

"Before I deserted last time—or was that the time before?" Mehmet said. "I can't remember which, but when I was in the army a few months ago, we got word that the Russians armed four units of Armenian volunteers. They put Armenian revolutionaries in charge of the troops."

"Russian Armenians?" Ali asked.

"Most are Russian, but they say some of these infidels have fled Turkey and gone over to the enemy. It's thought that the Russians are going to use them for some offensive, maybe in the Caucasus." He glanced at Souren, who kept his eyes fixed on the ground. "So that's why the government can claim that Turkey is justified in eliminating the rest of the Armenians now."

Souren wondered if his old friend Sarkis were one of those volunteers. A sense of pride welled up deep inside at the thought of his old friend fighting for the Allies and alongside fellow Armenians. How he yearned to do the same!

It was not difficult to guess which way the wind was blowing. All day long the prisoners speculated who would swing. As night approached, the hangman's noose seemed more real. Unable to sleep, Souren became engulfed in a wave of despair.

The thought of his aged mother at home alone became unendurable. He wrested his thoughts away from her, only for them to land on little Vartanoosh. Again and again her cries for help rang in his ears. *Why didn't I rescue her? Why did I just look from my room?* He pressed his hand to his face as if to cover his shame. *Maybe I would have gotten killed trying to help Bedros. But it would have been better than the cowardly death the Turks are now preparing for me.* After a long while, he finally quieted his spirit and pondered his alternatives.

How can I escape being hanged?

It occurred to him that the guards changed at four-hour intervals. They also wore uniforms not dissimilar from his own. This gave him a plan. He would wait for the changing of the guard. He'd get up, go over to the toilet, and reemerge with his railroad-issued pencil and pocket notebook in hand to stand near the door. He felt the pockets of his uniform to make sure he still had those items. He did. When new prisoners were brought in, he would ask them official questions in flawless Turkish. "Name? Age? Occupation? Offense that landed you here?" When the guards changed again, he would transfer out with them.

The new guards would not know him and would assume he had been given this authority. Some of his fellow prisoners might object. But, if they questioned him, he thought to himself, he would simply shrug his shoulders and remind them that it paid to be educated.

When the opportune moment came, Souren carried out his plan to the letter. Fortunately Bora was asleep, and none of his other fellow prisoners questioned him, and neither did the guards. At the second changing of the guards, he walked out with them, while the new shift stood at attention in respect for his pencil and paper.

Good-bye, jail, guards, and hangman's noose! Souren smiled to himself while strolling out and quietly whistling a Turkish military march. Winding through the streets, he went home. Sophia embraced him tightly, and almost immediately afterward, he went to bed, exhausted.

Suddenly, violent pounding rattled the front door, waking him. Souren jumped up and ran to Sophia. Pushing her into her bedroom, he commanded, "Hide in the armoire!"

The front door sounded as if it were being beaten down. But his initial fear somehow again made way to boldness. He opened the door.

A guttural voice yelled, "Halt!" Once again Souren felt the point of a bayonet in the hollow of his ribs. "No one is allowed to leave!" the policeman continued.

Realizing he had fallen asleep in his military uniform, Souren scowled back as he brushed imaginary dust off the brass buttons on his sleeves and firmly growled, "What do you want?"

The men were instantly taken aback at the uniform and the young man's tone. They lowered their guns, and one of them lumbered less aggressively forward.

"We are looking for a young Armenian deserter who is to be court-martialed," he said.

Souren again brushed his military sleeve to draw attention to his official status. He said there was certainly no such fugitive there but offered to help them search for the runaway reportedly hiding in the house.

He lit a candle, and the two followed him. They tore up all the beds. Chests were opened and the contents rifled. The soldiers neared the bedroom where Sophia was hiding. The officer threw open the door but came to a sudden stop. His eyes rested on a large portrait of Souren's brother-in-law, Dr. Otis Lamson, a distinguished physician in the United States.

"Who is that infidel?"

Souren knew he must draw the officer's attention away from her bedroom. "Why, Captain, don't you know? That is Shakespeare, the great American poet," he replied, purposefully botching the identity.

"Oh, of course!" said the commanding officer, hoping to appear knowledgeable in matters of classical Western literature.

"To be or not to be, that is the question," Souren recited in Turkish with a wry smile.

"Oh yes, I remember," said the Turk and followed Souren out of the room without going near the armoire in which Sophia was hiding.

Their search of the house complete, the soldiers departed, visibly disappointed at not having found the Armenian youth they had come to arrest. Souren ran up to his mother's room and threw open her hiding place. His mother's inert body fell out of the doorway. Her head smacked the floor and began to bleed. She lay motionless at Souren's feet.

"Mother!" He dropped to his knees and pulled her head into his lap. He wiped the blood from her face and forehead. "Mother!" he cried as he shook her.

Sophia's eyelids fluttered, and a wave of relief washed over Souren. He laid his mother on her bed and ran next door, calling for help. Maryam rushed in and immediately comforted her beloved neighbor. Another woman neighbor fixed the bed, and Souren helped lay his unconscious mother down.

He was still holding her cold fingers when she finally awoke and showed the desire to talk. Souren and Sophia both knew it had been too close a call. This was likely the last time they would have a chance to talk.

"The Committee of Three have issued communiqués that any action against Armenians is permitted as long as it feeds the committee's coffers and the Young Turks' military goals," she said. "They are free to wipe out any Christians who won't convert to Islam."

Sophia held the depressing view that eventually she and all Armenians in Smyrna would be given governmental deportation orders to march into the desert and either die of starvation or be shot. Souren still struggled to believe that Germany would not permit such a systematic economic and sectarian Genocide.

"The Germans I know in the orphanages and hospitals seem decent and fair-minded," he said. "Maybe German officers are the same and won't allow the deportations and killings."

Souren knew that his only hope lay in this possibility. In bidding farewell to his mother, he hugged her and spoke softly, "Somehow I will find the right general."

Brushing his military uniform, he crossed the street and called on Sister Henriette at the orphanage. He begged her to go with him to the German consulate with the plea to prevent the Turkish plans for deportation and the wholesale murder of the Armenians before it was too late. Sister Henriette had also long been troubled by the state of affairs and agreed to see if her status and connections would work. She and Souren made their way to the German consulate. After a short discussion with the consul, Souren was referred to the German military headquarters. When he arrived, an assistant to General von Sanders received him respectfully. But he said he was too busy to deal with him and so referred him to another department.

Unfortunately this department was headed by a Turkish officer. Without further ceremony, Souren was escorted out by two gendarmes and again thrown into jail. This time his jail was a dilapidated small room where, once again, deserters and criminals of all ages and colors were packed in standing rows, waiting to be sentenced. Exhausted and discouraged anew, he fell asleep leaning against the wall.

He woke with a start. It was morning. He'd missed his chance to escape. He was heartsick to find himself still surrounded by a bunch of prisoners. A guard handed out the morning ration of bread, but Souren waved him away.

He watched as a sentry walked in and called ten names. The sentry gave the brief explanation that those prisoners were apparently to be court-martialed in another part of the city. Souren saw this as another chance to escape. Sure, it was risky, but the alternative was the hangman's noose.

Pretending that he was one of those called, Souren fell into line. As the prisoners trudged along, he caught sight of his friend Ali, who silently saluted him with a knowing smile. Souren and the other prisoners walked single file toward the recruiting office, closely escorted by armed soldiers.

His steps slackened as a familiar thought crossed his searching mind. *An ounce of prevention is worth a pound of cure.* Souren could well remember his father bending over the pulpit with his right arm swaying upward and down as he inspired his attentive and devoted congregation. The memory worked like a tonic on Souren's tired nervous system. His dazed mind cleared, and his eyes searched for that "ounce of prevention" in the crowded, narrow streets of Smyrna.

A weary but ever-faithful donkey carrying his master rounded the corner just in front of the line of prisoners. To Souren, this was a splendid sight, for a donkey on this street could mean only one thing: a caravan of cud-chewing, stoical camels was about to claim the narrow street for themselves. Indeed, as Souren rounded the corner, he saw that pedestrians were pressed against buildings and stood inside doorways to make room for these beasts. The caravan was lugging ammunition—presumably from the wharfs to the railroad station, less than a quarter mile from Souren's home. Ammunition at the front was scarcer than men. Hence the camels with their bulging, deadly loads had the right of way.

The call to prayer rang out, "Allahu Akbar!"

Indeed, thought Souren. *Great was Allah who directed man to make the cobbled streets of Smyrna so narrow and so crooked with blind corners and alleys.* The march of the prisoners halted, and the men were pushed to the side to make room for the caravan.

Unexpected traffic ahead forced the caravan to stop. Souren saw his chance. He ducked his head to avoid being crushed against the protruding ammunition boxes on the back of an oblivious camel that seemed to welcome this unexpected pause. The space under the belly of the animal, between his front and hind legs, appeared as a door to freedom. No desperado had ever faced a more conveniently open gate for escape!

Souren's heart pounded as he anxiously looked both ways before lifting a corner of the heavy rug with the small fringe of bells that covered the camel's back. He stooped and quickly passed through the gap. His cheek rubbed against the camel's fur, the first time he'd ever been so close to one. His fear of being kicked and disemboweled by the surprised animal came second to his instinct to escape an even more likely death.

Catching his breath, Souren crouched forward and, with two steps underneath the camel, came out on the other side of the narrow street. His body still trembling as the caravan resumed its progress, he squeezed between a woman carrying a shopping bag and one of the new Turkish employees at the train station, who didn't recognize Souren in his military uniform. Souren was now slowly walking in the opposite direction of the line of court-bound prisoners. For him, freedom was again beckoning ahead.

As he passed the city hall, Souren saw that his name had already been posted on the wall. With a shiver of panic, now he knew for certain that he was on the list of fugitives expected to garnish the gallows that had been erected in the market area of the public square. Still, he mingled into the motley traffic with more confidence than fear. In fact, he felt almost bold. The successful escape and his convincing costume—a Turkish army uniform—filled him with considerable pride. He listened intently to the passing conversation among a group of soldiers. One spoke of a German commander in the nearby town of Gaziemir who was drilling Turkish forces for the Dardanelles. The success of an Allied submarine in penetrating as far as Canakkale and sinking a Turkish ship had instilled the fear of an imminent landing.

Souren lingered to catch more details. He caught enough of their discussion to sense that he might know of the general these Turks were talking about. He remembered vividly the German officer who had attended military concerts at which Souren had occasionally played. The evocation of Gaziemir and its music-loving commander echoed in Souren's mind. He pondered the possible prospects. He certainly could not go home. The authorities would be regularly searching his neighborhood and this time would discover his identity. That would mean certain death and also some terrible punishment for his mother. He felt that if he could somehow see that general, he could request a spot in the regimental band. The plan might have little chance of success, but it was all he could think of.

He walked to the train station, where his military uniform furnished him a free pass on the next train. When he arrived at the garrison in Gaziemir, he gained easy entrance. He made his way to the headquarters, a confiscated mansion owned by Armenian friends of the Tashjian family. He strolled in purposefully. His eyes darted around for the general's office. Spying it, Souren ducked through the doorway before he could be intercepted and stood before the general, who was bent over a map. The general looked surprised to see a young man in his office. Souren was relieved to see he'd been right, and the commander was the very same one he remembered as a fan of music. The general was rosy cheeked, handsome, and stately. He was about forty-five, and his benevolent smile took the edge off the forbidding monocle on his right eye.

Souren presumed the German officer spoke no Turkish or Armenian and wondered if he spoke English. Souren's parents' contact with German missionaries and the German consul in Smyrna had exposed Souren to that language. The only source of study had come from the German-English dictionary Sister Henriette had given him as a Christmas gift. Maybe this was enough. It seemed providential that his very life now depended on winning the favor of a German officer.

Souren saluted him with a quick nod of his head and a simultaneous click of his heels. "Excellency, *guten Morgen!*" He thought he saw a look of recognition from the general. He wondered if the German remembered him. While they had seen one another at a few musical events, they did not know each other. But after one performance, the general had personally expressed his pleasure in the rendition of a particular piece and had even stopped to shake the hand of each musician.

"I am the piccolo player you once met," Souren attempted to explain.

The general smiled at the boy's broken German and responded in French, which he spoke no better than Souren did his language.

"Mon general," Souren addressed him in French, "je suis un Arménien. Un déserteur."

Souren thought he saw the general's face register compassion and understanding. Hope swelled within, so he continued in French, "Remember the concerts in Smyrna you attended? I played the piccolo. We shook hands after the performance of Beethoven's *Moonlight Sonata*." Souren unbuttoned his coat and pulled out his piccolo. "Darf ich ein bisschen?" he added, wanting to win over the officer with knowledge of his mother tongue, albeit broken.

"Go ahead," the tall Prussian replied.

Souren performed a bit of the third movement from *Moonlight Sonata*. Some of the Turkish officials in the adjoining offices came out to listen.

"Who is that?" one of them whispered to another, though Souren could hear them well enough.

"A talented musician, it seems," the other replied. "At least he's earned a private audience with the commander."

"There's a war on, and he's granting auditions for the regimental band? Germans! So damn strange."

Souren did not look toward them but continued his concert for the general, who, obviously understanding no Turkish, could not hear his underlings confidently insult him in his presence. One of them called for a Turkish folk song. Souren ignored him and began another classical piece he was sure the general would recognize.

Smirking, the general held up his hand to signal to Souren his interview was over.

Souren stopped immediately. He felt his palms begin to sweat. The piccolo slipped from his hand, but quick reflexes allowed him to snatch it up before it fell to the ground. His heart raced. By now the other Turkish officers had returned to their desks. Souren stood before the general, wondering what he would do if he were denied a place in the band or, worse, if the general turned him in as a deserter.

They stared at one another for a moment. The general was pondering something, of that Souren was sure. He wanted to beg the man for help, to tell him of his widowed mother and of his escapes and of certain execution if he were captured, but he had to be careful not to invite any suspicion from the Turkish soldiers in the nearby rooms.

The general finally spoke. "What is your name, young man?"

"Herant," Souren replied. "Herant Tashjian is my registered name, sir."

"Report to the band leader, Herant. I think he could do with another piccolo."

Those words were music to Souren's ears. Indeed, a finer symphony had never been written! He thanked the general, saluted, and bid him good-bye in Turkish, just for the sake of any eavesdroppers.

As he left, Souren overheard the general say in German, "Sergeant Wagner, get me a list of deserters from Smyrna, and find out what you can about one named Herant Tashjian. And Sergeant, this is totally confidential!"

—⋙—

Since the German military mission of 1913, German officers had worked alongside their Turkish counterparts, attempting to re-build the Ottoman army into a reliable ally in the event of war. For their part, the Young Turk government used the Germans to bring their army forward and regain some stature in the world af-ter its humiliating defeats in the Balkans and against Italy in North Africa. Many problems manifested themselves in this symbiotic al-liance, not the least of which was language. German senior officers and Turkish junior officers and troops could barely communicate. In his interactions with the Turks, the general had been as often frustrated by the lack of adequate verbal communication as he was by cultural divides.

Tensions resulted from clashing mind-sets. A Prussian militaris-tic approach demanded punctuality and discipline. In his new com-mand in Turkey, the general was leading men whose conceptions of time and order were totally different from his own. To make matters worse, his Turkish interpreter was limited in German and often did not understand orders issued by the general. Because he knew no Turkish, the general was dependent on these inferior translations. There was no end to misunderstandings and mutual exasperation.

One evening, in advance of an important set of maneuvers, the general instructed the Turkish soldiers—through a translator—to report to a certain location at 4:30 a.m. the next morning. As he waited for the troops to arrive, the general grew angry and impatient.

"How in hell are we going to win a war if soldiers can't tell time?" he ranted to Sergeant Wagner. "What a bunch of idiots!"

He proceeded to punish the men and renounced the interpreter, who suffered not only the humiliation of his commanding officer's contempt but the soldiers' resentment as well. The poor fellow had not understood that the officer wanted the troops to assemble four and a half hours after midnight, not four and a half hours after sunrise, which was the Turkish method of telling time.

And so it came to be that a couple of weeks after Souren's appointment to the band, Sergeant Wagner handed him a slip of paper. Souren eyed him. He figured the man to be a little older than himself, perhaps in his midtwenties.

"From the general," the sergeant said tersely, then added something else under his breath. Souren did not understand his German, but he could read the man's face, which said something along the lines of, "Hey, don't screw this up!" Sergeant Wagner turned around and walked away.

What is he? Souren wondered. *Friend or foe?* The message ordered him to report to the general's office at 0500. Souren bounced back and forth between anticipation and dread. Was the general going to transfer Souren to a different unit because the authorities had discovered his deception? Would he have him arrested, and would he find himself yet again an imprisoned "deserter"? On top of those conflicting thoughts, Souren was unsure if he was to come at 5:00 a.m. Western time, as he'd been taught by the missionaries, or 5:00 a.m. Turkish time, which would be nearly forty-five minutes later. That night he didn't sleep. He stared into the darkness imagining a myriad of scenarios.

At two minutes before 0500, Souren knocked on the general's office door.

"Come in," a pleasant voice called.

Souren adjusted his uniform and passed his hand over his hair before replacing his cap. The general was not wearing his monocle. His arms rested between stacks of papers piled high on either side.

"Guten Morgen," the general said kindly, pleased with Souren's punctual arrival.

"Guten Morgen," Souren replied, caught between relief and panic.

"How is the regimental band, Herant? Are they good musicians? Are you happy with your commission?"

"Yes, sir, very happy, except..." Souren stopped. His German was muddled at best. The general waited.

"Except for what?"

"Well, you see, I can't read music. I play by ear. But so far, no one has noticed, because I rapidly memorize what I hear and just start playing along."

The general looked pleasantly accepting, which surprised Souren. Obviously, this meeting had nothing to do with his piccolo playing.

"Where did you go to school?"

"I attended the International College of Smyrna, sir."

"What sorts of classes?"

Souren happily rattled off his favorite studies. "Literature, French, English, mathematics, physics, biology, anatomy, physiology." He paused to remember more.

The general studied Souren. "What do you plan to do after the war?"

"I want to join the rest of my brothers and sisters in America and study medicine."

"A doctor?" the general said, seeming very pleased.

Souren explained that his brother-in-law, married to his oldest sister, was a highly respected surgeon in Seattle, Washington, who had promised to help Souren get into a good university. Souren continued and told the general that one of his brothers was a dentist in a town with a funny name—Kalamazoo. He explained that two of his brothers were engineers and that another of his sisters was an expert on Nathaniel Hawthorne. Every time Souren didn't know how to express himself in German, he'd switch to French or English. His German was limited to polite conversation, but his familiarity with French and English allowed him to express far more emotion and detail.

"Where did you learn German?" the general inquired. He leaned forward, folding his arms.

"My father and mother opened the girls' orphanage with the Deaconess mission," Souren replied with enough German for the general to comprehend.

"I've been to the orphanage in Smyrna. It is a fact that the Deaconesses' work extends around the world."

Souren heard the word "deaconess" and just pretended to understand the rest. He nodded. "One of my sisters attended the Deaconess college in Germany, sir. My parents were friends with the consul here in Smyrna when my father was alive."

"Can you guess why I've asked you here at this early hour?"

Souren understood the question. Again now, he was suddenly afraid. Was the general going to turn him in? Tell him he must flee because the authorities had told the general of an Armenian who was in their midst? All fear melted away when the general smiled warmly and motioned to Souren to sit down. The general explained that he needed a trusted, educated translator. He could protect Souren, and Souren could certainly help him. Souren could translate telegrams that were in Turkish and could also send telegrams. Moreover, he could help the general secure lines of communication between himself and his Turkish soldiers, whose language and ways were as perplexing now as they had been when the general arrived in Turkey the previous year.

The general told Souren he'd need to take a Turkish name for his own safety. He assured his new translator that an assumed Turkish name would do the trick.

The news that the general wanted to keep him on as a translator stunned Souren. The boy stood up in silent disbelief. The position he had been offered was beyond Souren's dreams.

"Well?" the general asked.

"Besherik," Souren answered without hesitation.

The general looked confused.

"I would like to take the name Besherik," Souren said. "That's the name I began using when you assigned me to the band."

"Very good. Besherik it is." The general jotted something down on a piece of paper and instructed Souren to exchange his military musician's coat for that of a regular soldier. "Just show this paper. If you have any trouble, come back, and I'll take care of things. Go ahead and bring your personal effects over now. You'll bunk with Sergeant Wagner."

Souren saluted the general and literally ran back to the band quarters. He grabbed his blanket and meager possessions, which included his trusty piccolo. Moments later, he entered the room where Sergeant Wagner was still asleep. He tiptoed to the empty bunk, sighed deeply as he lay down, and thought how incredibly lucky he was. His nightmare of desparately hanging on to the back of the fierce monster floated again into his mind. Less afraid now, he drifted into the first peaceful sleep he'd had in months.

Chapter Five

—⚋—

1915–1916

Telegraph wires clicked, and secret orders streamed out. Souren's unit was ordered to head to Selcuk, a new name for the ancient city of Ephesus, fifty miles from Smyrna. In 1914 the Young Turks had renamed the city to celebrate a conquest of the Seljuk Turks several centuries before. Souren and his new comrade, Sergeant Wagner, loaded the general's trunks onto the train. Souren was charged with the safe transport of the general's valuables, a job he took as seriously as the general did his command. Out of bitter experience, the general distrusted the Turkish attendants who had been assigned to him.

Souren stacked the trunks one on top of the other and took his station in the railroad car. Wagner jumped inside the same car and fastened the door from the inside with a chain and padlock. For the duration of the trip, the two men sat on a hickory chest next to a window where they could watch the countryside and keep an eye on anyone who came near the car.

After almost two hours, the train slowed down, and Souren knew they were approaching the station. He stared expectantly out the window, waiting to catch sight of the immense arched bridges that he knew stretched along the tracks.

"Almost close enough to touch," he said softly.

He recognized the ancient aqueduct that had been built to carry water from rivers in the mountains. On these massive structures, a vital stream of water flowed to the city's inhabitants.

As the train stopped, Souren heard one of the soldiers cry, "Hadji Baba!" Wagner unlocked the door and peered out to see what all the commotion was about.

"Hadji Baba!" One of the soldiers pointed toward the sky, to a pair of majestically soaring storks overhead, long legs dragging behind, necks folded, and wings outstretched.

Another shouted, "Aleikoumi es Salaam! Khosk gueldiniz, Hadji Baba!" (Peace be with you. Welcome, Father Pilgrim!).

Wagner elbowed Souren and gave a disparaging look as he tossed his thumb in the direction of soldiers hollering up to the pair of the elegant, angular birds.

"The Turks are very superstitious, Wagner," Souren explained. "They call the stork Hadji Baba, which means 'Father Pilgrim.' For them, it's either a good or a bad omen. If his beak is pointing down, as that one's was, he has said to them, *'Salaam Aleikoum!'* 'Peace be with you.' That is why the soldiers called back to him, *'Aleikoumi es Salaam.'"*

Souren continued, "The Turks anxiously watch for storks this time of year because they believe these birds are returning from their annual pilgrimage to Mecca. The position of the beak is interpreted as a prophesy about the coming years."

"We should ask them if we're going to win the war," Wagner added sarcastically.

"Careful," Souren warned the sergeant. "This is no joke to them."

The German cursed under his breath and shook his head.

The two began unloading the general's trunks from the train car.

It was raining when Souren stepped off the train and right into a puddle. He slipped on the muddy bottom, lost his footing, and fell, sitting straight down. Wagner, still on the train, laughed his head off.

Souren turned, ready to shout a string of Turkish profanities at Wagner, when the general approached. Surprised to see him, Souren remained sitting in the mud in a state of utter confusion.

"Take my things to the Austrian house. You know where that is, I presume?" With a wink, he turned around and marched off.

Over his shoulder, the general called out, "Get a few porters to carry these trunks, and don't leave them unattended while you're enjoying your little bath."

"Yes, sir!"

Souren stood up and cautiously made his way around the corner of the station to find some porters to haul the heavy trunks. By this time, Wagner was wiping tears of laughter from his eyes as he watched Souren walk sideways to hide his muddy backside, which looked like a wet, heavy sack of manure.

Souren signaled to the porters who were standing around the station, waiting for work. They were easy to spot because their lifelong job of carrying heavy burdens had left them permanently stooped. Deftly, each one fit a trunk in a loop made from a large leather strap, hefted it onto his back, and stabilized the weight by running the strap across his forehead and bending forward as he transported the burden.

They arrived at the two-story house formerly used by an Austrian archaeology team. The British had originally led and financed the unearthing of the ruins, but in 1905, when the political climate changed in favor of the Austrians, the Ottoman government suspended British archaeological work in preference to the Austrians. The house was abandoned by them at the start of the war but now was to serve as army headquarters. In a short time, officers had occupied the building and made themselves at home.

The next day Souren trudged through the mud up to the castle at the top of Ayasuluk Hill. He sat on a large stone jutting out from one of its walls, leaned back, and stared thoughtfully toward the heart of ancient Ephesus, nearly two miles distant. It stretched along the crest of the Bulbul and Panajir Hills in the lush Meander Valley, prominent from time immemorial for fertile land and harvests of succulent grapes, sweet figs, and amber honey. This was the Ephesus immortalized in the Bible, now reduced to ruins.

A steady rain penetrated Souren's shirt and trousers. He shuddered from the cold. Tents where soldiers sought refuge from the rains dotted the hill.

Souren shook his head and said, "How has it come to this?"

He knew he should be grateful to be alive and to have escaped from a court-martial. Yet, he was growing impatient to find the Allied lines and to join their side in this gigantic struggle of a world at war. He thought back on the night before, when he had comfortably filled his belly with schnitzel and mashed potatoes. Lucky for him, the German officers maintained their familiar diet even in war. Moreover, he slept under a roof and in dry quarters.

The town, in contrast, was not faring well. The villagers handed their sparse food over to soldiers. They couldn't refuse them without inviting reprisals against which they had no defense. Even if the locals had something left after the recent harsh winter, there would not be enough to feed the hundreds of soldiers encamped on and around Ayasuluk Hill.

The population of locals had likewise shifted, as the surrounding towns and villages had been home to many Greeks just the year before. But the boycott and the government's policy of intimidation—the same dark forces that had resulted in Nikkos's murder—had driven longtime residents from their homes and vineyards. Ephesus and its environs were now populated mostly by Turkish residents.

Souren stared beyond the three-cornered tents and out toward the plain, past the spot where ancient Ephesus rose to greatness. He saw only a marshy, mosquito-infested swamp that archaeologists believed had once been a harbor.

He sighed heavily.

The more he considered his situation, the more anxious he became. He'd read the telegrams to the general reporting the morbid fate of labor battalions—battalions that were designed specifically for the extermination of military-age Armenian men. Even some German higher-ups wanted Armenians deported from the Eastern Front, but the ones Souren knew personally, including his own commander, opposed the violent means.

Recently a telegram had come with news that an Armenian town called Van was under siege and holding out against Turkish forces. To keep up appearances, Souren feigned disgust at the Armenian revolutionaries purported to be leading the resistance against Turkish forces. However, inside he rejoiced and tried to figure out a way to join his countrymen. It was a seemingly impossible expectation, but he could not stop wishing he were fighting alongside his fellow Armenians, whatever the odds.

"So that's Ephesus?" Wagner asked as he made his way to join Souren.

Souren grabbed Wagner by the hand and hoisted him up the final step. Three days of steady rain had made the climb to the top a very slippery business. The rain had stopped, but thick gray clouds hung over the land.

"Actually, this is Ephesus, too," Souren replied.

"I thought this was Selcuk."

"It's only been called Selcuk for a year. A year ago, it was Ayasuluk. Before that, Hagios Theologos, because the apostle John was viewed as a holy theologian who was believed to have lived here. And before that, the place we are standing was considered part of Ephesus."

"So was the castle built as a fortress against the mosquitos?" Wagner joked.

Souren contemplated the large fortress behind them.

"Not exactly. It was built by the Byzantine Christians around the sixth century. And that was a church." Souren pointed to a spot farther down the hill. "According to a legend, Saint John is buried on that spot, so Emperor Justinian erected the basilica there. And according to tradition, Saint John stood on this hill and prayed for universal peace."

"It's hard to believe the sea reached those hills at one time," Wagner said. "But I guess that's good for us for right now because the British and French fleets can't shell our position." He chuckled.

"And you know what, Wagner?" Souren said, pointing to a mound with blocks of cut stones and huge column drums lying helter-skelter. "That's all that's left of the magnificent Temple of Artemis, one of the Seven Wonders of the Ancient World!"

Souren explained to Wagner that the goddess worshipped by the Greeks as Artemis, and by the Romans as Diana, had inspired construction of a magnificent temple that regularly brought thousands of pilgrims to the shores of Ephesus.

Wagner raised his hand and announced, "Okay, history class is over! Let's go to the tavern and dry out a little bit. I'm tired and cold! Time to be tired, cold, *and* drunk!"

Upon entering the dingy pub, Mustafa, the generals's secretary, called Souren to the corner where he sat alone.

"An order by the war department is circulating through every regiment, demanding that a Herant Tashjian be arrested and sent to Ankara for court-martial," he whispered hoarsely. "The strange thing is, the commander burned the whole batch of documents from headquarters that included reports about this man." Eyeing Souren with a look of suspicion, he added, "Besherik, why would he go through so much trouble to save one Armenian?"

Souren had never told Mustafa who he was, and tried to reflect a look of confusion about this startling disclosure.

"The government is hunting him down. They fear he knows too much about military installations in Smyrna and that he's trying to defect to the enemy. He's probably alive only because of our gracious commander. Tell him that if you ever meet up with him," Mustafa added.

"Sure," Souren agreed, staring right back. "If I ever meet him, I'll tell him."

Souren, shaking from the encounter with Mustafa, walked out of the tavern and through a light rain toward the ruins of ancient Ephesus. He wanted to escape his self-accusations of cowardice and selfishness.

Through the city ran a wide road paved with flagstones laid by Roman engineers. It was furrowed by the tracks of chariots. He passed the Celsus Library, not yet fully excavated. Souren eyed the Roman viaducts, castles, and fortifications, reminders of the city's past glory. He strolled past torn-down altars and temples, the remains of an ancient culture. He shook his head upon beholding Greek marble statuary, all decapitated by the invading Seljuk Turks. He paused to examine the huge wall of the city that showed traces of repairs from the Greek, Persian, and Roman eras. At a glance, the history of mankind's effort at supremacy unfolded before him.

Without thinking, Souren walked to the very spot that held delightful memories from his innocent school days. The faculty at the American school brought their pupils on an annual outing to Ephesus, and the afternoon was spent playing a fast game of rugby on a flat area within the fallen walls of the vast Artemision, as the once grand Temple of Artemis was known.

That was indeed a great day. The boys from the American school were allowed to meet the students of the girls' school and perhaps exchange a few words in spite of watchful eyes. The joint picnic took place in the open space of the ancient public square, once called the Agora. Souren lingered there, remembering the pretty girls and wondering what had become of them since. He thought of his friends who had been drafted. He remembered Armen and their hard-fought marble games when they were little boys. Pleasantly nostalgic, Souren roamed the area reliving better times.

He left the Agora, crossed the stone road, and climbed toward the top of Mount Prion, another splendid site that archaeologists had undertaken to restore. Into its side, an amphitheater had been built with the idea of getting a bird's-eye view of Ephesus. At a distance he saw a shadow creep out from under a huge boulder. It stopped every few feet, looked around cautiously, then picked wild berries from a bush.

Souren's curiosity led him to follow the creature. With measured and careful steps, he descended the ruins of the Grecian amphitheater and crept into the arena, hiding behind fallen marble columns without being seen.

To his astonishment, what he thought was a wild animal turned out to be a little girl in rags with long, unkempt hair tied in bundles with little red strips of cloth. She was digging roots with the long nails of her thin fingers. Souren lost his footing, slid, and stumbled on a boulder. She raised her head and saw him, ran, and crawled under the iron door of a stone cave that in ancient times had been a den for wild beasts. Now it contained a number of old statues locked away by the excavators before they reluctantly retreated ahead of the Ottoman army.

The space between the iron door and the stone wall was narrow, and Souren could not get in. But he could see the little girl crouched in a corner, scared like a trapped animal. He called to her in Turkish and then in Greek. She would not answer. He jarred the iron door and pulled the thick, rusty chain lock.

She screamed in Armenian, "*Mayrig, Mayrig!*" (Mother, Mother!).

"Don't be afraid, little girl," Souren replied.

He recognized her as an Armenian orphan hiding from the soldiers.

He implored her to come out. He told her that he was a brother Armenian and stretched his hand toward her to coax her from her refuge. She put a finger in her mouth and shook her head while her almond eyes shone in the dark cave like two diamonds. Souren must have done something to gain her trust, for she crawled out. The frightened eyes had slowly changed, and as she approached, Souren could see tears of relief for having found a kindred soul.

"*Agchigus*," Souren repeated. "My little girl. Don't be afraid. Where do you come from? How long have you been here? My name is Souren, and I'm from Smyrna."

The little girl at once recognized him.

"Souren?" She threw her arms around him, kissed his hands, and rubbed them against her cheeks. He could hardly believe what he saw. This was his neighbor's little daughter, Vartanoosh. She was more like a shadow of an old woman.

As he looked again into the cave, he saw that with great effort she had built for herself a safe and warm nest. He saw she had gathered some rags, a little hay and straw, and had put aside a few nuts and some red berries.

"Souren, have you heard anything about my father?" She explained to him that the soldiers couldn't have killed him. "He was always so good to everybody; even the Turks liked him."

Souren didn't know how long they sat reminiscing about life in Smyrna before her little tired head was on his knee and she was sound asleep.

He continued to come every two or three days to bring her food. Though her situation was a dire one, he felt some satisfaction in providing her with a blanket and a pillow.

One day when the two sat talking, Wagner stood on a fallen pillar and called anxiously for Souren.

"Return to headquarters immediately! The commander is very sick!"

Souren hurriedly told Vartanoosh to go back to her hiding place and assured her he would come again soon.

She scrambled back into her cave, and Souren sprinted to headquarters.

Souren entered the commander's room and saw him heaving in agony. He was burning up with fever and shaking with chills.

"He's been vomiting nonstop the last few hours," Sergeant Wagner explained.

"Malaria!" Souren announced.

"I know," the general muttered weakly. He opened his eyes, looked around, squinting. Recognizing his attendants, he asked for water and some quinine. Then he motioned his translator to come close. Souren leaned over the bed.

"I want a *real* doctor!" the general said in English to avoid being heard by eavesdropping soldiers. "Take my horse."

Souren understood. His commander did not want to become the patient of the Turkish doctor assigned to this unit. The man was rarely sober and made no secret that he detested Germans. Souren left immediately. He rode the commander's horse hard and fast all the way to Kusadasi, a port city twelve miles southwest of Selcuk. In less than two hours, he had returned with an army doctor, an Armenian who, after conducting a careful examination, reassured everyone that the commander was doing as well as could be expected.

"He must not be disturbed," the doctor emphasized. He left instructions with Souren on administering quinine, an antimalarial drug. He also told Souren to telegraph him immediately if the general were to take a turn for the worse.

Souren's expression turned from relief to fear.

"But I don't expect that to happen," the doctor reassured him warmly. He stared at the young man for a few seconds, thinking he knew this Turkish soldier. Souren shrank under the doctor's scrutiny.

There were other attendants and guards, but Souren remained at the general's door for three days and nights, ready to answer when the commander called. He ached at the prospect of losing the officer, who had become almost as dear to him as his own father. Souren could not help worrying about what would happen to him if the general either died or was removed from command and sent to Constantinople to recover. What if his illness were so serious he was sent back home to Germany to convalesce? The uncertainties plagued Souren's sleep and gnawed at his nerves each day.

The day the general began to sweat profusely, the men celebrated, for it meant he had entered the last stage of the attack. Souren stared in admiration at his beloved commander, who had by now kicked off his wool blankets. Eleven ugly scars, wounds received in Belgium, made him seem so much more human to Souren, while at the same time making him feel he was in the presence of the bravest man he had ever known.

By the fourth day, the commander had recovered considerably and was able to sit up. Souren, who had kept a constant vigil, had barely eaten in all that time. His fears allayed, he acknowledged the sharp pangs of hunger and happily strolled into town in search of a feast of fresh fruit, bread, and hot tea to celebrate this wonderful day.

The commander's official interpreter was a Turk who had studied in Germany. However, his family lived in a nearby town, so he often could not be found when the general wanted him, and the commander came more and more to rely on Souren.

"Your German is improving," he would tell him.

What he didn't know was that while Souren may have understood a German or French order the commander issued, he would not necessarily know the corresponding Turkish military terms. Sometimes, he didn't even understand an order given in German that he was supposed to translate to the regimental officers. In that case, he used the military terms he did know in Turkish. It would be no exaggeration to say that the less Souren understood a command from the general, the more emphatic and vigorous his translation of it. Mostly, he managed to keep a straight face when things went haywire, but he wasn't always so lucky.

One morning a telegram came announcing that Prince Schaumburg von Lippe would be arriving by train at three o'clock that afternoon.

"The prince is coming to inspect our section," the general informed Souren. "Meet him at the station, and give my regrets for not being there. Provide whatever he requests. Our soldiers are under his orders."

The commander, still weak from his bout with malaria, used his recent illness as an excuse to avoid this distraction from more pressing concerns.

"Wagner," Souren said, "I am going to meet His Excellency, the Prince. How shall I address him? How do you say, uh, 'those boxes' and everything? You know, uh—"

"Oh," Wagner replied, "that is easy. You salute His Excellency and say, 'Sind dies die ganzen Klamotten?'"

"Sind dies die kazen Gla—"

"Sind dies die ganzen Klamotten," Wagner corrected him.

Souren brushed lint and dust from his jacket, gave his shoes a new coat of polish, and made sure that the iron horseshoes on his heels would give the right clang when he saluted the prince. How strong and important those shoes made him feel. He landed a few goose steps to give himself confidence.

"Sind dies die ganzen Klamotten?" he repeated over and over.

His biggest worry at the moment was the little mustache he was busy shaping. He had tenderly watched it grow thick enough to be visible and to display its authority. He put a final touch of wax to his new crop of mustache and twisted the ends to make them curl "à la Wilhelm."

He looked at his reflection and said politely and confidently, "Sind dies die ganzen Klamotten?" He saluted his reflection and rushed to the station. He shook with excitement at such an important honor as greeting a German prince!

Just before the train pulled in, the station was cleared of inquisitive locals. Souren, a Turkish officer, and the stationmaster awaited their guest. The prince, with a cane in hand, stepped out of the train as if he were a celebrated monarch gracing his subjects with an appearance. He must have been disappointed at the small delegation standing on the platform. Souren thought the man looked like the picture of the Smith Brothers stamped on the box of cough drops his mother kept at home. Twelve German sailors and officers followed behind the prince. Souren offered the regrets of his commander.

A clamorous squawking turned the heads of all. One of the prince's attendants set two large cages on the platform and turned back toward the train car from which he had just emerged. The birds continued their noisy protest. The attendant stepped out again with another cage. This one held half a dozen canaries.

Souren glanced at the Turkish officer standing next to him and whispered in Turkish, "Is this man fighting a war?"

The sound of barking dogs drowned out the canaries and the parrots. The prince, an avid hunter, had come prepared for an expedition. The collection grew as more and more metal trunks, boxes, and bags—a collection of presents from every front he had visited—continued to be unloaded.

Souren approached Prince von Lippe with military precision. Clicking his heels and saluting, he said, "Excellency, sind dies die ganzen Klamotten?"

The prince stared back with a puzzled mien.

Thinking he hadn't been heard, Souren repeated himself with more authority and increased volume. Some in the prince's entourage chuckled. As for the prince, he slapped his thigh and threw back his head. His mouth opened wide, and he let out a loud, inelegant guffaw. The screeching and chirping of the exotic birds, the barking of the anxious dogs, and this caricature of a clown made Souren feel like he was at the circus, not an army headquarters.

A flush of heat burned his cheeks. They were laughing at him, but he didn't know why. He cast a sidelong glance at the Turkish officer, who merely shrugged. Souren looked down to quickly assess his uniform. He didn't understand what was so funny.

In broken Turkish, the prince thanked Souren.

Souren raced back to the commander.

"What's the matter?" the commander inquired. Souren had burst into his quarters, startling the general. "What is it? Has something happened to the prince?"

"Nothing. Nothing…" Souren was out of breath.

"He asked Prince von Lippe, 'Sind dies die ganzen *Klamotten*?'" Wagner volunteered from the doorway.

The commander smiled broadly. It was the first time since his illness that Souren had seen him this animated. It was unfortunate that his being the butt of a joke brought the commander to life.

"Wagner, why must you torment the boy?"

To Souren he said, "Wagner gave you the wrong word. Instead of 'Gepäck,' he had you say 'Klamotten.' Consequently, you asked the prince, 'Is this all the junk you have?'"

Souren shot an angry look at Wagner, but he and the general were laughing so hard that Souren gave up being embarrassed and joined them. With precision, he imitated the prince standing with his cane in one hand and his gloves in the other. He described the spectacle of birds, slobbering dogs, and the many boxes and bags of war curios that the prince had been collecting during his clandestine military inspections of defenses.

"Is this how he fights a war? I had to call twenty soldiers to move his junk!" This time Souren used 'Klamotten,' and the three men dissolved into renewed laughter.

—◊—

Kemal was the commander's attendant. He was punctual, alert, and always wore a crisp and clean uniform. He spoke very little German but did all he could to anticipate the general's needs, including memorizing the general's schedule. Each night, he laid out his uniform for the following day, making sure it was fit for the occasion. He was always at hand to bring the general his meals and drinks. When the commander fell ill, Kemal said prayers constantly for him.

One day the commander called in Souren and Wagner and told them that the lock on one of his trunks had been broken and twenty Turkish lira stolen. During his illness, only certain individuals had been allowed into his room.

Souren swore he hadn't robbed the general, who replied, "Don't worry. I'd never suspect you." Nor did the commander consider Wagner a thief. Mustafa, the secretary, was ruled out, which left only one person.

"Kemal!" Wagner said.

"Dammit!" the commander yelled.

"He's the only one who was ever in here alone with you."

"He's right, sir," Souren added. "I was outside your door all four days. Only Kemal had access to those trunks when no one was around."

"Make certain of this before you have him arrested," the commander replied.

Wagner, a born Sherlock Holmes, assured the general he knew how to get to the bottom of it.

"Leave it to me, sir. By tomorrow, you'll have your criminal and his confession."

That evening, Wagner invited Kemal to join him and Souren at the tavern.

"What's this?" Kemal asked.

Souren explained that it was Wagner's birthday and this was how Germans celebrated the occasion.

The unsuspecting Kemal eyed the food greedily. It was wartime, and this lavish spread defied blockades and bombings. He ordered a whole keg of cherry wine to be brought to the table, and he emptied one glass after the other.

At the proper moment, Wagner sprung into action.

"I'll wager that I can drink more than anyone else in the army," he challenged Kemal and Souren.

Kemal winked at Souren and said in Turkish, "Besherik, does this German think he can outdrink a couple of Turks?"

Souren nodded at Kemal and held up his glass.

Kemal threw a lira on the table and emptied his glass as if it were an act of patriotism.

Wagner followed suit and tossed two liras on the table.

Kemal laughed and poured himself another drink. After he finished, he tossed another lira onto the growing pile of coins. The contest continued until Kemal had dished out fifteen liras.

The following morning, Hallis Bey, the Turkish interpreter, who happened not to be at his village visiting family, held court and asked Kemal to confess, but the commander's attendant adamantly denied it, even swearing on Mohammed. Then, the interpreter called in the *chavoush*, a sergeant, an infamous man, who had the power to force one to divulge his innermost secrets against his will. Kemal quivered when the torturer entered the room.

He snarled at Kemal, "You can't fool me!" and banged both his fists against Kemal's head. "Tie up the bastard!" he bellowed. "And bring him around."

With a violent jerk, he pulled the prisoner aside and threw him on the floor. Kemal, unable to move, crouched helplessly. He covered his head with his arms and begged for mercy. The chavoush ordered his arms and legs tied and made him kneel. Then he delivered twelve painful lashes to the soles of poor Kemal's feet, which changed color and size with each powerful strike. Confessions and supplications followed amid crying and yelping.

That afternoon, Souren found Kemal scrambling up to the loft of an old barn. His bloodied feet could bear no weight, so he pulled himself up by his hands and scooted forward on his knees. Souren felt sorry for him. Yes, he had made a grave mistake by stealing from the general. But Kemal was sorry, Souren could see that much. That he was a thief did not enter into Souren's mind. Kemal was suffering and needed help.

During an agonizing week in his dark, filthy quarters, Souren took the prisoner water and food and also dressed his wounds. He who had been the general's attendant, who had worn a pressed uniform, was now nothing more than a pathetic liar whose confession had been beaten out of him. Later that month, Kemal was sent with one of the battalions to the Caucasus.

—◆—

It was Christmas Eve, a homesick Christmas, which made Souren revolt against the gods of war, in this case men like Kaiser Wilhelm, Enver Pasha, Lloyd George, Czar Nicholas II, and Georges Clemenceau, leaders who had jumped at an excuse to expand their empires. As Souren saw things, the world had gone crazy trying to wipe out a civilization wrought by centuries of arduous toil and patience, tearing ruthlessly at its very foundation with teeth sharpened by scientific efficiency. What he did not yet know, and could not even have imagined, was that this war would generate inventions to destroy on an unprecedented scale.

Wagner lay stretched out on his cot, talking about his wife and infant son, who were to have Christmas without him.

"My son was born six months after I left Berlin, and I have not seen him except in a photograph." He grabbed the wine on the floor beside him and finished off the last quarter of the bottle in remarkable time.

Sergeant Wagner was the typical German soldier, a sternly disciplined machine who would not hesitate to do whatever was required for his fatherland. But after enough drinks, he turned melancholy.

"I was one of the first to enter Liège under General von Kluck. We did horrid things to the Belgians. We tore down houses where machine guns were suspected. We didn't know if they were really there." He wept softly and then shouted, "Deutschland über Alles!"

Souren was unsure how to respond. He felt uncomfortable when Sergeant Wagner rambled on like this.

"How long do you think this war will last?" Wagner asked. "I wish they would blow up every goddamn thing! If I were Hindenburg, I'd gather my forces—all the artillery, ammunition, and soldiers—and make a sweeping dash to Paris. This trench warfare is consuming us all!" He paused angrily. "Lucky you're not married."

The sergeant took the treasured photograph from his pocket and held it. Souren stared at the child resting in his mother's arms while she smiled brightly into his innocent face.

"That's Fritz. They say he has golden curls, and his blue eyes are just like mine." Wagner was at that moment a proud, happy father. "And what a smart boy! He has already learned to say 'Papa.'" His expression suddenly turned dark, and his voice struck a melancholy tone. "But who knows when I will see him?"

Unnerved by Wagner's descent into depression, Souren tried to cheer him up. "No use worrying," he said naively. "The war will be over soon. Everyone says so. Let's go to the tavern and drink. Drink and be merry!"

"It is Christmas!" the sergeant hollered.

To Souren's relief, Wagner did not take much convincing. The two war-weary soldiers walked to the tavern, a dingy, dilapidated old shack, determined to celebrate.

"Here's to Fritz. May he never wear the uniform!"

Wagner emptied his glass in one swallow. He filled it again and raised his glass. "To your health, and may the war end soon!" He polished off the second glass.

The scarlet liquid, though innocent looking in the *bardak*, when emptied into their stomachs, made the two feel like kings and gods. They ordered more drinks to be brought to their table. Barbed wire, trenches, and machine guns had faded from their minds like ghosts. It was Christmas, and they were exceedingly happy.

Two Turkish soldiers stumbled in, already drunk. Souren and Wagner ordered the old, hunchbacked innkeeper to serve them drinks. It was their Christian holiday, and they celebrated it by sharing wine and ouzo, a sweet liqueur that tasted like licorice. Two street musicians joined the party, and everyone danced and sang to the strains of Oriental music. The last bugle call to retire rang in their ears like a black omen.

"Damn this war!" Souren murmured. Wagner nodded.

The two Turkish soldiers were helped out by the anxious inn-keeper. They cursed and departed noisily.

Before Souren and Wagner could leave, the commanding Turkish officer came in. He held the rank of major, was half drunk, and dragged along a young woman who was dressed in an exquisite Oriental costume under her *charshaf* and veil. Her silk headgear was braided in gold, and an open breast wore a large necklace of golden coins. On her bare, slender arms, she wore bracelets of precious stones worn in serpentine fashion. The tips of her ringed fingers and nails were tinged red from henna.

Souren and Wagner started to stand at attention, but the major gestured for them to sit back down. "Celebrating your holiday?" he asked Sergeant Wagner. When Wagner nodded, the officer ordered drinks and threw a handful of coins to the musicians. "Dance for my German friends," he said to the woman. "It's their holiday, and they deserve a gift."

She threw back her veil, took the tambourine from the musicians, and danced. Her whirling motions were graceful and emotionally expressive, but her black eyes were fiery and spiteful. She tiptoed, then knelt at intervals, banging her tambourine on her elbows and knees as if the wildest daughter of the Ottomans was trying to allure Souren and Wagner with her Oriental charms and voluptuous motions. Suddenly she became mad, furiously mad, and looked at her master in disgust. Just as quickly she changed her expression to a trance of total abandon.

The gypsy pulled out two red silk handkerchiefs. One represented the dancer herself, the other her soon-to-be-selected lover.

She took a corner of each handkerchief into her teeth and breathed on them, symbolically imparting life. She laid them on the floor gracefully. Then she danced around and between them.

She tucked opposite corners of both handkerchiefs into the waistband of her trousers so that they hung like bags at her sides. She reached into them and gestured to signify that the bags were empty. She pretended to receive gifts and to fill the silk bags with them. With a flourishing gesture, the gypsy released a corner of each kerchief to spill the imagined contents. Playfully, she kissed one of the fluttering kerchiefs, then slowly passed it between her breasts, down her body, and threw it in a wad at Souren.

The men whistled and clapped. Souren blushed. Wagner pushed him out of his chair in the direction of the hypnotizing girl. He had to join her. It would be bad manners if he did not. For his part, Souren yearned to dance with her, but he hesitated. He had never danced with a girl. It had been sternly forbidden in his home and at school.

The beautiful girl tantalized him as she waited, twirling her handkerchief in midair and staring straight into Souren's eyes. Had he not consumed several drinks in the course of the evening, he might not have mustered the courage to cross the floor and seize the dancer into his eager arms.

Next he was waking up on his cot, with uniform and shoes still on. Through the fog in his aching head, he remembered that they had danced, alternatively softly, then with fierce passion. For how long, he did not know.

—w—

It was after midnight. Souren hadn't slept much the last couple of days. Every time he closed his eyes, he saw his beautiful dancer. He could not get her off his mind, day or night. He relived the moments he could recall: her red hand tattoos; her blousy, silky trousers that sat low on her hips; her dark brown hair that had been coiled on top of her head; stray tendrils that had framed her perfectly oval face. Her large eyes had bewitched him, and he could not break their spell. He could not get her out of his mind.

The stress in his body became so tense that he had to rise from his cot and walk around. Not wanting to waken Wagner, he soon found himself strolling aimlessly outside, breathing deeply and bemoaning his misery. His agitation increased until he finally admitted to himself that, for the first time in his life, he had fallen in love. As fate would have it, the object of his fascination was a complete stranger, a woman of little virtue who made her living dancing in taverns.

As he walked along a row of residential houses, he was stopped by the faint sound of a cry. Just as he felt a chill breeze against his face and neck, he heard the sound again. He was certain this time that it was a young girl's voice.

The moon peeked out from behind the black clouds. The faint voice compelled him forward, so he walked in its direction until he stood a few steps away from what he recognized to be the Turkish commander's home, consisting of two contiguous buildings, one of which housed his three wives. He followed the voice, trying to confirm whether the lyrics were in Armenian.

"Is this real?" he whispered aloud to himself. "It's a Turkish officer's house. I must be losing my mind!"

Even so, he stood rooted at the spot because just then he heard another string of syllables in his native tongue. Souren made sure no one had spotted him as he crept still closer, close enough to hear clearly the soft, sweet voice singing an Armenian lullaby:

Lie still, Pallig
In your dreams so sweet
I'll pray while you rest and sleep in peace
On your silken tresses
On your rosy cheeks
I'll stamp in the morn a lingering kiss

The song was broken by sobs.

Souren's heart beat faster, and his throat tightened.

"My god, who is she? She must be Armenian. But how can she be in this Turkish military hellhole?"

The voice possessed a magnetic charm, and Souren longed to behold its owner.

He crawled under the fence that enclosed the property. Remaining close to the ground, he crossed over to a window where a candle flickered. Slowly and without a sound, he stood up and looked through the window. Startled, he dropped to the ground. He sat stupefied. He got to his feet again and peeked in at the figure he recognized as the gypsy girl. Only now, she rocked a cradle. Her red tattoos had faded from her fingers. Her hair fell in thick, wavy locks past her slender shoulders. The flimsy night-gown was transparent enough to reveal sculpted breasts and a tiny waist. Those fiery eyes from Christmas night were red and filled with tears.

She cannot be the mother of the child, Souren thought to himself. *She's too young. She's not a gypsy. Her skin is too fair.*

He watched her easing the child into a peaceful slumber.

She must be the servant.

When the young woman saw the baby was asleep, she wiped her tears with the edge of her nightdress, crossed herself, and put out the candle.

The following day, with his unit still awaiting orders, Souren was again able to take leave and return to the Turkish major's house. He kept a constant watch on it from a hiding place among the adjacent trees. He wanted desperately to catch a glimpse of the young woman. He yearned to get to know her. But at the thought of approaching her, he felt unworthy and inadequate and withdrew into hiding. In the afternoon, his patience was rewarded. He saw her come out, gracefully balancing a large pitcher on her shoulder. He watched her pass by on her way to the fountain.

She was frightened to see him come out of the grove from behind the bushes. He gently told her in Turkish, "Do not be afraid of me. I could never harm you."

She gave him a drink, and he thanked her in Armenian. With a faint smile on her lips, she made a flowing dance motion with her hand to indicate that she had recognized him from the evening at the tavern.

"Do you understand Armenian?" Souren asked.

She did not answer. She was paralyzed for an instant.

"Are there any Armenians still alive?" she asked petulantly, not trusting this Turkish soldier who was trying to woo her by speaking Armenian.

Souren continued, "I heard the charming voice of an angel in the night, and I am glad to have found her." He smiled. "I'm Souren Tashjian. I'm from Smyrna."

He quickly explained to her all that had transpired recently, his arrests and escapes, and the protection of the kind German general. He told her about Vartanoosh who lived in the cave among the ruins.

"I take her food. Go and see her yourself. She'll tell you who I am."

The exchange in fluent Armenian, as well as Souren's gestures and general comportment, almost persuaded her. She bit her bottom lip as if concentrating hard on an impossible equation.

"I must go," she said. "They are waiting for me." She hurried away.

During the next few days, Souren vacillated between ecstasy and depression. Wagner, no fool when it came to the torments of infatuation, threw friendly jabs at Souren, who uncharacteristically moped around.

When he could stand it no more, Souren contrived to meet her again on her way to fill her water jug, since he knew that to be a part of her daily chores. This time when he appeared from behind the trees, she did not jump, nor was her tongue frozen with fear and suspicion.

Not wanting to be seen talking to a stranger, she quickly told him, "My real name is Beatrice. The commander is keeping me to be the wife of his son, an officer on the Eastern Front." She spat out the last sentence with disgust.

He breathlessly told her that he wanted to know her story and they should find an opportunity to meet again. When she nodded approvingly, he told her of a spot he had discovered farther into the grove, away from the house, and then turned around and hurried away as if to hide a most precious treasure.

—⋙—

Souren was perplexed by this shy and sensitive young Armenian woman who could double as a lascivious tavern dancer. The contradiction did not make sense. He waited with fearful expectation for the explanation, but they did not get a chance to be together again until two days later. They met at the small clearing in the grove Souren had previously mentioned.

She started with a soft, low voice that he could barely hear.

"In our quiet village, the war was a distant report that did not affect our daily life. But one day a wagon driver came through town warning us of wholesale massacres taking place. We thought him crazy at first, but he insisted that Armenians throughout the eastern provinces were marked for annihilation. He had overheard some Turks at an inn talking about government orders to kill all Christians and to take their possessions.

"Some of our people believed him. Others went to the local administrator, who insisted it was all false rumors. Then the telegraph wires to our town were cut. Memories of the last massacre filled us with fear. We knew it was time to act. All able-bodied men gathered together. Plans were drawn for barricading the streets. That night we organized our defense, even though we knew it would be futile against the overwhelming strength of the Ottoman army. Still, we had to do something!

"Under cover of night, everyone helped dig trenches along the streets. We obstructed our windows and stored up food. One day, someone brought the news that a captured Turk admitted to secret plans to kill all the Christians in our town. The next day, when the Turks attacked, we easily repelled their assault. My father had a command post at one of the street corners. I stood by his side filling cartridges in his gun."

Souren admired the assurance with which she evoked the Armenian defense against attack from their neighbors. She obviously took pride in that part of the story. With a firmer voice, she continued describing the details.

"Within a short time, the Armenian organization had grown into a city government. The homegrown military defense took command of the situation. Rifles were few, as the Turks had confiscated them during the early days of the war. And there was very little ammunition at first. Some of the boys commandeered a warehouse and turned it into an arsenal. With a few of my friends, we went in and helped them.

"It was a place of great activity, where the most clever workmen of the city manufactured effective hand grenades, loaded cartridges for which the powder and even the primers were made on the spot, repaired rifles, and, in the crowning achievement of all, put together a cannon named 'Revenge.' We loaded it with plenty of powder, nails, doorknobs, and iron bearings from the looms. It made a terrific racket that served to at least intimidate the Turks, but without causing much damage. A rationing commission was established for the distribution of food. The women were in charge of it. There was also a police department, a health department, and even a legal court for the short duration of our siege.

"The Armenians resisted for seventy days, each day fighting more fiercely. But our resources were dwindling. I could see that our people became hungry and anxious. Mothers were worried for their young ones. They would gather them in the most remote corners of their homes and pray over them."

Souren was listening silently, transfixed by the pain she obviously felt at recalling her ordeal.

"When the Turks failed to break our forces, they brought heavy equipment to fire at our buildings. They would sneak up at night like rats along our streets and dynamite our houses. When all this failed to break the morale of the defenders, the Turks flew white flags. The two sides negotiated a truce.

"My father had been shot in the chest. My mother and I cared for him as best as we could. I felt his hand squeeze mine before his wounded chest rose in a last heave and he died.

"The truce did not mean anything to the Turks. It only gave them a chance to regroup and to wait for the arrival of a large force of the regular army that overwhelmed our city, mercilessly massacred the population, and plundered our homes, churches, and schools."

Beatrice's voice strangled to a murmur. He could see her hands tremble. He lowered his head and waited for her to collect herself.

"Before his death, my father had asked one of our American missionary teachers to keep me, since my mother had vowed to commit suicide rather than fall into the hands of the Turks. Before dawn the American woman, one of the teachers at the mission school for girls, sneaked into our hiding place and fled with twenty of us into the mountains. But my little sister was not with us. I had lost her in the dark. For two weeks we lived eating roots, grass, and leaves. By the third week, we were forced to go on, hoping to find shelter in some friendly village. The

Turks who had been looking for us, watching and hiding by the roadside, kidnapped us. What could we do? We had no weapons, and our protector could hardly fight off armed Turks, though she tried very hard to save as many of us as she could. Finally the American woman and four of us who had survived the terrible ordeal made it to the town of Konya.

"An old Turkish woman gave us a room in exchange for all the money the missionary had. We lived there and survived by making lace and fine needlework that the missionary sold at local bazaars. One day I accompanied her to help her. A man whom I had met before, a Major Husenedin Bey, saw me. He bought a handkerchief and asked my name. When we were on our way to our room, three of his soldiers overpowered us, and, despite my screams, they carried me to the major's home. Since then, he has been using me as a servant and tells me he will make me a bride for his son."

At this point, she broke down and sobbed convulsively, hiding her face in her hands. Embarrassed, not knowing how to respond, Souren simply put his hand on her shoulder and kept silent. After gaining her composure, she continued with her story.

"Among the businesses that the bey runs in this city is the inn where you and the German soldiers stopped the other evening. One of the attractions was the dancing of a gypsy girl called Anooshka. Men who could pay for a drink of *shurup* came in to watch her dance. The bey insisted that Anooshka teach me her trade. Now he has me dance whenever he hosts dignitaries. I hated it at first. But now, when I feel carried by the beat of the drum and the music of the piper, I can express my fears, my sorrow, my anger, my yearnings in all freedom. And they like it. They just lust at the body. They know nothing about the soul.

"Anooshka ran away with a rug merchant. That's why you saw me dance at the inn. I almost died of embarrassment when I discovered that you were not a Turkish soldier. Please, forgive me."

Souren assured her there was nothing to forgive. And there wasn't.

—⬩⬩⬩—

Days later, the commander left for the coastal town of Kusadasi to oversee the construction of defenses. The island of Samos lay a mile off the mainland at its nearest point. The Allies had occupied this strategic island, which had become part of the Kingdom of Greece in 1912. The British and French fleet enforced a blockade that extended up the coast to the Dardanelles, near the ruins of the legendary city of Troy. Their scout planes regularly flew over Kusadasi on reconnaissance flights.

Souren and Wagner watched the headquarters in Ephesus while the general was away. And though it was wartime, since their unit was now idle while awaiting orders, they were having the time of their lives.

Unbeknownst to Wagner, Souren met with Beatrice almost every day at the grove, under the shelter and seclusion of the vines. Emboldened at the success of their clandestine relationship, they extended their interludes from ten minutes to nearly an hour.

The couple spoke softly about the future and what they wanted to do after the war. An awkward silence ensued. Souren considered kissing Beatrice, but he didn't know if she would reject his affection. He saw her look down and was unsure how to interpret her body language. Suddenly, and without the least bit of self-consciousness,

Souren leaned in. Beatrice did too. Their lips barely brushed in a hesitant and timid manner. They quickly rejoined, anticipating a sensuous, pleasurable exchange, when the sound of a snapping twig broke the spell. Beatrice jumped up and saw Yagmur, the oldest of the Turkish major's three wives, running out of the grove. Without a word to Souren, she ran in pursuit of the nosy old woman who would surely report everything she saw to her husband.

The next morning, the major called Souren to his quarters.

"Pack your gear, Besherik. You are leaving for the Western Front on tomorrow's train! I could have you shot, you know!"

Souren overcame his trembling and stood stock-still.

"She is delightful, isn't she?" the major asked in a playful tone. But then he quickly became angry again. "She is too good for you, a lousy soldier sucking up to a German general. She is to be a gift to my son. Since I cannot trust you—"

"I promise—" Souren interrupted the major.

"Silence!" the major continued. "I saw how you looked at her when she danced. Do you think I'm blind? Your general is away. He can't protect you now. You leave on the next train! Do you hear me?"

Souren found Wagner at the tavern and told him about his secret meetings with Beatrice and how the Turkish major had ordered him to take the morning train out of Ephesus.

Wagner was never at a loss for a good prank on a Turkish soldier. He smiled at Souren. "You want to get back at the son of a bitch?"

Souren hedged. "Of course, but what do you have in mind?"

"The general has sent orders for his horse, dress uniform, sword, lash, and field glasses to be brought to Kusadasi for a parade. Apparently, the Turks feel the need to raise troop morale. You could go there. Tell him yourself about the rat Husenedin Bey."

Souren smirked and nodded approval. He liked this plan.

"I'll get a cavalry escort to make it authentic. And you wear the general's uniform so no one stops you."

"What if the general sees me in his uniform? I could get court-martialed!"

"I'll telegraph him and explain you'll get there a lot faster as a general than a mere foot soldier. There are several outposts between here and Kusadasi. The general will be pleased if you get there yet today."

As soon as he was out of the encampment, Souren put on the commander's coat. A dazzling sword at his waist, and field glasses dangling from his neck, he rode through the lines with a cavalryman following him.

Every few miles Souren passed outposts. When near enough to these posts, Souren would let the sword swing at the side of the horse, the clang of which alerted the sentry that a German officer was approaching. All came out of their dugouts and lined up in the sun, standing at attention. Souren returned the salute in an indifferent way and continued his pace.

Before arriving at Kusadasi, Souren took off the general's garb, put on his own, and assumed a more humble temper. He presented the general with his things and asked permission to tell him of a problem back at headquarters. The commander listened to his story. After Souren's panicked account, the general forcefully reminded Souren that he was part of *his* staff, not that of Major Husenedin Bey.

"I will send a message to the major and inform him that you have been ordered to organize a fife-and-bugle corps for all the regiments in Ephesus while I am in Kusadasi. But, Souren, you need to stay away from the girl."

Souren understood. His trust in the general to follow through gave him the courage to set out for Ephesus without fear of the major's revenge.

On his return trip, all Souren could scrounge up for transportation was a hungry, skeletal pony. Blue glass beads hung from its neck to ward off evil spirits. A villager, hoping to sell the gaunt creature, patted the protruding ribs as if he were stroking a solid, healthy steed.

Souren looked around to see if there was a better alternative. Who was he kidding? The army had requisitioned all the good horses. He was lucky to find what he had. He paid the man and mounted the pony.

This time, without the general's uniform, he and the cavalry escort had to stop at each outpost and state their mission, a time-consuming protocol they had avoided earlier in the day.

"Look out for the German general," they were warned.

No sooner had Souren reached the second outpost than a glint in the sky caught his attention. Far to the south, three specks hung unnaturally in space. Souren studied them for a while.

"Do you see that?" he asked the escort.

It was difficult to tell if they were actually moving, yet they seemed to slowly grow into winged shapes.

He heard them now—a faint, dissonant hum as they inched imperceptibly toward him. And now the new sound of a motor, much closer; Souren wheeled around to see another machine. This was the biplane he had seen on patrol several weeks before, with German crosses painted on the wings and tail. It had cleared the hills to the north, slowly climbing and banking in a wide arc to the southeast.

The three continued toward him, unswerving as a tram on rails. A small scout plane led the formation, followed by a large, ungainly craft with long, frail-looking wings. A second scout, similar to the first, brought up the rear. They were coming from the direction of Kusadasi. They must be British. Was the big plane for bombing? Perhaps he would see a fight!

Soldiers began pointing, some scurrying to find a safer place. Souren simply watched, mesmerized, not thinking of danger. He had heard reports of the British bombing a harbor or a bridge or a railway. The incidents had caused panic, but little damage.

Squinting into the brilliant sun, he scanned the skies to the east and south for the German. Nothing. He thought he could still hear the motor. The plane had to be close. But where had it gone?

The British were almost on top of the outpost. He could see the tiny pilots leaning over the cockpit rims, focused on something below. Massive pontoons for landing on the sea were attached to the undersides of the planes. He saw the translucent skin on the wings and the bright British roundels.

At that moment, the bombing plane tilted sharply to the right. The German was on him and already banking away. The machine gun fire filtered down among the sounds of revving engines and whining rigging wires. *Poomf! Poomf!* The British bomber was already stricken, marking the sky with a belch of smoke. It dived and circled slowly to the east. The scouts were slow to react and followed the bomber in its turn. The lead scout spotted the German and attempted to cut him off as he maneuvered for another pass. The scout overshot. The German's plane made a tight turn inside the bomber's spiral and fired again. Now flames licked out from around the motor and spread quickly. The bomber was finished. It rolled over onto its back and, shedding its fragile wings, plunged to the earth.

When Souren looked skyward again, it was the German being pursued. The lead scout had positioned himself high and in back of the German as they slowly circled. The scout was gradually gaining on him, hoping for an advantage and a clear shot. The second scout watched from a distance.

The commotion of the air battle awakened the local air defenses at Kusadasi. As the fight drifted in that direction, every gun seemed to open up at once—the cracking of artillery fire shaking Souren's insides. Flashes and dirty clouds of smoke appeared at random around the planes. The German had had enough. He used the distraction to dive steeply away. A shell exploded near the lead scout, lifting it sideways into a violent skid.

For a moment the plane seemed dazed, like a drunken soldier, but as the brown puff dispersed, the machine began rolling and staggering and then turned its nose downward, spinning and whirling in jerky turns, trailing a long ribbon of smoke, then crashing into the hills. The final scout dived away to the south and ran, companionless, in the direction of Samos.

Cheers rang out among the soldiers. Souren squeezed the pony's rib cage with his knees. It complied and ambled along.

—⋙—

Wagner was at headquarters waiting anxiously to get the news. He paid the escort for helping out with his caper and sent him away.

"Well?"

Souren dismounted the scrawny pony. "You are standing before the newly appointed drum major," he announced and took a deep, flamboyant bow.

"Perfect!" Wagner said. "I've cooked up some wild boar left by Turkish hunters. Let's celebrate your escaping the Western Front!"

Muslims considered the boar unclean for the faithful, but Souren and Wagner had no such scruples and feasted on the gamey meat that Wagner had prepared.

Assured that his general had already sent the message concerning his new orders, Souren returned to Major Husenedin Bey's home to present the same message. When the major answered the door, Souren saluted and began. He had spoken only a few words when the major waved him away and closed the door.

In ten days, Souren had the fifes playing melodies on the highways of Ephesus. And in two weeks, his musicians were heading the battalion on their marches and parades. He obeyed the general's directive and did not see any more of Beatrice. He also avoided the major as much as possible.

Every day, just before sunset, the battalion assembled in front of the ruins of the Temple of Artemis. The bugles played the retreat twice, and at each interval, the soldiers would shout, "Long live Talaat and Enver, pashas of the Ottomans!" The sound echoed and reechoed from the distant hills, reminiscent of the time two thousand years before when the silversmiths cried out on this same spot, "Great is Diana of the Ephesians!"

Telegraph wires clicked once again, issuing secret orders. Troops were instructed to prepare to move out the next day.

Souren wanted to tell Vartanoosh good-bye, so he raced to her hiding place. The farewell would be short, because the train was pulling out in less than an hour. She wasn't there, and though he wanted to call to her, he feared exposing her. He paced in front of the little cave for ten minutes, then headed back to the train station.

Wagner secured the padlock and sat down beside Souren. They were on their way to Menemen, twenty-two miles from Smyrna, and then on to the Dardanelles, where the Ottoman Fifth Army had pinned down invading Allied forces.

"Well, perhaps you'll finally see some action," Wagner said optimistically.

Souren watched the aqueducts disappear and, with them, any hope of ever seeing Beatrice again.

Chapter Six

—※—

1916-1917

A bent figure, burdened and defeated, walked aimlessly along the coast beyond the somber, misty city of Menemen. Damp, chilly gusts from the west threatened to steal his fez, but Souren clutched it tightly and leaned into the biting wind. He glanced up at the gray clouds overhead and moved his lips. Then he suddenly dropped to his knees and shook with sobs.

His hope upon leaving Ephesus was to get to the Dardanelles, where the British navy and soldiers of His Majesty's empire—including New Zealanders and Australians—fought to take the strategic Gallipoli Peninsula and to secure the famous straits. Their aim had been to sail into Constantinople and quickly put an end to the war.

The Dardanelles once had seemed to him to offer a chance to defect because the channel, at its widest point, was only two miles, and a mere mile at its narrowest. One mile between him and freedom! Souren had dreamt about it, fantasized about his getaway. He once had even imagined donning a British uniform and fighting alongside Armenian volunteer units, saving Beatrice, snatching his mother from Smyrna, and settling her in a nice home in America near his and Beatrice's home. Of course, there was Vartanoosh, too. Perhaps Beatrice would have taken the little girl with her. He and Beatrice, after marrying, would adopt Vartanoosh and raise her. She would call Sophia "Grandmother," and his brothers and sisters would be her extended family of aunts and uncles.

The latest war news had ended his escapist fantasies. Telegraph wires proclaimed a British withdrawal from the peninsula. After eight months of brutal fighting, the British had made a secret retreat. Turkish officers organized parades. Military bands struck up victory marches. The papers ran huge headlines. At the behest of the government, all of Turkey celebrated. Nearly a million men had fought in this long campaign that had left over one hundred thousand dead and five hundred thousand wounded. Under leadership of the Germans, the Turks threw back the Allies and humiliated the celebrated British Royal Navy.

"God, why? Why is this happening?" Souren pounded the earth with both fists. His pants soaked up water from the recent rain. A brisk gale yanked off his fez. Vulnerable and cold, he wept alone.

Not only was the war not going to end anytime soon, it appeared that the Allies might even lose. That thought at one time had seemed remote. How could God allow the defeat of the Christian Allied nations just as the Islamic government was organizing the massacre and deportation of hundreds of thousands of Armenians throughout the Turkish Empire? His mind raced from one injustice to another.

Clearly the tipping point had come when, in Constantinople, on April 24, 1915, 250 prominent Armenians were arrested. The government alleged that they had detained Allied sympathizers who were loyal to Armenian political parties and were posing a threat to the security of the empire. Coincidentally, the following day, the Allies landed on the Gallipoli Peninsula about two hundred miles northwest of Smyrna. He thought of his mother. The convergence of events surely would have caused much chatter at the orphanage and throughout the neighborhood.

The Allies had been knocking on the door of the Ottoman Empire, and the Young Turk leaders clearly intended Armenians to be the scapegoat. Following the total defeat by the Russians at the infamous Battle of Sarikamish in January 1915, the government had already turned on the Armenian minority, claiming all as guilty of sympathizing with the enemy. Now the Armenians would, of course, again be blamed if the Allies made it to Constantinople. His depression deepended. He recalled how word of the Allied landing had temporarily instilled hope in his mind and alleviated his fears of imminent doom. But his anxiety soon returned as it had over the Armenian quarters everywhere. The situation for all Armenians was deteriorating rapidly. He cursed the whole bloody mess.

Souren turned his face to the rain and swore out loud at Enver Pasha. The tyrant's history and character were well-known. Affectionately called Little Napoleon by his friends, in 1914 he had secured the title of Minister of War. Small in stature but mighty in ego, according to Wagner, he dressed meticulously, spoke German fluently, and had married an Ottoman princess.

It was his own vanity that caused him to launch an ill-conceived offensive against Russia, Turkey's archenemy. Wagner had chuckled as he told Souren the story. Enver had no military successes to his name, and with no more than a title and an inflated view of himself, he went the way of his namesake, Napoleon Bonaparte.

Like the French a hundred years before, Enver lost the battle against the Russian winter. Wagner said that German intelligence had learned that of the ninety thousand men marched into the Caucasus by Enver, nearly eighty thousand starved, froze, or succumbed to disease. So instead of a victory parade through the streets of Constantinople, the humiliated little tyrant slinked back to the capital raving against the Armenians, on whom he blamed his colossal defeat.

The main enemies of the Ottoman Third Army had been nature and the ignorance of Enver, but Armenian volunteer units recruited by the Russian military brilliantly defended a strategic pass and prevented a Turkish advance. Wagner confirmed what Souren already knew from his grandmother's history, that the majority of Armenians in these Russian units were citizens of the Russian Empire. However, according to German intelligence, a handful of Ottoman Armenians had defected and also fought alongside their fellow Russian Armenians. This provided the pretext for the minster of war, livid with embarrassment, to label all Armenians in Turkey as coconspirators. Enver's resounding defeat had handed the Young Turks the excuse that Committee of Union and Progress needed to undertake whatever brutal measures were needed in dealing with Turkey's Armenian subjects. Enver exposed himself as the oppressor he was.

In February 1915, Armenian soldiers in the Ottoman army had been systematically disarmed and relegated to so-called labor battalions, followed in April by the mass arrests in Constantinople. Five months later, Minister of the Interior Talaat Pasha—the only man more powerful than Enver—sent a telegram to governors and mayors throughout the empire ordering compliance with the government's decision to exterminate the Armenian population. Failure to do so would result in being charged as an enemy of the government. A couple of German command telegraph stations had mistakenly been included in the communiqué's distribution.

It now all flooded Souren's tourtured soul like an overflowing river. He held his head in disbelief as he recounted animated conversations back home that had nurtured the illusion that help was on the way. His mother and her guests had spent hours trying to soothe one another's anxieties by pointing to the nearness of the Allies and the impossibility that the British fleet could be stopped. But instead of a swift and decisive conquest, the Allies bungled the landings at Gallipoli and ended up bogged down in Turkey's "No-Man's-Land" for eight months. There would be no rescue of the Armenian nation after all. His whole world had unraveled.

Now soaked and prostrate on the ground, he swore again and again and cried until he could no more. Finally he rolled over and looked up at the clouds rushing by. As he slowly rose to his feet, he clasped his muddied hands in desperate prayer.

"God, please, please help me!"

—◊◊◊—

Several days later, in Menemen, Souren appeared in public on horseback with his commander. People recognized him as the interpreter and greeted him respectfully. Turkish junior officers struck up friendly conversation, believing he was one of them. These officers ate like kings, yet their troops lacked uniforms, were denied adequate food, and their teeth rotted and fell out for lack of good nutrition. Many died not from wounds but from disease. Souren harbored a grudge against the officers as incompetent military leaders. He also hated them as the enforcement arm of a government that was systematically emptying the empire of his own people.

His convincing disguise as one of the officers earned him a degree of freedom, which he used to extract what little revenge he could. He accepted invitations to drink, and even, from time to time, salutes. His esteemed role as interpreter to the German general afforded him many opportunities to mix with these Turkish officers from whom he accepted ingratiating compliments on his knowledge of German, and his intellect, to them proof positive that the mind of the Turk was as enlightened as that of any so-called infidel.

In those moments, his commander would quietly comment wryly, "Besherik, you do your people proud."

"Thank you, sir," Souren would reply.

As the weeks progressed, Souren even began to enjoy this public role. He started to feel like a free man again, until one morning when he ventured alone into town on his day off and noticed a crowd gathered in front of the courthouse. He drew close enough to see what transfixed the townspeople. Three deserters were about to be executed. Three guns discharged, and three bodies fell. An officer ordered some bystanders to drag the corpses to a nearby tree, where they were tied upright and left as a warning. Souren read the words written upon the victims' chests: "This is what happens to deserters."

The blood had already frozen in his veins. Wan and weak, he turned away from the gruesome sight. The soft cries of a few of the bystanders lingered in his ears. Those poor men were not even wearing shoes. They had probably escaped their ranks to go home and see their families, maybe even enjoy a hot meal. They may have fought valiantly somewhere in this godforsaken land, but they were repaid with bullets to the head. And they were Turks! What would be his fate if he were caught as an Armenian deserter?

Souren returned to headquarters and stayed away from town for several days, until he had to return with Wagner to purchase supplies. Wagner, who by now had grown to like Souren quite well, did not pull any pranks. He, too, had seen the soldiers tied to the tree and knew how such would haunt Souren.

—⁓—

One day an Armenian dentist from Smyrna came through head-quarters on his way to examine soldiers before they headed to Canakkale, a town on the southern coast of the Dardanelles at its narrowest point. Dr. Manoogian, although drafted, had been spared assignment to an Armenian labor battalion because of his badly needed professional skill. He asked Souren in Turkish if he could examine his teeth. When the two were alone, Dr. Manoogian, who had recognized Souren, told him that his mother was seriously ill with cholera. Souren thanked the dentist and hurried to see the commander to request a leave of absence.

"Sir, I must see her before we leave for the Dardanelles. It may be the last time. She's very sick."

The commander signed passes under Souren's assumed name. Travel on the trains and between cities required papers, but that alone would not protect Souren if he were discovered. The general, knowing the dangers that loomed, trusted that Souren would find a way. The young man was clever and cautious. Besides, he knew the city inside and out.

The following day, Souren left Menemen. He passed through each checkpoint without incident. Upon reaching the familiar station in Smyrna, he was careful to remain unnoticed by station employees.

While hiding in a recess of the hall, he watched Turkish soldiers inspect the baggage of travelers coming into Smyrna. Aware that many residents of the city were sympathizers of the enemy belligerents, the Turkish authorities had instituted a screening unit at the station to monitor the flow of arrivals. The inspection was intended to spot foreign spies, smugglers of weapons, and denizens returning from the countryside with food to be sold on the black market.

From his vantage point, Souren recognized a well-known Armenian couple that was returning home, probably loaded with victuals unavailable in the war-stricken city. Haiganoosh was a statuesque woman, massive and muscular, who cruised through the line without interference. The inspectors were too busy eyeing her form to pay attention to the two heavy bags she carried with ease.

Her husband, Avedis, was less assertive and had lagged behind. He was a man of small stature, tightly dressed in a Western suit with a celluloid shirt collar and a thin black tie, an outfit that reflected his bookkeeper occupation. The anxious glances he cast about and the brown leather case he nervously held against his chest caught the attention of one of the soldiers. Asked what he was bringing along, with a trembling voice, he started listing all the purchases he and his wife had made at the farms: two legs of lamb, five kilos of flour, two jars of tahini, three cuts of basturma, and a heavy bag of bulgur. Astounded by this enumeration, the soldier called over an inspector, who ordered Avedis to open his bag. The two men watched intently as his shaking hands awkwardly exposed the contents of the case. They burst out in uproarious laughter when nothing but freshly dug potatoes appeared. With resounding curses, they chased away the man with his potatoes, shouting at him to get the hell out of there and rush home to dream about his banquets.

During the exchange, Souren escaped notice and cautiously made his way toward home.

He approached the soldier standing guard at the entrance to his neighborhood and said to him, "I'm here to relieve you." The guard didn't care why he was off duty two hours early. He simply nodded at the soldier before him and started off in the direction of the bazaar.

Souren jogged down the street to his home. When he saw the house, the ache of homesickness swept through his body. As he climbed the steps of the porch, he wondered whether he should knock. His instinct was to walk through the door as he had all of his life. Now, however, he might startle his mother if she mistook him for a Turkish soldier. He noticed a curtain suddenly drawn closed. He stopped abruptly.

They know I'm here! The authorities are inside waiting for me! His mind raced. If he turned to leave, his mother would be questioned. If he just opened the door and went inside, he would be arrested. Far better he be captured than his mother put through an interrogation.

He knocked on his own front door.

A stranger's face looked out at him through the half-opened door. Souren noticed several other Armenians in his living room. He let out his breath with relief.

"I'm Souren Tashjian," he said to the stranger in Armenian. "Dr. Manoogian told me my mother is ill. I've come from Menemen to see her."

Souren rushed past the man and ran upstairs to his mother's room. He almost cried upon seeing her. She was pale and much thinner than he had ever seen her before. More troubling, though, was seeing how the war had aged her.

"My boy! My Souren!" she called weakly.

Souren knelt beside the bed and wept softly. Sophia held him close, stroking his head and patting his arm. "Thank you, Lord," she repeated over and over again.

Aware of the risk and that their time was short, they hurriedly exchanged bits of news. "Oh, I almost forgot," Souren said. "Vartanoosh is well. I saw her at Ephesus!"

"Praise God," Sophia uttered with a mixture of wonder and sorrow.

"What has become of Bedros? Have you heard anything?" Souren asked.

"He was sent to a labor battalion," Sophia sighed.

Souren winced at the dreaded news.

"Thank God you have escaped that horrid fate." She closed her eyes in silent thanks. "How will Vartanoosh survive?" she whispered.

Souren told his mother about Beatrice, who had been taken captive by the Turkish officer. "She promised to look after Vartanoosh. Poor thing lives like an animal in a cave. I did what I could for her, but if anyone found out that she is an Armenian in hiding—"

"You did the right thing, Souren." Sophia saw the expression on Souren's face when he spoke Beatrice's name, but, perhaps sensing it was painful for him, she did not inquire.

"Where have you been these months? Just Ephesus? I had feared you died on Gallipoli."

"I leave for Gallipoli tomorrow."

Her face grew ashen.

"I'll be safe. It's not the front anymore."

Souren explained that his general oversaw defenses and that he would be far from the front line should hostilities resume.

"I'm probably in the safest place in the whole country!"

That reassurance was enough to set Sophia at ease.

"They check the neighborhood every night," she warned him. "They've searched the house at least once a week for the last four months! So far, I and other older wormen have not been confronted because of the orphanage. I don't think they want to draw attention to what is going on by disrupting a foreign-sponsored orphanage."

"When do they come?"

"In the evening. Always in the evening." Sophia breathed heavily and asked hesitantly, "Have you heard about Armen?"

"No," Souren replied. "How is he? Where is he?"

"I gave part of the house to his family after Armen and his father were drafted. His mother and sister were traumatized and financially distressed and came to live with me. When Armen had returned from Gallipoli to recuperate from influenza, he stayed in your room and even wore your clothes. You two were always so close."

"Gallipoli?" Souren had a sinking feeling.

"He had a resolute and creative mind, you know, and the courage to carry out his plans—a determination to change things single-handedly." Sophia had a special place in her heart for Armen and spoke of him with great affection. "About a month after he came here, the fighting at Gallipoli was still raging. Armen watched thousands of Turkish troops, along with several Armenian slave-labor battalions, passing through Smyrna on their way to the front. Knowing their fate, he grew more and more agitated. One morning, the whole city was buzzing. People spoke of a revolution. At the train station and on official buildings, someone had anonymously posted placards, written in Turkish and Greek, calling the Turkish forces to revolt, for they were being sent to be slaughtered at the Dardanelles for the Germans. 'Comrades, the national revolutionary union is calling you! Rise and end the war with the Allies!' It was signed, "Revolutionary Union," and had the Turkish seal.

"People waited for a revolution," Sophia continued. "The army officers and soldiers seemed to welcome the news, and many had cherished the thought, but there was not one daring person to be found to make the break and start an uprising. They were like sheep, with not a bit of self-reliance or imaginative spirit. They would meekly follow and be slaughtered at Gallipoli.

"The next thing you know, soldiers surrounded our neighborhood. The soldiers came here looking for Armen. It was he that had called for a revolution! Poor Armen. They beat him ferociously, but he stood up under their blows and walked out of here upright and unshaken. Afterward, many Armenian families were exiled on suspicion. Innocent people were forced from their homes and sent to Konya." She paused for a moment. "Did you know, Souren, it was his father who, years ago, had been the director of the government telegraph offices at Magnesia. It was Armen's father who had given Talaat Pasha a job and helped him advance! The soldiers took his mother and sisters away, too."

Souren sat in silence. He could barely comprehend the story. If it hadn't come from his mother, he never would have believed that Armen would defy the military as boldly as he had.

"At his court-martial," Sophia said, "Governor Rahmi Bey asked Armen about his plans for his intended revolution. Armen expressed himself so fearlessly and dramatized the plight of the Turkish forces in such a way that the governor recommended that he be exiled instead of hanged, saying to the court, 'This young man is another Jean Valjean.'"

She paused briefly and then continued. "No one has heard from him or his family since."

Souren shook his head to make sense of this news.

"Armen intended to be a good soldier. He believed that change for Armenians was possible. He wanted to prove his patriotism. He tried to convince me to register instead of deserting."

"He left something for you. It's in my top drawer. Take a look."

Souren walked to his mother's bureau and pulled open the top drawer. He saw the speckled marble he had won from Armen and then given back to his friend at the Christmas party.

He slammed the drawer shut.

"I'm hiding! Armen didn't hide! He showed courage. He fought back!"

Sophia tried to reason with Souren. "Some say Armen's courage was only foolishness. The government punished nearly a thousand Armenians because of his actions. Dr. Post sent a report to the missionary board. Mrs. Reed read it and told me Dr. Post saw over ten thousand deportees in squalid conditions in Konya. The police guard them by day, but they are left without protection at night. That's when the villagers come. They rob the refugees of money and the clothes on their backs. Whatever they can get their hands on, they take. Girls are kidnapped and raped."

"We can't just sit here and let them do this," Souren said. "We can't walk to our deaths without a fight. Mother, what is going to become of you?"

"I'm doing quite well, considering. The missionaries manage to bring me some letters and even a check now and then from your brothers and sisters. That's how I am able to feed everyone here. I put some money back for you, too." She gestured toward a bookshelf.

"No, please, I'm getting along fine. Use it for our guests downstairs. They need it more than I do."

The young woman serving as nurse to Sophia entered the room. It was time for his mother's bath.

"I'll come back later," Souren said.

From the top of the stairs, he eyed a little girl stretched out across the lap of an old woman, presumably her grandmother. Nearby in a cradle, an infant cried off and on. With her left foot, the worn-out woman steadily rocked the crib of the inconsolable baby. An elderly man and two children sat in a corner looking dazed. The man who had answered the door still watched the street from behind the curtain.

Souren heard women in the kitchen preparing the evening meal. He realized suddenly how unfamiliar his home had become to him. He did not see family; he saw strangers. Gone were the fragrances of abundance. The comforting aroma of fresh bread, the whiff of tangy sarma cooking on top of the woodstove, beside a pot of chicken and a panful of pilaf, had been replaced by unfamiliar, less appetizing smells of rationed, inferior food.

He approached the man at the window and asked, "Who are you?"

"I am Garabed." He explained that he'd come through Smyrna on business and hadn't been able to return home. "I ran into missionaries who had just come from my town, and they told me that the Armenians had all been driven out in caravans. My brother, Hovagim, and his wife, Lucine, both had been killed. Lucine's body had been horribly mutilated, both of her breasts cut off. My brother's scalp was found a few days later."

Souren wondered silently at the eagerness with which the man talked about his tragedy.

The far corner of the dining room was occupied by what was left of the Sarkissian family. They told Souren they'd fled their home when the men whom the government had gathered in the church had been torched with the building. Armenians choked at the nauseating odor of burning flesh. They crouched in their homes and clasped their hands over their ears to block out the screams of grown men and their teenage sons. Sporadic gunfire punished those who tried to escape the flames. The same night, soldiers searched houses one by one to force out the remaining Armenian occupants and drive them into the Syrian Desert. No time to pack. No horses or mules to carry their belongings. They were herded like cattle.

"You can come back and reclaim your property after the war," local authorities promised before sending them out under the bayonets of gendarmes, who robbed and killed their charges rather than protecting them.

The Sarkissians described how they hid along hedges and back alleys. Mother and grandfather with three young children made it safely out of the town. They hired a Turk, a longtime friend of the family, to smuggle them to the coast. They paid him a hefty price for the danger he accepted, since anyone found aiding Armenians was subject to execution. The family lived for weeks in fear of outlaws and soldiers roaming the countryside. They worried constantly that the friend they had hired would be eager to turn them over to the authorities. They were at his mercy, but fortunately he shuttled them some two hundred miles to the outskirts of Smyrna, where he left them near the ruins of the ancient aqueduct.

The children's father and his two older sons had been killed months before, when Armenian men in town were called to register for military service. Instead of being issued a uniform, they were tied in groups of four and marched a few miles from town, where they were attacked with hammers, knives, and scythes. Yet another catastrophe befell the family, the grandfather explained, when the cholera epidemic sweeping through Smyrna ravaged his daughter's littlest one. They had buried the child only a few days before. His eyes met Souren's, who had no words to adequately express his grief and anger. He simply stared back in hopeless anguish.

"I thought I had seen the worst in 1895, when soldiers split my father's head with an ax. And for what reason? He was Armenian! In 1909, when my grandmother was burned alive with others in our village, I told myself I had beheld evil at its apex." He glanced over at his grief-stricken daughter and two grandchildren. "I have lived long enough to know I was wrong. What I saw this time was evil beyond any I had witnessed before. They're butchering the

Armenian men in the slave-labor battalions when they can work no more. They send women and children out on a march to the desert of Der Zor. No shelter! No food!" His voice caught suddenly, constrained with deep emotion. "They are set on killing us all!" He gasped and fell back against the wall as if he had been struck with a fist.

Souren took him gently by the arm and helped him into a chair.

The old woman on the couch spoke for the first time. "These are my grandchildren." She wore a fashionable hat with a downy plume and a brim nearly the width of her shoulders; once a symbol of her aristocratic bearing, now it mocked her situation.

"I am a widow and almost blind. I cannot provide for them." She pointed to the little girl lying in her lap and the baby fussing loudly in the cradle. "I seldom sleep. I sit here and rock my grandson while he cries for his mother to nurse him."

"Where is his mother?" Souren asked impulsively.

"The government here in Smyrna now is singling out the wealthy Armenians for deportation. They sent away my son and daughter-in-law No crime but that of being wealthy *and* Armenian. Their home was requisitioned. My son's factory taken. The children and I were told to find somewhere else to live. And so here we are."

The little girl reflexively sat up and tenderly cupped the aged face in her hands.

"Don't cry, Nana. Daddy is going to come and get us. He said so." She pressed her nose to her grandmother's and then kissed her on both cheeks.

Souren's chest constricted. His eyes burned with tears that he tried to hold back. He followed the noise coming from the kitchen.

"Souren!" One of the ladies greeted him and hugged him tightly after kissing him on each cheek. "Your mother has been so worried. Thank God you're alive. Thank God you're here!" It was one of the women from church. Her bright eyes and genuine smile warmed Souren. He was introduced to a couple of the other women whom his mother had taken in.

He thought he recognized the young woman sitting apart from the others. Yes, he was sure it was Yervant's wife, the beautiful girl who had rode in the grand parade several years before. Her dark tresses no longer shone soft and luxurious but were matted and stringy. Her rich brown eyes showed little sign of life.

Souren started toward her.

"Come with me, son."

Souren turned and saw Garabed standing in the doorway and followed him out of the kitchen. The two sat in a corner where Garabed could watch the front of the house. In a hushed tone, he related the terrifying story of Yervant and his lovely bride.

Though Yervant had been a supporter of the Young Turks and the beliefs he thought they espoused, they had turned on him—as an Armenian, he'd been singled out as an enemy collaborator. Soldiers knocked at his door one night, and he tried to calm his wife while also telling her to hide. She climbed inside the divan, a low built-in chest that ran along the base of the wall in their parlor and served as both a seat and as storage. Depleted by the shortages of wartime, there was room enough in the divan for her to lie down straight with her arms by her sides. Yervant covered her up with linen and rags. He closed the hinged lid and scattered several colorfully decorated cushions on it. The soldiers used their gun butts to strike the door, and as soon as Yervant turned the key, the soldiers pushed through and began beating him.

One of the soldiers reached above the fireplace and pulled out a rifle that Yervant had received from the government years previous during the Young Turk revolution. They accused him of planning to use it against the government. They beat him to near unconsciousness and dragged him out of the house.

Other soldiers began to ransack the place, looking for gold and jewelry. One of them noticed the evidence that a woman lived there. He began to seach the whole house: kitchen, bedroom, closets, and parlor. Finally he threw open the divan in the parlor and pulled out the rags Yervant had used to conceal his wife.

Garabed paused for a second and looked down and shook his head before continuing. When he saw the unmistakable locks of a woman's hair, the soldier grabbed them and jerked the frightened young woman out of her hiding place. The three men fell on her like a pack of wild animals. They muffled her screams by shoving a scarf into her mouth. She was raped over and over for the duration of the night.

News of Yervant's arrest spread quickly the following day, but no one knew what had happened to his wife. No one knew until Mr. Terzian found her about six hundred meters from the house. She was crouching beneath a thick growth of foliage, naked and bleeding.

"He wrapped her in a blanket and carried her here," Garabed said.

The poor woman had lived in fear of soldiers ever since, and Garabed worried that Souren's uniform might spark a fit of screaming.

"Your mother has gently coaxed the story from her, but the poor girl hasn't spoken since. We haven't heard anything about Yervant—where's he's being held or if he's even still alive."

Souren's hands shook uncontrollably. "I have to do something!"

"Shh." Garabed calmed him. "We have women and children here."

Souren regained composure with deep breaths and inaudible curses. "How long will you stay?" he asked Garabed.

"I'm not sure. I've been told to stay out of sight. The Danish consul, with whom I do a lot a business, promised to get me news as soon as he has any. In the meantime, I wait."

The two men paused. It was Garabed who broke the tension-filled silence.

"Live, young man—live!"

"What?" Souren asked.

"I know you want revenge. So do I! We'll get it first by surviving. We must find a way to live! All of us in this house and every Armenian still breathing in Turkey. We must endure, and after the war, those of us who have survived will reclaim our country. With the help of France, England, and America, we will throw off the damned Turkish yoke forever!"

Souren started up the stairs after the nurse signaled him that he could return to his mother's room. He didn't want to merely stay alive. He yearned to do something far more heroic and meaningful. Holding tightly to the banister and with a heavy heart, he gazed down at the refugees in his living room. The only thing between him and certain death was the cursed Ottoman-German uniform. They were all much more vulnerable than he was. He searched futilely for some bit of wisdom or truth to assuage his guilt.

Souren sat on the edge of his mother's bed and held her white-and-purple hands. He followed the bulging veins from her wrist to her knuckles. The skin on her fingers felt like thin paper.

"I have to go," he said, as if resigning himself to leaving. "There's only one train available tonight, and it leaves in about twenty minutes."

He longed to stay and take care of her, but that would only endanger her and those she valiantly protected inside their home. When he did finally tear himself away, he did so without looking back. He didn't even pause in the doorway. He feared that if he slowed down or stopped, he might never leave. He hurried down the stairs and out the back door. It was night, so his exit went unobserved by the roaming soldiers who would see his presence in an Armenian home as cause to investigate. He passed safely out of the area and turned toward the railway station.

No civilian passengers or even soldiers were allowed to board the train. Enver Pasha, with his staff, along with the austere Marshal Liman von Sanders, the German general who had transformed the ragtag Ottoman army into a valuable ally, were scheduled to depart on that train. All traffic within a radius of a mile was stopped. The streets swarmed with armed soldiers guarding the tracks at regular intervals of fifty feet. The general had warned Souren of this potentiality, and the two had decided Souren would pretend to be a member of the military staff.

"Besherik," the general had said, "if anyone can do it, you can."

At the station, Souren surreptitiously snatched an unattended briefcase and shoved it under his arm. He rushed around appearing to be the busiest man in the army, and no one dared stop him. When he saw several officers board, he followed them. Once on the train, he mingled with Turkish and German attendants and officers' bodyguards.

He sat on a German trunk and, in his broken German, talked with the German soldiers who thought he was with the Turkish officers, while the Turks assumed Souren, in animated conversation with the Germans, was attached to the German staff.

All was going quite well until a railroad official accompanied by Turkish officers recognized Souren as the Armenian employed by the British railway company. He stopped abruptly and demanded in Turkish to know what he was doing there.

Souren assumed a defiant German poise and yelled, "Was ist los?" (What is wrong?) and continued his conversation with the Germans as if he did not understand Turkish. His heart was pounding so fast and so hard, he thought for sure everyone on the train had seen right through him. His mind raced to find an escape in case he were pursued.

The railroad official apologized and walked off. Relief flooded over Souren like a giant wave churned up before an impending storm. When the train finally pulled away from the station, Souren felt a further sense of relief, but he didn't feel safe until he got off the train a few miles outside of Smyrna when it stopped to take on water. From there, he made his way back to camp on foot.

—w—

The scene at camp was chaotic. Regiments were sent back and forth, soldiers outfitted with uniforms, some for the first time in full gear. Many of these reinforcements came from far-flung corners of the empire, from the desert or from isolated villages high up in the mountains. Those villages gave little consideration to events in Constantinople, and even less for the Dardanelles.

According to the general's announced itinerary, by train they would go to the Port of Bandirma. A boat would take the troops from Bandirma to Canakkale. From there, the men would march sixty miles to Kumkale on the Asiatic side of the entrance to the straits. Some of the young officers were enthusiastic, but the soldiers dreaded being sent to the front.

With a serpentine movement, the steam-powered train chugged north across fertile plains toward Bandirma, on the Sea of Marmara. At noon the next day, under a bright and scorching sun, the men heard a roaring sound. Everyone in the car ran to the windows in time to see a black cloud approaching the train. Frantically, they rushed to close the windows.

"What is it?" Wagner asked.

"Locusts!"

A shadow fell, and the train was engulfed suddenly, overwhelmed on every side. The wheels of the train spun on the greasy rail. The engine puffed more steam in its fight against these stubborn insects. Giving up hopes of making any progress, it pulled to a loud, screeching halt. Several had made it through the windows, into the commander's train car. Souren and the attendants began stomping on as many of the dreaded insects as they were able. Wagner, who had never experienced a locust swarm, watched with interest and horror, for the sheer number of the creatures made his skin crawl. He motioned to Souren to come and see a curious sight. It was a pair of locusts in an apparent fight to the death.

"Once they leave the swarm, they start feeding on each other," Souren explained.

The stronger locust pinned its opponent on its back. The struggling locust tried to free itself.

"Flip him!" Wagner couldn't help himself. He coached the underdog. "Pull him down!"

The entangled insects pivoted in a circle, the stronger one holding the other down with his head burrowed in the victim. And just like that, he flew away. Wagner and Souren followed his flight. Then, looking down, they saw the dead locust, decapitated and perfectly still. Wagner waited for the victorious locust to alight and then smashed him violently under his boot.

"You son of a bitch! Who kills their own kind? Who kills their own?"

All Souren could do was cringe at the terrible symbolism.

"Hey," someone shouted. "We've got ourselves a couple of deserters! See them running away?"

Again, the men crowded at the windows.

The locusts that had landed were devouring every blade of grass.

"There have to be thousands of those bastards!" Wagner said.

"More like millions," Souren corrected him.

"And two soldiers among them," Wagner mused.

A pair of rifles sounded with sharp reports, and the two deserters dropped right under Souren's window.

The general had not been in the car when the insects enveloped the train. But now Souren heard him screaming what he was certain were profanities. Souren had never heard these German words, and could not hope to translate.

"Fresse—ihr seid Idioten! Ihr blöde türkische Scheissköpfe seid Hurensöhne! Verdammt, verdammt—ach du Scheisse!"

Souren turned to Wagner.

"He's very mad," Wagner said drily.

"Besherik! Besherik!" the commander yelled.

Souren sprang from the train car and made his way through the thick layer of insects.

"Yes, sir!" he called. He still hadn't caught sight of the commander but could hear the sustained string of profanities.

The commander stepped over the coupling and joined Souren on that side of the train.

"You tell them to stop shooting the goddamned deserters! We don't have enough men as it is! They can't shoot them every damn time—the idiots!"

"Yes, sir!"

"And tell them to get those goddamned bodies back inside. Morale will plummet if we leave them here."

Souren, Wagner, and the commander's attendants, as well as the guards who had shot the men, gathered close to the bodies, everyone trudging through a thick covering of the hated insects like it was a blanket of heavy snow.

Souren told the Turkish guards to get the bodies back on the train.

"If you put those bodies on the train, then you will get the locusts too," one guard pointed out.

Souren repeated this to the commander, who agreed and told the men to leave the bodies where they lay.

The group of soldiers stared in disgust as they watched nostrils, eyes, mouths, and ears fill with the burrowing, insatiable locusts that were now devouring the dead bodies. Just beyond them, the swarm gorged itself on every blade of grass with a sinister grinding noise.

An order went out for all the men to grab shovels and begin cleaning off the tracks. It wasn't until a southern wind finally carried the locusts away two hours later that the train whistled and was again on its way.

—⁂—

When they arrived at Canakkale, the commander and his staff headed the division and marched to Kumburnu. Everyone's belongings were loaded into two large flat-bottomed sailboats. Souren was assigned to supervise the transport of their equipment and supplies. He felt a strange combination of excitement and panic. These were the straits the Allies had failed to penetrate. The waterway was still densely fortified, and the captain, a veteran Greek sailor, zigzagged to avoid the thick underwater forest of mines. He became quite friendly when Souren talked to him in Greek. On the stimulus of his pipe, he proudly pointed out the landmarks by which he was guiding his craft through the danger zones. In a few places, tugs assisted their passage. They were halfway through the straits when a terrific explosion knocked Souren off his feet. He rose just in time to see the body parts of German sailors and officers floating by amid debris of their twisted and splintered motorboat. Nauseous and frozen in place, he stared wide eyed at the human clutter. *My God, the insanity of this all just gets worse,* he groaned to himself.

"There is Mudros." The captain interrupted and directed Souren's gaze toward the harbor of the historic island of Lemnos. A row of puffing smokestacks marked the entrance to the storied Hellespont. Souren recognized the sorry remains of the wrecked tramp steamer *River Clyde*, the famous modern ship of Troy from which intrepid sons of Australia had landed after the ship was beached.

If only, Souren thought to himself. *If only they could have prevailed.*

Gallipoli's No-Man's-Land had lost its horrors except for some fragments and shell holes. Its profound dead silence was broken by activity in the dugouts. The officers had found a supply of cold food, marmalades, and jams left over by the British in their hurried evacuation of Gallipoli. Some of the soldiers had acquired good khaki uniforms whose buttons were imprinted with the British Royal Crown. All their water kegs were inherited from the belated expedition of the Narrows.

Some of the new arrivals bragged about throwing the British into the sea and regretted not having been part of the action. But those who had fought were glad for the relative quiet at the front.

In a dingy barrack, Souren sat down at a long table with dozens of other soldiers to a meal of bean soup in a thin broth. He decided to eat before his three-mile trek back to the general at camp. He tore a large piece of coarse bread in half and glanced around at the other men, who were noisy and jovial.

He stopped suddenly, sure he heard someone speaking Armenian. He wondered for a moment if he was hallucinating. Casually, he looked up from his meal and realized the soldier directly across the table was rambling in Armenian.

"He's crazy!" one of the Turks informed Souren.

"Tell him how you discovered the British were gone," a soldier coaxed the lunatic.

"He's the one?" Souren asked in surprise. He didn't look like a dependable messenger, yet this babbling man, labeled insane by his fellow soldiers, was also heralded as a hero of sorts. Spared the slave labor battalions because of his skill at making and reparing boots, he also had been a sentry on duty at Gallipoli. While scouting one morning, he was the first to report that there were no soldiers in the enemy trenches. On the strength of this news, the Turks gradually pushed forward to find out that, overnight, the British had evacuated their troops right under their enemies' noses.

Souren couldn't help but hear and comprehend the man's ravings. He was talking about his family. Instinctively, Souren put his hand over his mouth in horror.

"My sisters! My sisters!" he wailed in Armenian. "Where have they taken my sisters? They killed my parents!" The man was weeping now. He pushed his soup away and beat his head on the table.

"He goes on like this for hours, but he's harmless," one of the soldiers said. "He's probably homesick. A man can lose his mind in the army! He was a skilled cobbler, now look at him."

Souren tried to affect an expression that would not betray that he understood the man. The Armenian spoke of a man passing through the unit and telling him that his family had been deported.

"While I was serving my government at the front, that same government treacherously killed my parents and carried away my sisters!"

The spirited singing and bursts of laughter drowned out the sorrowful voice.

Souren got up from the table. He rode back to camp with renewed determination to find a way out of this mess before he, too, became a raving lunatic.

—𝔴—

The British maintained a presence off the coast on the islands of Lemnos and Tenedos off the coast near the entrance to the Dardanelles. They must have noticed the movement of troops on the mainland, because a heavy bombardment began. Souren and Wagner watched with field glasses from the dugout. First came a sinister hiss. Then, a huge shell would plow up the ground. The land was sandy, and a good many of the shells would not explode after impact. Others whistled overhead, throwing sand and dirt on them and burning their noses.

The British were in the habit of teasing them every morning with a bombardment, but their scout planes were nothing more than annoying. Souren and Wagner got to the point that they could identify each plane by the noise of its engine, and gave a pet name to each aircraft. At night, however, the air raids were dreaded. The sputter of an engine shrouded in darkness and waiting to drop its bomb whittled away at morale and robbed the soldiers of their sleep.

They had been in this godforsaken spot for a week, living in dugouts like ants. The commander had a room, all covered with pine branches, on top of the hill. Souren put up his tent half buried in the ground near his door, thinking the war was nothing more than a game of hide-and-seek, where camouflage was the secret. Camouflage could lead the enemy to believe there were no soldiers or fortifications when there were, and it could suggest all the forces of Hindenburg and the guns of Krupp were at the ready when there were none.

Souren received an order to ride with the commander for an inspection of the coast. Wagner called him over to prepare him.

"Souren," he said, "you need to learn the precise terms to translate the general's instructions when you accompany him today." Pointing to the trenches, he said, "*Sheissen Graben*. Let me hear you say it."

"Sheissen Graben," Souren repeated with ease.

Wagner then suggested the horse Souren should take, and Souren agreed. Only when it was too late did he realize that the horse hadn't been broken. He bounced up and down, trying to follow the commander and his Turkish staff, vowing to have his revenge on Wagner.

As the party of officers rode along the waterfront, soldiers jumped from everywhere and lined up for inspection. Souren began the work of translating between the general and a Turkish soldier.

"Suppose the enemy is landing," the general asked. "What are you going to do?"

The sergeant major said, "We will shoot them all!"

"No, that is wrong. Let them approach the coast. Then shoot them if they do not surrender. In this way we may get news about the enemy."

The commander turned to Souren. "Ask the sergeant the whereabouts of Company Four."

Souren translated the general's question, and the sergeant pointed to a trench and replied in Turkish, "Behind that trench."

Souren said to the general, "Herr Commandant, hinter den sheissen Graben."

The commander was puzzled and asked Souren in English, "What do you mean?"

In English, Souren answered him, "Behind those trenches."

"Oh, yes, I see." He smiled. "But you see, 'sheissen Graben' translates as 'shithole.'"

Souren realized that he was ever gullible when it came to Wagner. "Twice in one day!" he murmured under his breath. "This is the last time I play the fool!"

And it was—but not because he avenged himself on Wagner. Upon arriving back at camp, Souren learned that a unit under Wagner's leadership had been transferred up to Suvla Bay, from the Asiatic side of the straits to the European side. He could not decide what bothered him most, losing his wisecracking German friend or missing his chance to get back at Wagner.

—⁂—

Sitting in front of his tent one evening, Souren watched the flares and played an Armenian song on his piccolo. It was called "Groong." He disguised the iconic song by playing the melody in the rhythm of a waltz. It felt unnatural to play the slow, melancholy ballad in the three-four time of a German waltz. He thought of the lyrics as he piped out the notes, searching for comfort in his loneliness.

I have left my farm and all my belongings
I've gone far away, my soul aches as I sigh
Oh, dear crane, stay awhile—let your voice touch my soul
Oh, crane, do you have any news from our country?

Souren noticed movement in the distance. He jumped to his feet. A figure darted behind a tree.

"Who's there?" Souren called.

The mysterious figure showed his head, crossed his index fingers, and kissed them in fear and supplication. Souren cautiously approached him. It was a young lad dressed in rags. Souren noticed bruises all over his body.

In Turkish the stranger asked, "What is that song?"

Souren paused. "Do you know it?"

"I think I recognize the melody. Are you Armenian?" he asked, no longer speaking in Turkish.

"Yes," Souren replied without censoring himself. The sound of his native tongue, tinged though it was with odd pronunciations— obviously an Anatolian accent—made him instantly susceptible to trusting the stranger.

The young man fell at his feet and embraced him. Hardly able to take enough breath to talk, he told Souren that he had been severely beaten and thrown into prison, below in the dugouts.

"When I heard the sound of your music, I sneaked out while the guard was asleep." He stopped to look around and then whispered, "I am an Armenian, but no one knows. I am known as Hussein." He winked playfully.

Souren could not believe his eyes or his ears. He offered the boy some of the beans and bread left in his tent. Hussein hungrily devoured his portion before hurrying back to his cell.

"I will come again in the morning."

When Souren expressed concern for his safety, Hussein said confidently, "I'll be fine. The guards change shifts regularly. I'll slip out during the confusion."

The next morning, just as he had promised, Hussein appeared while Souren was eating his breakfast. He had set a place for his new friend, whose eyes landed on the fruit. Swiftly, Hussein emptied the bowl of raisins into his pockets like a thief. Souren watched him drink his coffee and chew huge mouthfuls of bread. Feeling Souren's eyes on him, Hussein raised his tin cup toward him and smiled with gratitude for his compatriot's generosity.

Souren shrugged, a little embarrassed by the amount of food he was fortunate to get. He learned that this prisoner was known in his company as Hussein the Arab Brigand, or Chakigi-Hussein. Periodically, he would gather all the army blankets he could carry, desert the army, and sell them. The last time he deserted, he took his gun and ammunition and stationed himself on the highway, where he held up soldiers and asked for their passes, which he would tear up. He would then proceed to rob them. When recaptured, he got by with only a minimum number of lashes. He was young and at least somewhat admired because his actions were so daring. Besides, he was a soldier and the company tailor, both of which the army desperately needed. Desertion dwindled ranks, and those who remained to fight often wore tattered tunics and trousers. A tailor like Hussein, though bent on desertion and theft, had his place in the Ottoman army nonetheless.

One night when all was quiet, Hussein came to Souren's tent and told him the reason for his last lashing. The company's Turkish imam, Hoja, was to go to Ezine, a city forty miles away, with the company's money to buy some supplies and material to be tailored for him. He ordered Hussein to accompany him. The imam rode a beautiful, spirited horse, while Hussein was given a lifeless animal that could not keep up. When they came to a stream on the road, Hussein stopped and pointed his gun at the imam and commanded him to hand over his money, which he did. He then took the imam's horse and gave the imam his, and ordered the imam to follow him. They rode in this fashion for two hours, and just before they reached the city, Hussein changed his mind, returned the horse and the money, and told the imam it was all a joke.

The imam promised on Mohammed not to mention the incident, but when they returned to camp, the imam became furious and told of the holdup. To the officers this was a serious offense, yet also a hilarious one. Hussein was treated relatively leniently, only beaten and put into a cell for three days without food or water.

"Hussein," Souren said, "why do you do such foolish and desperate things? They would shoot you if they knew that you were an Armenian."

From first sight, Hussein and Souren discovered they had things in common. Hussein became attached and devoted to Souren. He knew better than to talk to Souren in the presence of others, but he would leap to his feet to salute every time he saw him, which made Souren feel stupid. Souren fed him daily, and with more calories, the boy regained his youthful complexion.

"How would you like to be part of my unit?" Souren asked. He thought Hussein would jump at the chance to get out of his cell.

Instead, Hussein asked, "Who is your commander? Maybe I know this Turk already."

"Oh, he's not a Turk. I'm an interpreter." Souren explained how he had come to be under the protective aegis of his kind commander.

Hussein impulsively barked out, "Curse the Germans!"

Souren drew back in surprise. "You don't understand. He saved my life."

"He saved your life? Well what about the rest of us?" Hussein shook with anger. His face had transformed into a grotesque expression that reminded Souren of the masks worn by the witches at a school performance of *Macbeth*.

"My home was Urfa."

Souren cringed. "Urfa," he repeated in a low, somber tone.

"Yes, Urfa, nearly a thousand miles in that direction," Hussein said, waving his hand eastward. "My father was the leading tailor in the city. I used to help him after school. When the war broke out, the Turks threatened the Armenians, telling us that if we became Muslims, we would not be deported like the rest. Armenian refugees had been coming through our city for months. Witnessing their heartbreaking condition, we knew that neither conversion nor giving up our weapons would save us. Massacres followed, and the government arrested hundreds of Armenians. My father used to tell my mother, 'If anything happens to me, you know where the gold is hidden.'"

Souren had heard previously some of what happened in Urfa. Hussein now filled in much more frightening detail. Under the leadership of a brave fighter named Megerditch, Urfa's Armenians set up barricades and dug trenches. Only three hundred men had weapons. Groups of ten were positioned in thirty locations to give the appearance of a well-armed resistance. Urfa's Armenians stripped their homes of metal, bronze, iron, and copper, transforming once-tranquil residences into arsenals where shells were cast and grenades assembled. The hospital was made ready for emergencies. The older women manned huge kettles to feed the fighters. Young girls and boys carried ammunition and supplies to the trenches. During sixteen days of bitter fighting, the Armenians stunned the Turks by repeatedly repelling their assaults.

Finally, the government had had enough. Fakri Pasha, the commander who had failed to defeat the defiant Armenians holed up on their mountain at Musa Dagh, was called to Urfa, and he came to settle the score. At Musa Dagh, the Armenians had defiantly held out against repeated assaults for forty days and were finally resuced by a French battleship. But this time Fakri would prevail against the Armenians.

He called on the German captain, Wolfskeen, and directed him where to aim his cannon. For four days, a relentless rain of shells devastated the Armenian neighborhoods.

Souren remained silent and let Hussein continue his story.

"When we received word that my father had been killed, my mother went to his hiding place and collected the gold. She sewed the coins into the hems of a few blankets and into our jackets. I watched her tie up her hair and hide a few pieces in the coiled mound of hair on the back of her head. She tied her scarf under her chin. Picking up my baby brother, she delivered instructions for us to be ready to leave. It wasn't long before soldiers strutted through our decimated neighborhood with rifles pointing, ordering us out of our homes and to the local caravansary with a large courtyard. Mother insisted that above all, we must stick together. I turned aside for only a moment to gaze at the shattered, smoldering buildings, and when I looked back, she was gone. My sisters and baby brother, too. I yelled, 'Mayrig! Mayrig!' That's when a Turkish soldier grabbed me and threw me into a line with other refugees. For hours I ran up and down the lines searching for my family.

"The soldiers kept us moving under the sharp lashes of their leather whips. They struck old women whose step they deemed too slow. They ripped open the flesh of a pregnant woman who had fallen down.

"Frantic to find my family, I was able to hide behind a large stone. For days, I watched as one caravan after another passed out of Urfa. A steady rain pounded the ground on one of those days. I saw a little boy holding on to his mother's wet, muddy skirt, his eyes darting around in fear. I was jealous of him. I wanted to be walking with my mother, too.

"Soon, no more caravans, and I knew that meant no more Armenians were left in Urfa. They were either dead or walking to their deaths. The knapsack with the bread and dried yogurt my mother had given me was long empty, and so was my stomach. I took the gold coins from my jacket and made my way to a village in the same direction as the caravans had gone. There, I purchased bread and cheese from a kind Turkish woman who looked at me with pity. She gestured southward. I slept on her roof until nightfall. I thought it best to travel under the cover of darkness.

"Maybe I could have found my mother, brother, and sisters if I hadn't run into a band of robbers who beat me and robbed me of my clothes and money. Before I regained consciousness, a Turkish officer spotted me. He was looking for deserters, and I became his latest prisoner. Along with the rest, I was put on a train and shipped to the front. As the others slept, I contemplated the situation. I stole papers from a snoring Turk. Since then my name has been Hussein, an Arab Turk. I hate Germans, and I live to exact revenge for my family!"

Souren still said nothing. What could he say? He was determined to help.

The next morning, he took some tattered uniforms to the commander, telling him that they needed mending. The commander, fastidious about military attire, agreed and asked Souren to find someone to do the work.

"I know just the person, sir," Souren answered.

"Well, then why didn't you take them there in the first place? Why bring the old uniforms to me?" The commander knew Souren very well by now.

The general possessed full knowledge of the deportations going on throughout the empire. He and his fellow German officers often argued with their Turkish counterparts about the government's anti-Armenian and anti-Greek policies. The forced march of the elderly, women, and children infuriated the likes of Souren's commander. Besides, the mass killings of the fighting-aged men meant fewer soldiers, and the precious few railroad cars and tracks that were available in Turkey should be used for the war, not ethnic cleansing.

At Souren's request, the general signed orders to have Hussein sent to him to become a member of the headquarters.

"I still hate the Germans," Hussein declared upon learning how he wound up as the company tailor.

"They aren't all killers!" Souren insisted.

Somewhat grudgingly, but more than a little grateful, Hussein moved into a small building that became an army tailor shop. With his turbaned head and fluent Turkish and Arabic, no one suspected he was an Armenian. He did exceedingly good work, and the commander was pleased. But woe to any clothes sent by the Turkish sergeant major or the imam. Hussein made them look like inflated balloons, and when they complained, he made them as narrow in the waistline as that of an Egyptian belly dancer.

Hussein and Souren spent more and more time together, and though Hussein was war hardened, he burst into tears when they talked about Armenians who were still alive. Souren told him of his brothers and sisters living in American. Hussein, too, had a brother there. What if Souren's family contacted Hussein's brother? The pair spent hours planning a way to contact their relatives. Souren floated the idea of a telegram. Hussein wanted something more tangible and exciting.

"If only we could muster a boat!" he said.

"But that might make trouble for the commander," was Souren's knee-jerk reply. He quickly added, "Besides, there are no boats."

One night during a long strategy session, the two decided they should swim across the bay and hope an Allied boat would pick them up. The idea was perfect, except for one thing: Hussein remembered he couldn't swim.

"You can't swim?" Souren asked, surprised.

"I didn't grow up by the sea!" he retorted defensively. "You'll have to do it, and then you will come back with a motorboat and get me."

The next day, Hussein sewed a pocket into Souren's trousers, where he put two English sterlings in case Souren needed a bribe to secure the necessary boat.

"Where in the world did you get those?"

"I killed a Kurd who had killed a British prisoner of war. He took the poor soldier's money, so I robbed him. A fitting way to spend it, eh?"

He repeated his brother's name and the city he believed him to be in several times, making sure Souren would remember.

"This is our only chance, Unger Souren." He identified Souren as a fellow freedom fighter by calling him an *unger*. Souren felt a visceral surge of pride and keen anticipation.

"I want to make it look like I drowned," Souren said, "to protect the commander from any responsibility."

"I'll take care of it," Hussein reassured him

"If they think I've escaped, they might go after my mother."

"Don't worry so much," Hussein cajoled.

Souren crept through the encampment. He crawled under the barbed wire and made his way across the sandy beach. He laid his clothes under a rock and quietly waded into the water. Oh! How cold the water was. Souren was a few hundred feet from shore and getting warmed when he looked out and saw warships bristling with guns. The sea was black and menacing under the night sky. He had never been afraid of water before this moment. He had grown up swimming with his friends in the crystal-clear Agean. But in the dark, in frigid waters, after having deserted his post, he trembled from fear and from the cold.

His limbs grew numb and virtually immobile. His skin hurt. As he began kicking, his foot brushed against something solid. The floating body parts of the German sailors he had seen in the straits weeks before haunted him now. These waters concealed naval mines triggered by contact.

What if the mine explodes? Souren reproached himself as a coward. "Nothing is worth doing without risk!" he said aloud through chattering teeth and a pair of lips so cold he couldn't articulate the words properly.

He wanted to cry out to Hussein, but what could he do? He sure as hell couldn't swim, and if Souren said he wanted to come back, Hussein would urge him on with something like, "Unger Souren, do it for Armenia!"

He recognized, though, that swimming over a mile in these conditions was physically impossible and headed back to the beach. After walking silently past a disappointed Hussein, he grabbed his clothes from under the rock and made his way back to his tent to thaw out.

"The commander is looking for you," one of the soldiers called from outside the tent.

Some Turkish officers had arrived unexpectedly, and the general needed Souren to interpret for him. Less than thirty minutes after his failed escape, Souren was exchanging war plans and best wishes, even a few jokes with which each party wished to impress the other. If Souren failed to understand the German joke, he substituted it with one of his own. The officers would look into each other's faces and enjoy themselves. Dark coffee was served in little dainty cups. Then they saluted and departed, satisfied.

Early one morning, Souren was ordered to the town of Ezine to run errands—a great opportunity for tension relief. Hussein needed supplies for his tailor shop, so he was allowed to accompany Souren. Once out of their section, their imaginations took over. Hussein rode an Arabian pony and was dressed like a warrior sheikh, with an open-breasted coat, a turban on his head, a bandolier on his shoulder, and a rifle on his back.

"Let's go and drive out the Turks," he yelled.

He was wild with joy for his temporary freedom. The two stopped occasionally for some target practice. Hussein was a much better marksman than Souren. They sang Armenian patriotic songs the entire way to Ezine. Then Hussein carried the pack and followed Souren as his bodyguard. Souren was wearing a German coat with leather puttees. They decided that his name was to be Hassan Effendi, a Turkish lieutenant, and when they stopped at any place, Hussein was to address him as his officer.

Late at night they saw the light of a village. They rode up to a coffee shop and sat down on the porch. It was Bairam, a fasting day for the Turks. The mosque, filled with devout believers, was aglow with lights. The proprietor of the coffee shop wore a green turban and a short colored apron as he served coffee on the porch. Inside the little shop, a dozen men were smoking their hookahs, sitting on divans with their legs crossed under them. They were talking about a great event that was to take place shortly. Husendin Bey, an officer, was marrying an Armenian infidel girl, and the whole village was dressed in gala array and celebrating. Souren's curiosity grew more and more, and he asked more and more questions. The bride, he learned, was Beatrice—and Husendin Bey was the son of the commander who had almost gotten Souren sent to the front. The news electrified his imagination, and his joy and restlessness were boundless. He filled Hussein in, and Hussein agreed they had to rescue her at any cost.

Souren paid the bill and crossed the street to where they had left their horses. Hussein made a big show of crying in alarm, "Effendi, they have stolen the bag of tobacco!" even though their tobacco was well and accounted for. He hurried back to the coffee shop and hit the proprietor in the chest with the butt of his rifle. "Your shop is a nest of robbers," he yelled. "You must find the thief!" Hussein made everybody stand up, and searched them. Then phase two of the plan kicked in: He asked the whereabouts of the *muchtar*, the mayor of the village. He directed the proprietor to lead them there.

The streets were dark and dingy. Lamps flickered on the corners. In contrast, the muchtar's house was aglow with lights from dozens of candles. Food was spread lavishly on low tables, and two rows of men were seated on carpets, legs crossed, facing the women and girls, who were seated on the other side of the large room. There was music and dancing that allowed Souren and Hussein to enter the hall almost unnoticed. Souren told Hussein to cover the room with his rifle by standing at the door. He met Beatrice's eye, and she looked at him in recognition.

With great authority, he ordered the men present to remove their pistols and daggers from their belts and hold their hands up. He kicked the weapons to the corner and told them they were looking for a thief. Then he held the bridegroom-to-be by the wrist and angrily scolded him about this thieves' nest. Beatrice, understanding Souren's intentions, ran to the door. Souren gradually backed up, still aiming his revolver at the men, until they were out the door. Then the three disappeared in the dark.

Souren vaulted Beatrice up onto his horse. He had to persuade Hussein not to kill anyone.

Hussein glowered and yelled at Souren in Armenian, "Don't you have any Armenian blood?"

Fortunately, no one understood. Hussein joined Souren and Beatrice, and the three rode toward headquarters by a different route than they'd come.

Beatrice was the same fearless and game daughter of misfortune. She clung to Souren tightly, and he could feel the throbbing of her heart. They could not exchange any words, but they could read each other's thoughts and worries. *Now what?* Where could they go in an enemy-infested land? Husendin Bey would be furious, and before morning, the news of her escape would spread. They would be doomed if found. Beatrice would stay with them through thick and thin, she attested, and all three pledged to stay together or die.

As they approached their unit, they stopped for breath. *Now what?*

How would Souren tell his commander that he had kidnapped the major's future daughter-in-law?

Hussein stood close to the fugitive girl, looked at her intently, and then said in radiant joy, "Why, here is our tailor! We are the same height, and no one knows me in the headquarters."

So they decided to keep Beatrice as the soldier/tailor and call her Hussein, known in the regiment as the brigand soldier. The real Hussein would pose as a Turkish attendant in Souren's quarters, with the name of Halil.

They mounted again and stopped at Souren's tent. When Beatrice was dressed in Hussein's uniform, she made the perfect soldier. Halil fixed a new uniform for himself from one of Souren's old ones, and they retired for the night, as if unaware of anything. For two months, life presented no unusual excitement. Beatrice did good work. No secret organization ever kept its secrets more sacredly than this triple alliance.

With repentance and love, Beatrice urged the two men to find other opportunities to rescue Armenian girls who had been forced into bondage. Meanwhile, Hussein wanted to leave the regiment in search of his mother and sisters. It took all of Souren's energy to contain them both.

—⚏—

The general received telegrams regularly. Sometimes, particularly those in Turkish that Souren translated, they sent him into fits of anger. Other times he'd crumple them up and toss them into the trash. One day, however, he received a telegram from German headquarters that caused a new reaction: sullenness. He had nothing to say about it, but Souren could tell it had made him sad. Over a period of two weeks, the tall, muscular general began to sag across his shoulders. His steps were heavier. He frequently waved off meals and spent more time than usual poring over maps. Periodically, Souren saw him pull the folded telegram from his pocket and read it.

"I must go back to Germany," he announced to Souren one afternoon before another inspection of the coastal defenses. "My brother—" His voice quaked briefly, so he started again. "My brother, the commander of a German regiment, was killed, and I must go and take his command."

He looked down before saying to Souren, "Also, this just came today." He tapped a piece of paper in front of him. "Every Armenian within fifty miles of the front is to be sent to the interior."

Souren suddenly felt like he was back in the frigid waters of the Aegean, passing dangerously close to a volatile mine. He stood in speechless stupefaction.

His worst nightmare was about to come true.

"Souren," the general went on, "I deeply appreciate the loyalty and the honesty with which you have served me for the past two years. I feel that we have become friends." The general cleared his throat. "I know that you want to come with me, both to get out of this hellhole and maybe for us to continue to work together. With the onset of what now seems to be a systematic ethnic cleansing of Armenians here, I worry about what would happen to you should your real identity be discovered."

A gush of relief sent blood coursing again throughout his body. He stopped shivering. Clarity replaced confusion. He waited to hear what the commander would propose.

"I suggest you come with me to Constantinople. I will try to obtain permission from the German military for you to study in Germany. Once there, you will be safe."

"I don't have any papers," Souren reminded him. "How will I leave the country without the proper documents? Officially, I'm a deserter."

"Let me see what I can do." The general excused Souren, who tried to quell his own joy out of respect for the general's personal grief.

—m—

In three days, the general's orders came. The Turkish members of his staff hosted a big celebration in his honor. TheArab Turks in particular had grown to greatly respect and admire their chief. They all wore their turbans and danced the Bedouin dance and sang while they whirled torches over their heads. Two soldiers on the shoulders of two others, with shield and sabre in hand, danced the war dance. The chorus and songs of the desert with the accompaniment of the sheikh's music made for a memorable spectacle. Amid shrieking and swaying to the dull, monotonous beat of tom-toms and the wailing of shields, the sheikhs danced in honor of their beloved commander. They started at dawn and continued into the darkness, similar to the dance of the conquistadors and adapted to the rituals of their religious beliefs.

The next morning, back at headquarters, mules, cars, horses, and camels were loaded up. Beatrice and Hussein accompanied the caravan to the city of Canakkale. Souren gazed at his friends with sorrowful eyes. In spite of their previous vows, now they were being forced to part. With the general's transfer, a new commander, with his own body of junior officers and assistants, was to replace him and his staff. Hussein and Beatrice were to be left once again to fend for themselves. Hussein was unafraid at the prospect. Beatrice planned to join a gypsy troupe. Gypsies, long a Turkish institution, were not bothered by the government.

For the parting occasion, Beatrice had transformed her old bride's dress into that of a gypsy. She could make her fiery eyes spell hatred and revenge, but now as she gazed at Souren, they were tear filled with love and sorrow. Her red lips could read a fortune, utter a prayer, or broadcast anger like the eruption of an emotional volcano at the Turks she despised. But now she lovingly read their fortunes.

When she came to Souren, she stroked his hands and said, "Be good, my liberator, and within six days, six weeks, or six months, destiny will bring us together."

Souren was a torment of mixed emotions. How could he leave Beatrice and Hussein in this situation? His love for Beatrice was too strong, and the three of them had become like the Three Musketeers, *all for one and one for all,* in a sea of terror and unfathomable tragedy still unfolding. Yet now was his only chance to escape in a way that also held the promise of the rescue of his mother and the chance to join the rest of the family in America. There was no real choice. He had to go.

Finally they bade one another good-bye. Souren and Beatrice embraced tightly and softly wept together before she finally turned and walked away. Souren turned to Hussein, and they strongly shook hands and clinched arms and then hugged. Hussein looked at Souren and smiled. He told his friend that his blood was boiling and that Souren would hear about him as a terrorizing brigand on the track of his parents.

Chapter Seven

—w—

1917-1918

Souren watched Constantinople come into view from the bow of the agile torpedo boat. Straddling the narrow Bosphorus Strait, the city built on seven hills joined East and West—Europe and Asia. Aya Sofia, a magnificent basilica built by Emperor Justinian, served now as a mosque, with four minarets marking its conquest. Directly opposite stood the Sultan Ahmed Mosque, which dwarfed the Byzantine masterpiece in size and opulence. Six pencil-thin minarets and the signature flat dome of Ottoman architectural prestige established Ottoman dominance and permanence in this once-Christian capital.

Along the coast, several veiled women of the sultan's harem sailed by in their imperial caïque, inlaid with gold and ivory; it was a long, narrow skiff that the royal family used to cross the Bosphorus Strait. The women traveled comfortably on velvet and satin cushions between the European side of Constantinople and Sultan Mehmed V's winter palace. Two German battleships floated aimlessly in the harbor, a result of coal shortages brought on by war.

Souren and the general climbed out of the boat and made their way up a steep stone stairway. The commander took three steps at a time. It wasn't that he was in any particular hurry, just that his six-foot-three-inch frame allowed for long strides. Behind him, Souren kept up. When they reached the top of the stairs, they found themselves at the foot of the Galata Bridge, which was bustling with pedestrians and horse-drawn carriages. Donkeys pulled carts back and forth from the Turkish neighborhoods of Stambul to the European neighborhoods in Galata and Pera by way of the Golden Horn, the tributary that separated old Stambul from the European residents. A few horse-drawn coaches waited for new arrivals.

"Grand Palace Hotel in Pera," the commander called to the driver. It probably was an unnecessary order, since all German officers stayed at the same historic hotel. Souren and the general climbed into the old carriage.

"You'll stay at the barracks and wait to hear from me." He eyed Souren. "You shouldn't have any trouble. I let the German officer there know you would be arriving. It'll only be a couple of days. You'll be fine."

When they stepped out of the carriage together, a Turkish woman caught Souren's eye. He didn't look because she was beautiful, though she was. His eyes followed her because he had never seen a Muslim woman in any color besides black, and surely had never seen a Muslim woman's hair. Yet this woman wore a red velvet dress and had pulled tendrils of bleached auburn curls from under her traditional black veil, letting them dangle in European fashion around her face. She wore makeup on her lips and eyes. He did a double take when he heard her call out in flawless German to the general. She introduced herself as Halide Hanoum and engaged the general in animated conversation as the two strolled toward the entrance of the hotel.

Souren looked back a couple of times trying to make sense what he had just seen and heard, but it was futile; he really did not know what to make of it. He had never seen a modern Turkish woman. Having heard of her was one thing. Seeing her was quite another.

Souren was not looking forward to staying in the barracks; he felt safest when he was in close proximity to his general. Here in the capital where Talaat and Enver ruled the empire, he worried about being discovered. He slipped his hand into his breast pocket and made sure his papers were still there. They were. He smiled to himself. In a matter of two or three days, he would no longer need these documents. He would escape Turkey and land triumphantly in Germany. He wasn't at all sure of conditions there, but he imagined things as he hoped them to be. Of course, if the general were assigned to another theater of war, Souren might find himself in France or Russia. Still, he considered his chances of survival better anywhere than Turkey.

Weary and a little disoriented from the tiring trip, Souren decided to take a room in a small, dingy hotel. He would worry about finding the barracks tomorrow. After checking in, he dropped off his valise in his room and went downstairs for dinner. The city may have thus far avoided the destruction visited on the Gallipoli Peninsula, but the people suffered the privations of war. Souren toyed with the slice of hard, tasteless bread on the plate in front of him. Tonight there would be no meat and only a bitter concoction of chicory pretending to be coffee. Dried apricots sat untouched on his plate, as well as a handful of raisins and a few olives. Souren was too afraid of cholera to take a chance on ingesting contaminated fruit. Tea and coffee were too expensive. So was milk, which meant no yogurt or cheese on this particular day. He imagined the feast his general was no doubt enjoying at the German officers' hotel.

Only a few more days, he thought to himself and pushed away his plate.

A commotion on the stairs distracted Souren from his insipid dinner. He saw a Turkish officer awkwardly climbing the flight of stairs, pulling his prosthetic leg along one step at a time. Souren could not see his face because the man kept his chin tucked close to his chest. A pang of sympathy swept over Souren. He had seen so many men mangled and deformed by the machinery of war. Thousands of them had been put back together, but their grotesque scars and mutilated bodies caused onlookers to turn away in pity and fear. Out of respect, Souren looked away from the pathetic sight. A moment later, he got up and stepped outside.

The mist of the great Bosphorus Strait swept up from the coast. *The sultan lives just a few miles from where I'm standing*, Souren thought defiantly. *I'm right under his nose, and he doesn't even know it!*

"Soldier, let me see your papers."

Souren turned around at the sudden interruption.

A sergeant approached with an outstretched hand. Souren pulled his travel papers from his breast pocket with all the confidence of a free man.

"The goddamned Germans got us into this war!" the sergeant complained when he read them. "Were you at Gallipoli?"

Souren looked down at the shiny medal pinned to his breast pocket. His award had come during a perfunctory ceremony meant to boost troop morale. Men who had seen no action received medals for nothing in particular.

"Yes. I mean, no. That is, I was stationed at the Dardanelles after the British retreat." He could hear himself stammering out of embarrassment. He had seen no medals decorating the uniform of the beleaguered veteran soldier inside the hotel.

"Oh," the sergeant said. He was visibly disappointed. "I thought that was how you'd won that medal."

Souren shoved his folded travel documents into his pocket and walked back inside the dreary hotel. The door to his room was ajar. He pushed it open and looked inside. An officer slept in the bed—Souren's roomate for the night. He was the same one Souren had watched struggle up the stairs. An artificial leg was propped against the wall with two familiar objects on the floor next to it. One was a small tin plate, the other a partial jaw made from vulcanized rubber. Souren had seen enough of the walking wounded to identify that small collection of prostheses.

He curled up on the floor and dozed off. Before dawn, he woke at the sound of the soldier's morning ritual. He watched the officer deftly hook his prosthetic jaw in place. It covered the gaping hole that was his face before a piece of shrapnel had shredded his cheek and splintered the bones. Souren eyed the galvanized tin that had been painted to match his skin. The fit and color camouflaged his grotesque visage. From across the room, the soldier's face appeared fairly normal.

"Maybe my children will be able to recognize me," he said, looking across the room at Souren. He slurred his words trying to speak through the crude contraption that served as part of his jaw.

When he reached for his wooden leg, it slipped from his hand and banged to the floor. Souren leapt to his feet and retrieved the crude device. The officer grimaced in pain when his tender stump bore the weight of his body against the hard, ill-fitted artificial leg.

"What happened?" Souren couldn't help asking.

The officer shrugged. "We were commanded to attack. When we climbed out of the trench, a grenade exploded next to me. Two of our men lay motionless on the ground, and when I looked at myself, my leg was missing, and my eyes were filling with blood. One of my buddies had a look of horror. That's when I realized that part of my face was missing too."

A long pause ensued. Souren tried to think of something appropriate to say, but it was the officer who broke the painful silence.

"I think it would have been better to have died than to be like this."

The next day Souren walked reluctantly to the barracks. Still two hundred yards away, he thought he recognized the two noncommissioned officers strolling out of the gate. He was sure they were Bedros and Berj, two childhood friends who had been in his Scout troop long ago. Souren signaled them, and the two stopped in front of him. He smiled. The round boys had grown into strong, handsome men.

"What is it?" Berj asked. "I haven't got all day."

"Berj, it's me."

"Souren!" Bedros recognized his old friend's smiling eyes.

"Besherik," he whispered.

The three were careful not to draw any attention to their little group.

"I'll meet you at the coffeehouse across the street," Souren said and walked away.

Berj and Bedros loitered for a few minutes and then made their way to the rendezvous.

The noisy street and the steady chatter of patrons drowned out their private conversation. Souren learned that the two men served as horsekeepers. Not only did they train them, they washed, brushed, and shoed the animals too. They were most fortunate. The only Armenian men the Turkish military spared from the deadly labor battalions, at least temporarily, were those with a critical skill needed for the army's effectiveness.

Souren explained all he had experienced under the protective aegis of his general and how he was leaving Turkey with him in a matter of days. Berj and Bedros wished their friend the best of luck in his new life. Conversation turned to Smyrna and their families and friends. Each told what he knew. Souren bore the most useful information since he had been home more recently than the other two. Poor Berj and Bedros hadn't seen Smyrna since they were drafted in the summer of 1915. They peppered Souren with many questions, and he was able to answer most of them. He could not, however, give any definitive news of their relatives.

"Armen was deported," Souren said.

"Enlisting in the army didn't save him after all," Berj reflected solemnly.

"Are you staying at the barracks?" his friends asked.

"I'm supposed to. The general said he sent a message to the German officer here."

"Oh no! That officer is an idiot. He is not to be trusted," Bedros sighed.

"What should I do?" Souren looked to his friends for help. The last thing he needed was to find himself sent to a Turkish barracks and be subject to an impromptu interrogation as to what he was doing there. The situation could prove dangerous.

His friends looked at each other and then back to Souren.

"You'll stay with us, but don't come through the gate."

Souren received instructions to sneak in through a back entrance near the horse stalls. They would wait for him and convey him safely through the maze to their sleeping quarters.

After the other noncommissioned officers had retired, the three crawled among them unnoticed. They were lying on the floor like sardines, their shoes and coats made into a bundle that served as a pillow. Usually, noncommissioned officers enjoyed the wartime luxury of a cot. However, large troop movements caused overcrowding at all the barracks in the capital.

Before dawn, Souren climbed out of a window.

This same routine took place the following three nights. Souren would show up at the designated location in the evening. His friends would meet him, and the three would weave their way unnoticed among the sprawling mass of soldiers. Each morning before dawn, Souren slipped out a window.

The last time Souren jumped through that barrack window, he did so with great anticipation. He thanked his old friends and wished them well before he rushed to the Galata Bridge for a pre-arranged meeting with the general.

Souren saw his beloved commander smoking a pipe and looking pensive. The general motioned for him to come and sit. As he did so, he set down his valise. The proprietor brought a second cup of tea. Souren grasped it and inhaled the sweet, luxurious fragrance. Tea, which was plentiful before the war, had become expensive and in some places even hard to find.

The general commented on the coal shortages and the paralyzed shipping in and out of the capital. In the distance they could see the two German cruisers. After evading several British fleets in the Mediterranean Sea, the German cruisers had sought refuge in Turkish waters, entering the Dardanelles and sailing up to Constantinople. The general recounted that in 1914, before Turkey had entered the war, global maritime laws stated that belligerent ships had to leave a harbor after twenty-four hours. And just like that, the German strategy to force Turkey into the war as its ally had worked.

"It's strange, the way these things go," the general said, looking at the cruisers. Souren wondered why the general was choosing this moment to be so reflective. "Souren, did you know that Djemal Pasha wanted Turkey to enter the war on the side of France? It was Talaat and Enver who preferred an alliance with Germany. And when our Admiral Souchon guided the cruisers through the Dardanelles, there was no turning back. Turkey purchased the ships, and, well, there they still sit. Once-glorious German war machines now idle on the Bosphorus."

The general continued, "I always thought that Djemal had a rich but complex and conflicted personality. It's impossible for such persons to think and act with consistency. They are a tangle of contradictions but put on a good face. But they remain enigmas who surprise themselves and others with grand and generous gestures motivated by the most depraved and sordid considerations."

Souren listened, surprised at the disclosure of Djemal's character by the general. He had served under him at the first Battle of the Suez Canal as a colonel and so spoke from a position of authority.

"Do you recall seeing the Turkish woman who met me outside the hotel?"

"Of course," Souren replied. "Halide Hanoum."

"Yes, that's correct. Apparently, she reformed the education system here in Constantinople and now is on her way to Syria to meet with Djemal Pasha. I learned that she is to be overseeing the so-called education of orphans—Armenians and Kurds. Here we are fighting a war, and Djemal has employed even teachers to conquer his smallest subjects. He believes Ottoman culture will forge unity and prevent independent ethnic groups from causing the fabric of Ottoman society to unravel. None of it will matter if the war is lost!"

"Djemal and Halide Hanoum are running an orphanage?" Souren asked.

"A few orphanages," the general corrected him. "Educating and converting the children of the parents they've massacred. Leave it to the Turks!" the general said with disgust.

The two sat in silence for a few minutes before the general asked, "Where did you say your family is from?"

"My mother is from Mush," Souren answered. "My father came from Caesarea. They moved to Erzurum. That's where some of my siblings were born."

"Well, the Russians are in control of the Caucasus. Enver has sent his best officers, best-trained soldiers, and vital supplies to Europe. So Turkey can't even protect her own borders. The soldiers remaining are unfit, untrained, and without enough weapons. It's a goddamned mess."

Souren wondered if the general were telling him their destination. Could he be headed to the Eastern Front? He felt a sense of jubilation at the thought of being close enough to the Armenian contingents fighting in the Caucasus to possibly escape to their ranks.

The austere German officer tapped his pipe against his teacup.

"General von Falkenhayn swore to bleed the French army white at Verdun. We lost over a quarter of a million men. Then, the British attacked at the Somme. German casualties soared to another quarter million men. It's a goddamned mess," he repeated, this time shaking his head. "Wilson has been reelected, so I imagine the Americans will declare war soon enough. And Italy has joined the Allies."

Okay, thought Souren, *perhaps we're headed to the Western Front.* He tried not to fidget. He was anxious but dared not press the commander for the details of their departure. A torpedo boat idled nearby.

After another pause, suddenly the general said, "Now, about our plans for the future."

Finally, Souren thought, and relaxed for the first time since he'd sat down.

"We've been working together for a long time. We've become friends. You've always been loyal."

Souren nodded hopefully as the general tapped his pipe on the table.

The general looked at Souren. "I wish I could keep you as my interpreter, but I'm very sorry to tell you that this will not happen."

Souren starred back at him wide-eyed and felt his heart race. Were they to go somewhere else? Would the general stay here in Turkey after all? If he weren't his interpreter, that would be all right. He would do whatever the commander demanded. A swirl of confused thoughts made him dizzy.

The general explained that although Marshal Liman von Sanders was willing to submit to headquarters the request for Souren to accompany him, von Sanders was convinced that the proposal for a German high officer to take a Turkish soldier to Germany would be judged totally unworkable.

He added, "The German army is too damned structured to suffer any breach for personal reasons."

Souren fell back, crestfallen. He was close to tears but too proud to express deep emotion in front of the general.

The sensitive general saw the deep disappointment of his young friend. He put his hand sympathetically on his arm and told him, "Souren, my friend, I cannot take you with me, but I will not allow you to be swallowed as a laborer by the Turkish army, nor will I leave you vulnerable to the government's campaign to rid Turkey of its Armenians. If you accept, then I will arrange for you to come under the protection of a German officer with whom I have served in the past and in whose word I trust. He knows your story, and he has promised me he will take you under his protection provided you remain loyal, which I assured him you would. His name is Lieutenant Hesselberger, and if you come tonight to the lobby of the hotel at seven o'clock, I will have him meet you there. You will recognize him because he doesn't look German. He doesn't like to be known as Jewish, but his father is, and you will recognize him by his short stature."

Souren looked down at his feet. *Hell!* he thought. *But what choice have I?*

He turned to the general. "Thank you, and I accept."

The general stood up and, with a final look at Souren, said, "Besherik, this is to wish you good luck. You are a most remarkable young man." He tightly grasped Souren's hand as he said it and then turned on his heels and walked briskly toward the anchorage of his ship.

Souren sat there for some time. He slumped in his seat with his chin against his chest, his eyes filling with tears. He knew an important turning point had just occurred in his life. *What the hell now?*

—◊◊◊—

A few days later, Souren boarded a special train with his new commander, First Lieutenant Hesselberger, an adventurer of war, and his assistant, Professor Behn, apparently one of the leading sculptors of Germany. As a special train took them away from Constantinople, Souren contemplated a bleak future. Things were obscure until Hesselberger explained to Souren that they had been ordered by Berlin to be pirates of the seas and continuously harass the Greek islands near the southwestern coast of Turkey.

The ultimate destination was the Bodrum Peninsula on the Aegean coast, but it would be several weeks, maybe even a couple of months, before they reached it. Several stops had to be made along the way to pick up the rest of the crew, weapons, and supplies. After the four hundred–mile trip to Aydin, the train cars would be traded for camels, since that was the end of the railway line.

Hesselberger had been a professional hunter of wild beasts. He proudly showed Souren a number of African jungle pictures of tigers, lions, and elephants lying slain at his feet. The first lieutenant was small, wiry, and exceptionally alert and active. Souren could not help but find humor in the little man who took down the mighty creatures of the jungle.

Professor Behn, as he demanded to be addressed, struck Souren as arrogant and haughty. He had just come from the Western Front and, though he was no more than a sergeant, swaggered around in a uniform of his own design that sometimes fooled others into saluting him as an officer. His authority, however, did not come from his preposterous uniform. He claimed special status by his association with Hesselberger, for whom there was no shortage of respect from the Turkish underlings and the German sailors in his unit. The prestigious Iron Cross First Class pinned on the left side of the first lieutentant's uniform proclaimed the kaiser's appreciation for exceptional leadership and unwavering patriotism.

Hesselberger and Behn touted the German way of doing things, whether it regarded food, beer, literature, or music—even waging war. Germans, the two men noted, were, generally speaking, superior to people of other cultures. In present circumstances, their only misfortune was being allies of the Turks, whom they considered entirely inferior except when it came to tobacco. Behn preferred the Saloniki tobacco, which Hesselberger pointed out was probably better thanks to the Jews who worked in the tobacco industry there.

"The Armenians are industrious and intellectual," Hesselberger said to Souren, "but they can't get along. Your people would be wise to accept their role in the Ottoman Empire and quit trying to establish a homeland. Look at the Jews of Germany. We have embraced being both of Jewish and German nationalities. Armenians could learn something from the Jews."

"The Armenians have some excellent art," Behn added. "It's really quite surprising when you think about it."

"How is it surprising?" Souren asked the supercilious professor.

"Surprising because you are an Oriental race. Not that Orientals don't create beautiful art, but it isn't the same as European. The proportions are all wrong. That's why Oriental art lacks a certain civilized feel. Japanese art, for instance, is flat, whereas Western art has depth."

"Armenians aren't Orientals. We are Indo-European, descendants of the Hittites."

"Is that so?" Behn replied. "Tell me, why is it that your people focus on religious subjects? If Armenians aren't building churches, they are painting pictures of them. It seems quite narrow, if you don't mind my saying so."

"Armenian art is sacred. We were the first nation to become Christian, and most Armenians are very attached to our faith in one way or the other." Souren felt a certain pride as he stared back at Behn.

The Germans let the subject drop in favor of their first preference of conversation, which was always lined with braggadocio: their hunting exploits in Africa. They loved to compete in telling the most extravagant tales of courageous acts, the down-to-the-last-second shot of the furious beast before them, be it an enormous rhinoceros or a mountainous, enraged elephant. In each case, the one shot placed in extremis strategically in the eye of the wild animal was supposed to have dropped it on the spot a meter away from the smoking gun.

By the time they reached the end of the railway line with several of the crew they had picked up along the way, Souren had already wearied of his new assignment and wondered how he would ever survive the egos of two such narcissistic men as these.

At Aydin, the vali, or governor, offered them dinner, an old-fashioned Oriental feast. There were at least twenty different dishes. The lieutenant exchanged some formal conversation but avoided any specifics. He had previously said to Souren, "We don't have any confidence in these people."

Early the next morning, the vali supplied thirty-five camels for their march to the coast of Anatolia. They loaded the camels with machine guns, one-piece artillery, and all of their supplies. The camel driver led the caravan, sitting on an old donkey hitched to the first camel. At times a contrary camel would stop and break the rope. When the cowbell attached to the first camel ceased to ring, they knew that a part of the caravan had become unhitched.

Behn, who had never ridden a camel, tottered up and down and from side to side. From the dizzying height of several feet, he observed, "While you can easily make the camel get down on all fours to climb onto his back, it does not make a very comfortable rocking chair if you have to sit on a load of machine guns."

Their progress was slow, about thirty miles a day. It was Souren's duty to telegraph ahead to the town or village where they were to stop that night for supplies and lodging. It was a matter of strict German policy in Turkey to take on supplies for double the number of horses, camels, and men. Thus, they would receive more than they needed. The surplus was then sold and the spoils divided equally among the soldiers so they could buy luxuries like soap and tobacco. Those who had anything left over sat down to a long night of poker. Souren did not care for cards and spent his time playing his piccolo or daydreaming about seeing Beatrice again someday.

They had been traveling for more than a week when they met a group of Armenians who were being driven out of the coastal area supposedly on suspicion of espionage. Hesselberger allowed the desperate people some of the vital supplies of his unit, but one of the Turkish cavalrymen who guarded them insisted they not be fed or given water.

Hesselberger sternly confronted the officer. "They will die before they reach Konya at this rate. Unless, of course, your plan is to let them die out here."

Souren wanted to grab the Turk by the throat. Once again he felt tortured that he was powerless to assist his suffering people. Konya marked the end of the Anatolian Railway and the beginning of the Bagdad Railway. Armenians in western Anatolia were driven on foot or sent by rail to Konya to await deportation to Syria. The Germans had developed the rail system for a direct link from Berlin to the Persian Gulf. Now the Ottomans were capitalizing on this infrastructure to remove Armenians, which incensed the Germans, who needed the railway cars for troops and supplies. Souren felt that Hesselberger was mostly thinking of this valuable and wasted resource, not the Armenians, as the little lieutentant unleashed his anger against the whole of Turkey when he saw soldiers rounding up the women and the elderly as if they constituted a danger to the empire.

The Turkish officer knew this German officer had no real authority over him. He had his orders. He simply cursed back at the

German and boldly stomped up to a barefoot woman and began to beat her. Souren and several others in his unit yelled out that he stop. But he ignored the men. Grabbing the woman forcefully by the arm, he yelled at her to get back to the column. The gendarmes resumed roughly herding the exiles away from Hesselberger's caravan and drove them mercilessly onward.

Souren felt sick to his stomach. There was nothing to do but to watch this pitiable group of Armenians, who carried no luggage with them and for whom there were no provisions, walk obediently under the blazing-hot sun of western Anatolia.

Hesselberger knew what Souren was thinking and stopped him before he acted foolishly.

"You can't do anything for them. I'm sorry. Leave it alone."

Souren felt the hatred take hold of his heart. His temples ached. His veins coursed with desire for revenge. The only sensation stronger than this was pain of utter helplessness.

A few hours later, after the military caravan had continued its march to the Aegean Sea, one of Turkish soldiers called out, "Gavour!" and laughed.

Souren jogged forward to see the woman whom the Turkish soldier had been beating earlier that day. She was naked. Her genital area was severely torn and bloody. Her breasts had been cut off. At most she was twenty-five years old. He noticed her pretty mouth, with its well-defined lips, hanging open. Her brown eyes with long lashes stared up toward heaven. Rivulets of fresh blood soaked her chestnut hair.

Instatnly sickened by the sight, Souren ran into a nearby thicket and vomited violently. Tears streamed down his cheeks. Sobs choked him. He convulsed with dry heaves that would not stop. His body fiercely rejected the horrible sight with round after round of involuntary retching. Finally Hesselberger walked up and handed him his canteen and patted him on the back.

The lieutenant ordered a few Turks to bury the body. When one of them refused, Hesselberger berated him. During the confrontation, Souren grabbed the soldier's spade and started to dig. He frantically tore away soil and stones.

"Hey," Hesselberger said quietly, "don't blow it."

Souren, grateful for the reminder, slowed his pace and dug with less fervor. Why should a Turk care about one Armenian? He regained his outward composure and prayed silently for this woman's soul, for her family, and for himself.

That night they camped in the open under clear moonlight. Souren considered the crescent moon, symbol of the Turkish flag, an omen for the refugees he had seen earlier that day.

—⁓—

In the morning, the camel driver and two of his attendants mixed straw and dark flour meal and rolled them into balls the size of a cantaloupe. The camels sat on their knees for their daily meal, opened their mouths, and swallowed each ball in one gulp, yet they seemed to chew it for hours. If there was any water, they drank a twenty-four-hour supply at one time.

Again they were on their way, following invisible trails until the caravan arrived at the village where they would camp for the night. Souren had telegraphed ahead, but when they rolled into town, the muchtar had neglected to gather supplies and had made no arrangement for the men's lodging. After being scolded by

Hesselberger, the muchtar's men hurriedly opened a Greek church for the soldiers and spread rugs for the men to sleep on.

The muchtar said to Souren, "You can tell your officer that I am tired of soldiers!"

But as soon as he found out that the men had authority to secure whatever they wanted, the venerable father stroked his beard and served them pilaf.

The camels were loaded before dawn each morning. The first part of the day was manageable, but as the sun rose higher, the heat rapidly intensified. Sometimes, the convoy leader would fall asleep and ride on serenely, his faithful donkey plodding forward on its own. But he would wake up instantly if anything went wrong, and if given a little tobacco, he would fill the valley with song, with no apparent worries about the war.

After weeks of grueling travel, the Aegean Sea finally came into view. The fresh sea breeze inspired and refreshed Souren. On Hesselberger's orders, they occupied a number of half-ruined houses on the waterfront.

One of the other interpreters to the lieutenant, a jeweler from Constantinople, invited Souren to a game of poker. "We need a fourth man," he said.

Souren was about to decline the offer, as he had never played before. But playing could make him out to be more of a comrade and enhance his security.

He hesitated long enough for the man to assess the situation and come back with, "A few hands. That's all. Whiskey, cigars, and poker. C'mon! Join us for a pleasurable diversion from this cruel monotony."

Souren acquiesced without much enthusiasm. The fellow interpreter smiled and patted him on the back. "Let the games begin!"

He led Souren to a dilapidated house. At a round, rough-hewn, rickety table sat one of the Greek prisoners, two Turkish soldiers, and two German sailors.

"I thought you said you needed a fourth man," Souren said.

"I did, but I guess you make seven. All the more in the pot!" His voice rang with glee.

Souren sat down and eyed his opponents by the light of the flickering candles, whose flames bounced around in the breeze stealing through the shattered windowpanes. He looked out and saw heaven's stars blinking in the sky. All of a sudden, he felt lucky and reached for the shot of raki at his elbow.

"Ante up, boys!" the interpreter called.

Souren's knowledge about card playing came from two divergent sources: his father's thunderous denunciations from the pulpit, and Sergeant Wagner.

Gambling was considered a sin. It went hand in hand with drunkenness and prostitution, his father had told him. Moreover, poker was a vice that landed families in the poorhouse. Men who could not resist the temptation would play until they were broke, hoping their luck would change. Their wives inevitably showed up at the parsonage crying because they had no money to buy food for their children. Souren vividly recalled a distraught women cursing the evils of gambling and alcohol as she sat in their parlor back home. As a young boy, he swore to himself and to God that he would never gamble or drink. He didn't know what a prostitute was at that age, but he also swore off that sin in the event he should ever encounter it.

Now that he was a military-hardened soldier, and while he still had no intention of visiting a brothel, he was willing to smoke a cigar, drink some raki—that ubiquitous Turkish liquor—and play poker. Souren noticed it actually felt good to let go of previous inhibitions and enjoy the company of others late into the night in a dense fog of acrid cigar smoke.

Although a novice, Souren had often carefully watched Sergeant Wagner play poker. Wagner took down so many formidable opponents that the Turkish soldiers either refused to play him or sought him out just to see if he could be vanquished. He never was, and his legend grew. Souren admired his friend's cool-headed ruthlessness at the table. He bled his opponents dry from one town to the next as their unit made its way across Turkey. When Souren asked him to reveal his secret to winning, Wagner held up two fingers nearly an inch from Souren, as if he were to poke out his eyes.

"The eyes," he said with all of the confidence of an older brother sharing an important life lesson with his younger sibling.

"But you need a good hand, don't you?" Souren countered.

"Not necessarily. Poker is all about deception. It's about making the guy across the table believe what you want him to believe."

"How do you do that?"

"I watch his eyes. I don't know what it is. A look, you know? And his neck."

"The neck?" Souren was confused.

"When the heart is racing, the blood pulses through the neck. You can watch it throb and know you're about to claim another victim. An anxious man with a losing hand cannot control a racing heart."

Three hours after he had sat down, Souren's pile of money had grown considerably. He liked his odds and stayed longer than he had planned. He wondered to himself about the many fools who had lost their precious wages and left their families hungry, all because they did not understand that this was a mind game, not just a card game. He laughed to himself.

One of the Germans cut the deck, and the interpreter started to deal. The men picked up their cards and anted up.

The interpreter started the bet high.

"I'm out," one of the Germans said.

"Me too." One of the Turks set his cards facedown on the table.

The Greek prisoner matched the bet and raised it considerably. The other Turk folded. So did the other German.

The interpreter made polite conversation and smiled more than he had in the hours leading up to this moment. Souren tried to decide if he smiled because his hand was bad or if he couldn't stop himself from gloating over certain victory.

Souren tossed in enough to stay in the game. The interpreter raised the stakes.

The Greek folded.

It was just Souren and his fellow interpreter left, the one who had cajoled him into having a little fun. Souren tried to get a look at his eyes, but the man glanced from his cards to the pot or up at the ceiling. He was relaxed and commenting on the game in a casual, friendly manner. Souren trained his eyes for a moment on his opponent's neck. Was it throbbing? He could not tell.

By now, the room reeked of stale cigar smoke and body odor. The breeze had ceased. Stink and tension hung in the air. The candles burned. His opponent's jocular mood irritated Souren. He did not seem like the same person. *Dr. Jekyll and Mr. Hyde*, Souren thought, recalling the story he had read at school. But what did it mean? Was he bluffing?

The interpreter drew one card and raised the bet. Souren looked at his dwindling cash. If he stayed in and won, he would walk off with at least three times what he had sat down with. If he folded, he would walk away broke. He drew two cards and tossed in the last of his money.

"I raise you again," the interpreter said in a tone so friendly and so likable that Souren wanted to reach across the table and punch him in the face hard enough to *make* his neck throb! His heart began to beat wildly. He could only stay in if he borrowed the money. He had a good hand. He knew he could win, but he began to doubt himself, and as he did, large beads of perspiration rolled like tears down his forehead. His eyes itched. He reached up and wiped them.

"Let's keep this game going," said the interpreter. "I'll loan you the money."

Souren felt blood pulsing in his neck and throat. Even his wrists and the backs of his knees thumped in unison with each panicked heartbeat. Was his the winning hand? He would never find out. He folded, and when he did, the fellow interpreter smiled broadly and deftly slipped his cards into the rest of the deck. He gathered his winnings and bid the others farewell.

Such is the price of deception, Souren mused to himself as he, too, said good night.

—⁓—

The next morning, Souren and his companions received orders to proceed with the caravan on to Bodrum, an ancient stronghold built by the Romans that lay just across from the Italian-occupied island of Cos.

When they were about sixty miles from Bodrum, Souren saw a saddled donkey grazing in a field where some traveler must have left it. Tired and sore from riding a camel, he got the attention of an attendant.

"Bring me that donkey," he commanded.

The scruffy animal appeared to be quite old. The saddle sat on a swayback, and a dilapidated bridle with one dangling rope had created a scar on its nose. Its eyes were half closed, while flies buzzed around it. It wasn't a fine mount by any measure, but it would be a better ride than the camel. At the order, the attendant looked at Souren strangely for a moment but did as asked and fetched the creature.

Souren dismounted the camel and climbed onto the donkey. When in the saddle, his feet were only two feet from the ground. He took hold of the rope and motioned to the attendant to take care of his camel. He had to slap his new ride on the flank several times before it began to move.

As he and the donkey fell back in line with the camel caravan, Souren wondered why the attendant had looked at him that way. *Did he think I was too presumptuous? Who did the creature belong to? Could it be an Armenian? No, not now. It would be almost impossible for an Armenian to still have a donkey. Had the owner been killed and the old animal left to just waste away?*

The thoughts evaporated with a sudden commotion up ahead. Several heavy crates had come loose and fallen off one of the camels. The whole procession came to a halt while a group of soldiers rushed about and the bundles were again put up on the camel and secured.

Over the next two days, Souren rode the only donkey in the camel convoy. At camp the evening of the second day, the owner of the donkey caught up with them. He saw his donkey and asked around for who had taken it. He was directed to Souren. The old Turk was probably in his seventies. He was short and thin, with a tobacco-stained white mustache and beard. Wearing only a dirty, tattered shawl and olive-green turban, he obviously was also quite poor.

"Pl-Please sir, that d-donkey is my only p-possession and my only way to travel," he stammered. "I need it."

Souren scowled and looked the man up and down for several seconds. "Okay. Take the damned thing, you old fool." He spit out the words in angry disgust. "Why did you leave it unattended in the first place? You should consider yourself fortunate that I found it and saved it for you. We could have shot the beast and cut it up. What are you doing out here anyway?"

The old man stepped back, wide-eyed in surprise. His hands shook as he looked fearfully at the uniformed Souren. He started to speak but then thought better of it. Keeping his eyes on Souren's face, he bowed a couple of times while backing away. He then turned and, with a limped run, hurried to fetch his donkey quietly grazing a few yards away. As he rode off, he looked back at Souren with an expression of either sadness or pity. Souren could not tell which.

The expression on the attendant's face when Souren had asked him to fetch the donkey reappeared in Souren's mind. Then the several recent impatient exchanges he had had with Behn and his anger at a couple of soldiers for not following simple orders fast enough also came back to him. Suddenly, he was tired. He didn't feel like the evening meal. He went to his tent and lay down.

What's the matter with me? Who am I becoming? Am I now the hardhearted brute? He felt as if his father now was looking down at him sadly and shaking his head. *Here I am, safe and well fed, and yet I act like this. Why, damn it? This godforsaken war, even when I can't fight it, is still eating me alive. I don't like who I am. Lazy, angry bastard! I can't let it get to me like this. I just can't. I can't.*

His head now aching and temples pounding, he tried to pray. "I beg you, God, please don't let me blunder into what I have despised and thought I never could be." He tossed and turned for what seemed like hours and finally drifted off.

—⁓—

Their final base was opposite the island of Kalymnos on the Aegean Sea. From ancient times until the last part of the seventeenth century, this picturesque cove had been the indomitable nest of dreaded pirates. From here, the notorious seafaring bandits attacked merchant boats and then retreated to the concealed refuge in the bosom of nature.

All along the beach were one-roomed demolished shops, resembling pigeonholes. Professor Behn occupied a room adjacent to Souren, who had set up his quarters in a vacated bakery. Here and there were a few once-beautiful stone houses, all empty and ruined from the bombardment of a year ago. Behind the row of abandoned shops, rugged hills rose up like a wall. One could reach the beach from that direction only by riding a nimble donkey or by making a treacherous downhill climb on foot.

The entrance to the cove was no more than a hundred feet wide. To the right of the entrance was a short, rocky mountain. On the left end, a narrow strip of land extended about a quarter of a mile and was punctuated with an ancient Roman fortress, now the newly established barracks. Here Hesselberger's men had a good view outside the insulated cove and kept guard day and night. Between the narrow entrance to the cove and the beach, an islet rose up out of the water. It was chosen as the perfect spot for an artillery implacement in case an Allied torpedo boat pursued the pirates toward the cove or ventured too close. On account of its almost inaccessible location to the hinterland, Hesselberger and his pirates were relatively safe and independent.

It took nearly two and a half months to shape the place. Trenches were dug and landing piers constructed. Hesselberger kept very busy recruiting and training volunteers—deserters and outlaws from all over the coast—in the modern art of piracy.

The lieutenant, after receiving a top-secret assignment, took some of his men on a two-day operation. He set aside one day for drilling his new recruits. These reckless mercenaries were willing to attack and loot, but they lacked discipline and cohesion. Hesselberger determined to train them hard before launching a strategic attack just north of the cove. Souren went along on this mission. His assignment included running messages and guarding the temporary base of operations during the raid. A recent telegram explained that a resident on the island they were targeting for a raid was spying for the Allies. Hesselberger had orders to strike fear into the hearts of all who lived there. He estimated a group of twenty-five men would do the job.

The plan was to have motorboats tow rowboats part of the way. Before attracting the attention of the townspeople, the motors would be turned off and the rowboats freed to row quietly to shore. The men would land in the dark of the night at different points under the guidance of the Greek prisoners. The prisoners had been captured for just this purpose and were threatened with the death of their families if they refused. The men would then sink all the fishing boats they could find, while another group would attack the Italian barracks and cut the telegraph. Then they would be free to pillage and return to their boats that same night.

Souren had grown tired of associating with thieves and killers and was disgusted with them and with himself. They who hit unsuspecting civilian targets in the dead of night had the nerve to call him a coward behind his back. He heard of it from one of the men.

"They say you are too afraid," the Turk had said to Souren a couple of weeks before.

"I have my orders," Souren had replied.

Hesselberger's orders came originally from Souren's commander before he left Constantinople. He had explained to the lieutenant that Souren was Christian and could not participate in the raids as a combatant but would make an excellent interpreter and guide. He also assured Hesselberger that Souren was a valuable asset because of his good relationship with the Turkish soldiers. Hesselberger honored the general's request, but it wasn't long before the ruffians under his command cast a suspicious eye on Souren as a gutless interpreter.

The second day of the special operation, Hesselberger and his party of irregulars left after breakfast. They would return, Hesselberger had said, at 0400, about an hour or so before dawn.

In their absence, Souren hatched a plan. He would prepare a feast for the men, who would be ravenous after their exploits, only they wouldn't know what they were truly eating. The scene of their triumphant return was always the same. The men would joyously spread out their booty and tell stories of the hunt. Brass and gold candlesticks gleamed in the firelight. They showed off coins, jewelry, clothes, and even family mementos of no value to a thief.

"Cowards!" Souren shouted aloud to no one but himself.

He climbed onto one of the donkeys and headed into a nearby town. With his own money, he planned to purchase enough food for each one in the whole group to eat himself sick. The merchants cringed when they saw the soldier come into their shops. They knew he would tell them to bill the sultan. But Souren surprised them by paying for each purchase in cash and at full price. No surprise was greater than his going to the butcher and leaving with fifteen pounds of wild boar. The locals, all Greek Christians, had never sold pork to Muslim. Among themselves they decided he must have been sent by a German commander, for the Germans loved to make schnitzel, even during war.

Back at the campsite, Souren built a fire. After carefully seasoning and marinating the pork, he ran the sharp end of the spit through the cuts of meat and placed them over the flames. He prepared potatoes with parsley, oregano, and olive oil. He sang as he cleaned and chopped carrots, onions, and tomatoes. A big pot of bulgur sat bubbling. Souren laid out several loaves of fresh bread and a small mountain of feta cheese.

Right on time, at 0400, he heard the voices of the victors and saw them coming through the thick brush with their spoils. The light of the fire shone on the table laden with a feast. The display of food caught them all by surprise.

The soldiers rushed at Souren, who handed them steak after steak, telling them that it was a cow that was accidentally shot and then sent to them. The hungry men devoured great quantities of juicy, tender meat rolled up between slices of thin bread.

"Besherik," they said, "it's okay to be a coward if you can cook like this!"

All of a sudden, one of the soldiers yelled at the top of his voice. Souren cringed as the man declared he'd discovered a signature long, coarse boar's hair. Souren pulled him aside and tried to convince him he had found not a hair but a thin piece of gristle. It was too late. The alarm electrified everybody. Soon, all of the men were vomiting. They were polluted! They ran to the water's edge, filled their mouths with salt water, and gargled. Souren watched them frantically scrub their teeth on the sleeves of their uniforms. Souren marveled at their revulsion at having eaten perfectly cooked pork. The bandits who had brandished guns and knives and fallen upon their innocent victims now cried out in fear of Allah's wrath. He had humiliated them now and took great satisfaction in the chaos he had created.

Lieutenant Hesselberger, who had gone back to his tent, arrived on the scene to rebuke Souren briskly by reminding him that, inasmuch as his conduct was attracting attention to his status, he was putting himself at risk of being discovered as an Armenian boy.

When they returned to the cove, the men who had eaten, or even touched, the boar meat were shunned for fifteen days, not allowed to mingle or eat with the others. During that time, they were condemned to sleep on the floor, away from the clean.

As for Souren, the men who had before trusted him no longer sought his company. He didn't care. He wasn't one of them. He counted being ostracized as a relief from the unending farce. Only Hesselberger and Behn were speaking to him now.

Chapter Eight

—ⵀ—

1918

Asmall caravan of three dilapidated wagons creaked forward. Two were drawn by tired, bony horses, the other by a shaggy old mule. The first wagon displayed bright red-and-green clothes that hung on the sides to dry. From inside, the sounds of children could be heard arguing and laughing. The occasional wailing of an infant briefly drowned out all other noise. The second wagon carted show animals, two dogs and a bear that was muzzled and transported in a cage. The third and most decrepit wagon was stacked with painted lumber for erection of a stage and benches.

The band of gypsies was looking for an audience. They set up camp about a mile from a cove. They'd heard from the locals that soldiers were nearby and hoped to fill their benches with an eager audience that had been deprived of the niceties of life and were weary of their isolation. The gypsies advertised their show by going to nearby villages and performing short skits. One child beat a drum, another blew piercing notes on a zurna, a popular woodwind instrument, while a few other children performed simple acrobatics. The two dogs wore dirty red fezzes and walked on their hind legs.

Souren and the men assigned to him were rolling boulders and driving posts. He'd received orders to oversee the building of a pier, acting as head engineer since he was the only one of the enlisted men with any formal education. Due to Souren's knowledge of the sciences and fluency in languages, Hesselberger trusted he'd accomplish the task quickly and efficiently. Besides, the lieutenant was leaving with a group on a training run, and he wanted to make sure idleness did not lead to trouble while he was away. Souren had proven himself a good soldier ever since the pork incident. Most of the men he had "polluted" were mere transients, mercenaries who worked until they got enough loot and then moved on.

When the gypsy children wandered onto the beach, they quickly captured the attention of an eager audience. Souren and his men stopped to watch the children and dogs perform. Before they left, the little gypsies announced the time and place of their show.

A few hours later, Souren sat down on one of the wobbly benches along with two dozen other spectators—some villagers but mostly soldiers. Souren welcomed the diversion from the monotonous life on the edge of civilization. He was a city boy from a busy metropolitan town that pulsed with energy. He missed the coffee shops, the promise of theaters (though his religion-bound parents had forbidden him to enter), the reeking camel caravans bringing news from faraway lands. He longed to smell once again fresh bread from Smyrna's bakeries. He missed the secondhand merchants like Ali who provided him with the latest gossip about those inhabiting the mansions around this pearl of the Orient.

Suddenly, a pretty dancer swept to the center of the stage. She was not as dark as her fellow gypsies, nor were her feet calloused and leathery. She wore a silk dress with a red bodice and a green-and-red skirt. She transported the audience into a world of grace and poetry, peace and harmony, a world where war could momentarily be forgotten.

Her dance had started with short, syncopated movements of her head and hands. As the rhythm of the instruments accelerated, she took possession of the space around her with the rapid steps of her light feet and graceful sweeping motions of her body. She danced in a way that expressed abandonment and delight in being alive.

After a sequence of rapid swirls, the pace slowed down. Her movements became languorous and tender. She responded to the sound of the drums with wide and lithe motions of her arms. She rose up on the balls of her bare feet and ran a few steps before stopping and twirling her body. Her skirt spun but revealed nothing above her ankles. Her glossy, long hair mimicked the red-and-green silk as she drew her head into full circles several times.

Her hips shook to the rhythm of her zills. The drum and zurna, which had fallen silent, joined in again. The gypsy girl kicked forward three times with her right leg. Then she crouched low and slowly swayed back and forth, rising only a couple of inches at a time.

The dancer smiled coyly at her audience just before she bent backward. The spectators cheered when she did this. She reached her arms back farther and farther until her fingertips brushed the stage. She then drew herself upright with breathtaking grace and ease. Fully extended, she finally turned toward where Souren was seated, her hair swirling around and her willowy arms swaying high over her head.

Souren had been hypnotized by the beauty of the motions. The dancer's precision and sense of purpose made her every move alluring. He was enraptured. Suddently, it all seemed so familiar to him. Now, the oval line of her face etched itself against the mountains lit by the setting sun. Suddenly and involuntarily, he stood up as if thunderstruck. He looked sharply into the eyes of the dancer. Yes, Beatrice was right there a few feet away from him!

He fell into a trance, wondering if he was fantasizing what he wished to be true. But he noticed that, while continuing her act, the eyes of the dancer now lingered on him questioningly. He knew that he had also been recognized.

A sinking feeling eclipsed his bliss. Conflicting emotions overwhelmed him. He slumped down as swiftly as he had jumped up.

The last time he had seen Beatrice dancing, she was the property of a Turkish general. He remembered the angry flash of her eyes. Those fierce eyes had shone with provocation and pride! Now she was dancing not like a slave but with all the expressiveness of freedom and self-assurance. When they last said good-bye, she had thought that Souren was leaving Turkey. Instead, he was still here, the interpreter for yet another German officer. Nearly two years had gone by. He had not made good on his plans, and he was still doing nothing to help stop the destruction of the Armenian race in Turkey.

The dancer responded to a crescendo of slurring notes on the zurna accompanied by frenetic beats of the drum. All at once, the gypsy, zurna, and drum stopped on the same beat.

The audience erupted in ecstatic applause. They wanted to watch this lovely dancer again, but what the people got instead was a muzzled black bear sporting a tattered and dimpled red fez.

The well-trained animal stood up on his hind legs and saluted the soldiers, who received the comedic gesture with roars of laughter. The soldiers responded by tossing coins into the hats carried around by three gypsy children. One of them, a young boy, approached Souren and surreptitiously slipped a piece of paper into his hand.

—⚊—

As Beatrice's note had instructed him to do, Souren stood hidden in a thicket of dwarf pines a few hundred yards from the gypsy camp. He heard music and laughter. He saw the campfires. He was anxious to hold Beatrice. At last, his dream was coming true.

He watched a shadow move away from the dark side of the lead wagon. He could make out a graceful form finding its way toward his hiding place.

He quickly recognized the shock of dark hair bouncing with every step. As she came nearer, he tried to control his breath, to repress his heartbeat gone wild by pressing his fist against his chest. He saw that she was wearing traditional gypsy attire, a long, flowing dress of red-and-green silk that shone in the semidarkness. He felt the urge to shout his love for her. Instead, he remained paralyzed until she was but a few steps away.

And suddenly they were in each other's arms, body against body.

"*Sirelis, sirelis,* my love, my love," Souren whispered against her cheek. He felt her body tremble. He found her mouth and kissed her passionately. She did not resist but shivered at the sensation of his tongue seeking her mouth. His hands caressed her breasts through the layer of smooth red silk. She kissed him more intimately. Slowly, Souren's hands traveled to her narrow waist, then around to the small of her back. Finally, they rested on her hips, which he gently squeezed as he kissed her on the side of her neck. He did not want to talk. He worked to memorize every curve of Beatrice's body. He longed to kiss her inch by inch and in that way that would sear her into his mind forever. He kissed her full lips again and stroked her silky hair. He still could not believe that she was here.

But there was much to share. Beatrice told Souren that after he had left for Constantinople, she began traveling with these gypsies. She had passed through Smyrna over a year ago. She told him of the strange coincidence she felt of strolling his hometown just weeks after telling him good-bye. But the city that once teemed with the traffic of thousands of pedestrians and long caravans of camels had been immobilized by the wartime blockade. Smyrna was no longer a thriving economy famed for welcoming commerce from the East. Gone was the crowd of wealthy Europeans shopping and enjoying elegant Sunday picnics. Several factories were in ruins from bombs dropped by airplanes or from artillery barrages from British ships. Soldiers patrolled the streets, the railway station, and the wharfs.

She described the random searches of homes and property that left the Armenians in a constant state of terror. "I met one woman who had been hiding her son in an upstairs room for a year," she told him. "During a search, soldiers discovered him. He wore a dress and scarf, but they knew who he was and dragged him out and killed him in front of her."

The whole city was on edge. She explained how she had found a beggar who spent his day on the streets and made extra money by telling strangers what they could never find out on their own. The old Turk explained how many Armenians accused as spies of belligerent nations had been jailed and that over two hundred others had been deported. But even after this the governor, Rahmi Bey, had ominously called a group of twelve of the city's remaining prominent Armenians to his home. He threatened the entire Armenian population in the city unless he was given additional names of those collaborating with Turkey's enemies.

He accused these unknown traitors of atrocities and treason and said that the government in Constantinople was insisting he remove all Armenians from Smyrna. He told them that if he did not receive the names of at least thirty Armenians guilty of the treasonous activity, every last Armenian would be permanently deported.

"Did they do it?" Souren asked.

Beatrice tried to contain her emotions. "Yes," she said. "The bishop of Saint Stepanos Cathedral gave the governor thirty names but insisted all of them had only lived very quietly. Many of the men bravely volunteered themselves. To protect the rest of the Armenian community, they insisted the priest put their names on that list."

Souren teared up at Beatrice's appalling descriptions, but he felt pride that some of the Armenian men had willingly sacrificed themselves.

Aware of his sadness, she quickly changed the subject. "But what about you, my love?" she asked as she tenderly stroked his face. "Where have you been, Souren? What adventures have you to tell me? Why are you still here? Have you become a spy for the Allies? Is that why you are still wearing the uniform of our enemies?"

She looked at him with hopeful eyes and squeezed his hand.

"I haven't had the opportunity to escape, Beatrice. I was set to leave with my commander but—"

He saw her expression change as she released his hand.

"I have been thinking how to escape, or that at least I would foil an attack, you know, when our unit is sent to terrorize the Greek islanders' villages—" He desperately wanted to calm her growing chill.

She drew back and then moved away from him. With the fire in her eyes he knew so well, she hissed, "And who am I kissing? My courageous and beloved liberator or an Armenian bystander?"

Tears now filled those beautiful eyes. "General Antranik is in the Caucasus leading too few Armenian volunteers alone against the Turks, and you are *thinking* about what you're going to do? *Thinking?* Our freedom fighters, deserted by the Russian army and without hope of Allied reinforcements, are dying, and you are still hiding out here and *thinking?*"

Souren shrunk back, dumbstruck at Beatrice's words. He felt as if a pair of strong hands had grabbed him by the throat and were squeezing hard at his neck.

"I cannot understand this!" she muttered. Tears streamed down her face. "Is there nothing more for you to do but go back to those disgusting troops and *think* more about what you can do! This is not enough, Souren."

Beatrice stood up and wiped the tears with her arm. She looked down at Souren for a moment, then turned and hurried toward the camp. In his last glimpse of her, Souren saw Beatrice lift the heavy tarp and climb into the back of the wagon.

He got up and stood alone in the darkness, devastated at the shift from ecstasy to dejection.

That night again he tossed and turned, cursing himself for being alive, and praying for a chance to win back Beatrice. He rehearsed what he would say. He longed to explain to her his genuine intentions to flee his unit and find his way to fight with the Allies. He had not been able to tell her that he had arrived in Gallipoli with that in mind, but that the British had already retreated, so he had no chance of escaping this way. What could he do?

As Souren lay wide-awake hours later on his cot, the escape path he had contemplated by bits and pieces over several weeks now began to crystallize. Hesselberger and his group of irregulars were again away for a few days. The timing was good. He determined that he would go back in the morning and explain to Beatrice how he would now escape, that he was not just a "thinker" and would no longer delay his leaving. It was the only way he could regain the love and respect he felt he had lost.

He got up. Restless, he walked the beach. There was no moon. His foot struck something in the sand, and he stooped to find a broken bayonet. With this discovery, finally he could launch his escape plan. The darkness emboldened him. Using the bayonet, he carefully opened holes in the hulls of each of the troops' boats on the beach. With surprisingly little effort, he pried the weapon into the seams between the planks. He twisted the bayonet until he broke off a large piece at the bottom of each boat. He did this to all the boats except for the commander's, which he left intact. That would be the one he would use.

Excited and nervous, he went back to his room and waited for dawn. He couldn't wait to tell Beatrice that today he was escaping. She would throw her arms around him and forgive him. She would kiss him and promise to pray for his safety and success.

As the first rays of light crept over the horizon, he raced to the gypsies' encampment. He saw no wagons. No horses. Just flattened grass where carriages had been parked. Wisps of smoke rose from smoldering coals of a campfire. His eyes followed the dirt road, but he saw no sign of Beatrice. The gypsies had moved on. Beatrice became only a fleeting dream once again.

Feeling weak and filled with self-loathing, Souren walked back to the cove. He was considering what to do next—should he go forward as planned?—when he heard Professor Behn call to him. The telephone station had sent a telegram. Souren glanced at it— he had his answer. He began reading it to the professor, as he did all telegrams that regularly came in Turkish and for which he was depended upon to interpret. But instead of translating the actual message into German, Souren substituted his own report.

"Good news! Russia and Italy are begging for peace. We are advancing on the British, and through the help of our gallant German brothers, we are going to turn the British fleet into a scrap heap!"

The professor jumped up and began pacing back and forth excitedly. "The war is to end soon! Victory is ours! Wow!" Throwing his arms in the air, he proclaimed, "Let's celebrate!"

"Professor," Souren said, "why not call the soldiers and tell them the news? Ask them to dress up? This is an amazing holiday!"

The professor agreed that this was indeed a good idea. He had Souren gather the soldiers, who soon lined up in front of them.

Professor Behn dressed as an officer for the occasion and launched into a patriotic address. Souren once again translated this to suit his own fancy. He raised both the kaiser and Enver Pasha to glories they could never achieve as mortals. Then, he ordered the soldiers to fire a volley in honor of the amazing shared German and Turkish victory over the Allies. Afterward, the professor awarded to each soldier a medal, a German coin on which was stamped a pirate with a sword and dagger on the deck of a boat with the inscription "Gott mit Uns" (God with us).

"Professor," Souren said, "the men have not had a decent meal for months. Why not give our junior officers a leave of absence and send them to the villages to get some lamb for us? When they get back, we can have a feast and celebrate the way such a historic victory deserves."

The professor again readily consented. The soldiers were relieved from duty and sent on the agreed errand. The rest of the troops were already drinking heavily, laughing and joking and congratulating each other. Behn joined in eagerly. Souren feigned enthusiastically participating also in the festivities. Well after dark, the entire unit, soldiers and officers alike, were drunk and asleep.

Souren slipped away and began removing the bullets from as many rifles as he could locate. The task was made easier because the troops had arranged their guns in groups of "victory pyramids," with the butts of the guns resting in a circle on the ground and the barrels and bayonets intertwined at the top. After he had collected as many bullets as he could, Souren walked beyond the edge of the encampment and threw them far away. He then returned to his room and wrote a letter to Lieutenant Hesselberger. In it he told of his long-held desire to do something to help his people, this being the reason for his escape. He expressed his appreciation for the years of protection he had received. He promised that whatever his future held, he would do nothing to risk the lives of these particular troops that the lieutenant and Behn commanded. He sealed it and then lay down on his cot to wait out the night.

As morning broke, he was the only one without a hangover, just as he had planned. "Now, boys," Souren said to a small group of groggy soldiers, "it will take at least another day for our new provisions to arrive. So let's grab some hand grenades and fish. A feast without the first course being fish, particularly when we are so close to the sea, would not be right."

He instructed three of the bravest of the troops to come with him down to the beach. Souren told the soldiers to fetch a few hand grenades and then to haul the commander's boat into the water. While the men busied themselves, he went back up to the encampment and stepped inside his room. He gathered his money and his medals, along with the envelope containing the letter to Lieutenant Hesselberger. He laid it all on his cot and closed the door on his way out.

Souren stood on the beach and stared at the entrance of the cove—a narrow passageway between two rocky headlands that led to the open sea. He surveyed again the barracks on the left side. On the right rose the rocky peak called Kodjabash. He had already made a few mental calculations, and they stood up to what he observed now. Resolute, he climbed into the commander's rowboat with the soldiers and stood in the rear.

In order to save every ounce of his energy, Souren had the soldiers do all the rowing. He saw several schools of fish and directed his oarsmen toward one. They chased the fish toward the entrance to the cove. As instructed, one of the soldiers stood up in the boat and cut the wick of his German hand grenade. Then, he took the cigarette from his mouth, at the ready to light the wick and throw the grenade into the water.

"Ready, fire, Ahmet!" Souren called. Ahmet's aim and timing were perfect. The hand grenade exploded uder the sea. The fish were now floating on the surface with their bellies turned up. At Souren's instruction, the soldiers jumped into the sea to harvest the catch and throw the fish into the boat. Just then, he took hold of the oars and, to the water-treading soldiers, said, "Good-bye, my friends!"

At first the water-treading soldiers couldn't believe he was actually rowing away from them. When they did, the gap between the boat and themselves was too large to close, so the soldiers swam back to the nearby rock outcropping. They yelled at Souren that he was approaching the forbidden zone and might be fired upon. Souren kept rowing with all of his might. The boat was large and cumbersome and meant to be rowed by two men. Time was short, and every second counted. The soldiers were still in such a position that they were out of the line of sight of the encampment and so far away that their shouting could not be heard on the beach.

By this time, the sun was a full red ball above the horizon. The placid sea meant easy rowing. Once outside the cove, he was in danger of being seen by soldiers in the garrison perched on top of the steep bank. He pulled the boat to his left to avoid direct gunfire by seeking the protection of the rocky peak on that side. As soon as he thought that he was far enough out to sea that he would again be seen by those in the garrison, he cut across to a small islet on his right.

By now enough time had passed for some of the troops to discover their rifles were empty. They found and loaded new ammunition, and shots rang out. With no time to dodge them, Souren rowed on. The islet was too small to offer much protection. He heard the bullets whistle past him before breaking the surface of the water. One hit the boat, but luckily above the waterline. Every splash the others made meant he had not been hit again. Both feet propped against the back seat, he pulled with all his strength, stretching fully with every strike of the oars.

To steel himself against fatigue and fear, he pretended that he was racing and would bellow, "Go, Souren! Go! You will make it. Keep it up! Row! Row for your life!"

The strain broke one of the oarlocks, and Souren fell backward into the bottom of the boat. Bullets sailed overhead. He struggled to take off his belt as quickly as he could, summoning the sort of speed one conjures up at moments like these. He wrapped and tied the belt in place of the broken oarlock and kept on pulling the oars until he reached a small island. It was nothing more than a pile of rocks jutting upward out of the sea. Straining to distinguish what lay ahead of him through the bright glare of the sun and the dazzling reflection on the surface of the water, he could make out the island of Kalymnos, the closest piece of land in the right direction. As nearly as he could figure, it was at most a couple of hours away. Inspired by this, he set out again, rowing furiously.

He had started like a racehorse but did not seem to be making much progress. The shooting from the garrison had stopped, and because of his previous night's precautions, no boats were pursuing him. But every stroke seemed to make the Turkish coast bigger and bigger, like a giant octopus trying to extend its reach. He looked around. The Greek island seemed no closer than it had an hour ago. He began to wonder if he was rowing the wrong direction. He panicked and checked his course. Yes, he was rowing away from the cove and toward the Greek islands.

His arms grew stiff and began to cramp. His back ached. He thought he needed let go of the oars for a rest, but when he looked down at his hands, they were still clutching the handles.

"Let go! Let go!" he told himself. But he could not release the oars. His hands, blistered and bloodied, had become glued to them. He wondered how long he had been rowing. The hot sun beat down. No clouds shielded him from the searing heat. Overcome with exhaustion, he fainted.

When he regained consciousness, he found himself again in the bottom of the boat. As he got back in the seat, Souren noticed a deserted island, just another pile of rocks. A lighthouse lay in ruins. Seabirds and wild pigeons screamed at him. He considered landing on the island but thought better of it.

"What if they are watching my progress and find another boat and come after me in the night?" he said out loud to himself.

He grabbed the oars. The instant his hands touched the wood, he flinched in pain. He could not make himself let go of the oars before, but now he could not grasp them. His hands were too stiff. He plunged them into the water. The salt stung his wounds, but he didn't mind. The dried blood had softened, and he extended his fingers. As he did, the torn flesh reopened, seeping blood. He flexed his hands a few times and then again grabbed hold of the oars.

He was nearly mad with thirst. He had not thought to pack water or food. He noticed his piccolo in the bottom of the boat. It had fallen from his pocket.

"I brought my piccolo, but I forgot water!" Souren laughed out loud. Then cursed his stupidity.

He rowed what must have been another hour before slumping forward, completely depleted. Deliriousness took over.

"Souren!"

He jolted upright, heart pounding with fear.

"My boy, don't be afraid. It's me."

He saw his mother sitting on a rock, tenderly protecting and rocking his cradle. Around her were the bodies of massacred infants. Several had been decapitated. Some had no hands. Their ragged stumps poured dwindling trickles of blood. He saw several infants who had been pierced through with swords.

"Who are they, Mother?" he asked.

"Our little ones of the Turkish butchery." She had her hand on his cradle and steadily moved it back and forth. She was singing a lullaby.

"Their parents?"

"All dead," she replied.

Souren wanted to turn away, but he couldn't. He stared in horror at the tiny corpses. He tried to count them, but each time he thought he had finished, more appeared.

"I gave you the name Souren Barkev like a code. As your two names say it, you will be saved from the sword that has cut down these poor babies," his mother reminded him.

"I'm trying, Mother. But I am so tired. I think they may try to come and get me if I stop."

"Souren," a stern voice bellowed.

Souren turned to see a distinguished figure now kneeling next to his mother. He was dressed in a Russian uniform and decorated with several medals. He looked at the children lying dead on the ground and said, "Do you know who I am, Souren?"

"Yes. You are General Antranik Ozanian, great protector of Armenians." Antranik had an imposing, muscular frame, and Souren considered him to be tall for an Armenian. His gray hair was combed back over his forehead, which greatly accented his thick, curled mustache.

"You defended the city of Mush during the massacres ordered by Abdul Hamid II and helped save some of my mother's relatives," Souren went on, captivated. He was looking straight at one of his heroes. "A few years later, over two thousand Turkish soldiers went after you and your band of fighters. You hid in a monastery near Mush—my mother told me this story many times when I was a boy!"

Souren felt giddy. He recited, with great excitement, the story that had made Antranik a hero among Armenians.

"The Turks surrounded you and your men when you came to defend the Armenians suffering under the Ottoman government. The Turkish generals demanded you surrender. But you tricked them," Souren continued with delight. "You dressed in the uniform of a Turkish officer and walked among them speaking perfect Turkish, all the while allowing your men to slip out a few at a time. When the Turks sent a messenger to negotiate your surrender, no one was left in the monastery. You are a legend, General!"

"Souren, I am outnumbered again, and this time I cannot simply slip away. I now stand and fight. You must go to the Allies and raise a band of volunteers and help me subdue the Turks. The Germans have trained you. You must do as you have learned, except you will not molest harmless people.

"Go! Now!" the general commanded.

"I will, sir. Yes, I will," Souren said.

Souren reached for the oars. The ache in his shoulders sent a searing pain into his chest and sides. He willed himself to push on across the vast sea, toward the island that seemed to float beyond his reach. He struggled for half an hour before once again collapsing. His chest heaved. The inside of his mouth was dry. His tongue swelled. His lips felt like thin, brittle pieces of paper that tore a little bit each time he opened his mouth and gasped for air.

"Oh God! I need water. Help me!"

"If you row, you will find water," a gentle voice comforted him.

"Beatrice?" He could hardly believe his ears or his eyes.

He turned to see that she sat near the bow in her red-and-green silk dress. Her bare feet were crossed at the ankles. Two long braids fell past her shoulders. She smiled lovingly.

"Is it really you, Beatice? I thought you detested me. I thought I had lost you."

Tears rolled uncontrollably down his cheeks.

"How could I abandon you? You have proven to be a brave and courageous man. Row, Souren! Row! When you succeed in crossing the sea, you can tell the Greeks about the planned raids. The Turks won't dare raid the islands once they know you've escaped to tell about it. You have the chance to save so many innocent lives in this alone. With Greek and Armenian volunteers, you can also land anywhere on the Anatolian coast. It will force the Turks to send some of their soldiers here to fight you. This will help relieve the pressure on Antranik's forces."

"I promise, Beatrice! I promise!"

"I will wait for you in the grove. Do you know where I mean?"

"Where we first kissed? At Ephesus?" Souren marveled again at her beauty.

"Yes, and we will make love again. But you must row to the island. When you reach it, you must tell all about what has happened to our people. So row now, Souren. Row on, my brave love."

He closed his eyes and winced in pain. It felt like a knife had split open his gut.

"Beatrice, I am so thirsty! I'm so tired!"

Without warning the boat was struck by a ferocious wind squall. A wave crashed over the bow, and she was gone!

Souren thought she had been swallowed up in the sea, and he cried out hysterically, "Beatrice! Beatrice!"

Holding onto the side of the boat, he stood up, readying himself to jump in after her. But when he got to his feet, his mind cleared enough to realize that the boat was now taking on water. He frantically started scooping with his hands. Then another wave hit. Again water poured in, even more than the last wave. Hurriedly he pulled off his boots and filled them and dumped the seawater over the side. He repeated the process as rapidly as he could.

"Faster! Faster," he urged himself on.

When the third wave hit, in a fit of rage, he cursed and slammed his boots down at the water in the bottom of the boat.

"I will not die this way!" he screamed. He clenched his mangled hands and shook them at the mighty Aegean Sea.

Exhausted, he fell back onto the seat and stared at the water and boots sloshing to and fro. Then he saw his piccolo, which also bobbed from side to side. He grabbed this only object of value left in his possession. He reached back to lob it into the sea, when all of a sudden, a massive beast rose up out of the waves next to the boat. So large was its body that Souren could not see the coastline of Turkey. He recognized the hideous creature's huge sharp tusks and the warty snout. He remembered its foul breath that smelled of death. He shuddered in fear and horror.

The monster snarled; its hate-filled eyes glared down at Souren. "You will not make it, you fool. Even now you are dying of exhaustion and thirst, and your end will come before you reach that island. It's farther than you think, and you possess neither the strength nor the will to continue."

Souren threw his hands up over his face. The monster snorted, and a putrid odor torched Souren's nostrils.

"You thought you had fooled me. Did you think I could not find you?" The beast pitched forward and let out a terrifying screech. "Filthy gavour!"

Souren clasped his ears to keep out the sound of pure evil. He opened his parched mouth to scream, but he could not.

A curtain of mist rapidly enclosed the adversaries. The sun no longer beat down on his face, but the sea continued to churn violently beneath his boat. Souren shivered uncontrollably from the cold. He tried but could not draw a breath. Was this the end?

An impulse from deep within him finally rose upward. Somehow he clenched his hands into fists. He felt the will to live again rising from the depths of his heart. From the very marrow of his bones, courage welled up anew. He summoned every bit of his strength to finally speak, and after all of his effort, one word escaped his lips.

"No-o-o-o-o-o-o!" he wailed.

The mist immediately evaporated. He now saw that in his right hand he was holding a sword. He lunged forward and drove the sharp blade into the monster's black heart. The beast writhed before disappearing below the waves with a heinous, demonic scream that reverberated across the expanse of the sea.

Souren's eyes opened with a start. He lay sprawled out, cold and soaked in the bottom of the boat with his piccolo in the tight, bloody grip of his right hand. He struggled and managed to lift himself back into his seat. A sharp pain shot through his spine. He panted like a horse that had galloped for miles—he was certainly as spent as that. Each heavy gasp burned his lungs. He glanced over at the eastern horizon and then turned his eyes to the west. He had no idea how far the wind squall, which had by now had blown itself out, had driven him during his tormenting semiconsciousness, but he knew that only a couple of hours of daylight remained.

"I must make landfall," he said out loud.

His own deprivations and fatigue could no longer matter. Ignoring his spent body, Souren Barkev took up the oars and pulled the boat forward.

Chapter Nine

—※—

1918

The sun slipped quickly down the western horizon. Souren wanted to avoid reaching land before dark. He needed to arrive on an unknown shore under cover of darkness. His arms dropped to his sides, and he slumped forward in the boat.

"Don't close your eyes!" He tried to steel himself against sleep. In his weakened state, his head seemed as heavy as a boulder. "Stay awake," he commanded himself.

He knew night was falling, but he could not muster the strength to lift the oars out of the water. Fear was no longer a potent-enough force. Death most assuredly awaited him. His hope for reaching freedom was dwindling as rapidly as the setting sun.

Just then voices floated over the water. Souren pulled himself up. He thought he saw three men in a boat.

"Another hallucination," he told himself. He closed his eyes and involuntarily slumped again.

The voices grew louder. Again Souren sat up. This time, he rubbed his eyes and splashed seawater from the bottom of the boat on his face. Yes, he saw another rowboat with three men wearing fisherman's caps, and he could hear their voices. Greek voices, it seemed.

He called out in Greek, "Hello!"

The men quickly redirected their boat toward a deserted island that Souren had not until then realized was behind him only about a quarter mile away. Only moments before lying exhausted and without hope in the bottom of his boat, Souren forced his hands to grasp the oars and began rowing toward the men, who were obviously trying to escape him. Souren pursued them, for they were his only chance to land somewhere. He had forgotten that he was still in uniform and appeared to them as an enemy soldier.

Souren followed the fishermen. They jumped out of their boat and ran ashore and hid behind some rocks. Souren glided his boat onto the sandy shore and stumbled out. He held his bleeding hands over his head to show he was surrendering.

"I'm Armenian!" he cried out in Greek with despair in his voice. "I have deserted my Turkish unit. I want to surrender."

An eerie silence dragged on. Souren turned and staggered back across the sand to his rowboat and tied it to the Greeks' boat.

He then called to them in hiding, "When you are ready to go, we go."

An old man finally stepped out from behind an enormous boulder. Cautiously he approached Souren.

"Who are you? Where have you come from?"

"I am Souren Tashjian. I stole this boat and rowed from Gumusluk Cove." He motioned toward the Turkish coast.

The old fisherman studied Souren. He saw hands covered with blood, bare feet, a military uniform that consisted of a Turkish coat and German pants. The old man was now more curious than he was afraid. He scanned Souren's rowboat for weapons. He smiled when he noticed the belt serving as a makeshift oarlock.

He turned to Souren and said in broken Armenian, "Perhaps you are telling the truth."

Souren recognized the challenge of a test and replied in his native tongue, "Please, take me to Kalymnos. I want to surrender myself to your military authorities."

The fisherman called out to the other two men still hiding. "If we bring a spy to Kalymnos, we'll be shot," he said in Greek in a hushed voice to the others, obviously thinking Souren couldn't hear or understand him. Souren thought the others must have believed him, though, because when they looked at him again, they smiled. Souren got into his boat, feeling confident of their goodwill.

No one spoke for nearly an hour. Souren sat slumped in his boat and felt the tug of the lead boat as it towed him. His bones ached. Blood still oozed from his ravaged hands. He looked as if he were bleeding to death from a mortal wound. Though he had drifted between sleep and consciousness, he sensed sudden slack in the rope to which he was tethered. Souren realized they had changed direction. He had figured that they were taking him to Kalymnos. But now he saw they were rowing toward another deserted island. He realized that perhaps they intended leaving him there. Souren waved his arm toward Kalymnos and pleaded with them in Greek and then in Armenian to turn the boat that direction, but they ignored him.

While the other two rowed, the fellow tasked with keeping an eye on Souren pulled out a short, sharp dagger and held it in his lap while seeming to flash a sinister smirk in Souren's direction. Souren anticipated trouble. He straightened up and repositioned himself on his seat. He did not know what he was going to do, but he knew he could not idly sit. He contemplated untying the rope connecting the two boats.

Suddenly the man with the blade dropped it. His eyes widened, and he slowly raised his hands in front of him. The others stopped rowing and did the same.

Souren had no idea what was going on. Before he knew it, all three men had their hands in the air and began stammering in Greek, begging for their lives. He followed their eyes to his hand that happened to be resting against his pants pocket. Jutting from the bloodied handkerchief in his pocket was a metallic-looking polished wooden tube, appearing from the fishermen's perspective to be the barrel of a handgun. Souren remembered hastily pulling the two sections of his piccolo apart and stuffing them with his handkerchief into his pocket. Now, providentially, the longer piece was protruding menacingly, and the fishermen were mistaking it for a pistol.

Taking immediate advantage of this unexpected turn, Souren yelled in Armenian, "Take me to Kalymnos, or I'll blow your heads off!" He moved as if to pull the "gun" from his pocket.

"Okay. Yes, yes!" The older Greek defended himself by explaining to Souren, "You are in the uniform of a Turkish soldier. We thought you were the enemy. We did not want to take you to our island if you were. But no, I do believe that you are Armenian. I have many Armenian friends in Turkey. I do business all along the Anatolian coast. I've never met a Turk who spoke Armenian the way you do." The old fisherman showed a toothy smile. "Please, son, don't draw your gun. We Greeks are your friends."

Souren kept his hand on his pocket and his eyes on the fishermen as long as he could. When they neared Kalymnos, he finally collapsed. His body succumbed to physical and emotional exhaustion. When he came to, he was still in his boat. It was almost dark. He looked up to see the three fishermen standing on a dock, telling an animated story to a small, eager crowd that had gathered to gawk at the stranger. News spread rapidly that an Armenian disguised as a soldier had escaped and somehow managed to row away from Turkey.

—⟶

Souren was miraculously again on terra firma, alive and in a safe territory. Fate had been merciful to him. Weak and barely able to walk, he stood up and looked around.

"Thank you, God! Thank you!" he said to himself.

He was approached by three uniformed men. He could tell by their uniforms they were bersaglieri—Italian military police. Souren knew that the Italian navy had occupied this island, and several others in the Aegean, six years earlier during the year-long war with Turkey. It took only thirteen days for General Giovanni Ameglio to end four centuries of Ottoman rule, and the Greek majority of the population welcomed the Italians. General Ameglio promised the inhabitants that the occupation was only temporary and that they would be allowed to carry on their customs and traditions, free from the yoke of Ottoman Turkey.

The officers were now standing around him. He tried to smile at them, but they averted their eyes.

"I came to see your commander. We are allies. I am Armenian. I have escaped from Anatolia."

They talked among one another. Souren did not know what they were saying, but he could tell his uniform was the cause of trouble. He turned to the old Greek, hoping for help.

"*Armeno*," the old man said to the soldiers.

Souren would later learn that by now, the whole world knew of the slaughter of the Armenians in Turkey. Their devastation was making headlines in newspapers across the globe. These soldiers nodded when they learned Souren was Armenian. He thought he even discerned compassion in their eyes.

At length, the island extended its famous Greek hospitality to its newest arrival. Young girls brought quilts from their dowries, and old grandmothers brought baskets of fruit and pastry. Souren had escaped from "enemy" country and was a curiosity. Besides, they were anxious to hear news. Many had relatives and friends on the mainland. They clamored for his attention, several talking at once.

"My husband had a business in Smyrna. We have not heard a word from him in three years," one woman shouted.

"My son is in the army. Do you know anything about..." The stranger's voice was drowned out by a sharp order of an Italian sergeant.

The townspeople obeyed immediately and made way for Souren to be escorted to the Italian garrison, which was nothing more than an old bar. The sergeant ordered that tables be pushed into an alcove with a fireplace to make room for Souren. An elderly Greek woman washed Souren's hands. She clucked her tongue while shaking her head at the sight of the torn flesh and of exposed ligaments in his palms. A beautiful Greek woman stood by, holding a bucket of water. Souren counted the pleasure of her quiet company worth the agony of having his hands washed free of dirt, dead skin, and dried blood.

He felt relaxed for the first time in what seemed like years. *Finally, I have achieved my purpose. I am free and among friends.* In his mind he began to plan his future activities.

That evening Souren enjoyed an Italian-Greek feast with such food as he had not tasted since before the war. No more German schnitzel and potatoes. Now, he ate food familiar to his palate—olives, eggplant, lamb shish kabob, and stuffed grape leaves. Memories from childhood accompanied the aromas and flavors he knew so well. After dinner, two bersaglieri began playing the guitar and mandolin to accompany the singing of their folk tunes.

It was quite late before Souren sank into a deep sleep lying atop a lumpy mattress that had been thrown across three bar tables.

In the morning he awakened with his body still aching. At first, he did not realize where he was.

"*Buongiorno!*"

One of the Italian soldiers he had met the night before greeted Souren buoyantly.

Souren winced with every move he tried to make. The soldier helped him down from the tables he had slept on and seated him in a chair. He placed in front of him a plate of bread, goat cheese, black olives, and fruit. Souren was most grateful for the hot cup of tea handed to him.

In the company of this bersaglieri, Souren walked over the hills to the main port of Kalymnos. His legs felt wobbly. His back, shoulders, and arms were stiff. The soldier did not slow down for Souren, who grimaced with every step.

Beyond the physical pain he endured, Souren felt excited and feverish with hope. He was finally among allies.

"No one in the world can be as happy or as fortunate as I am right now!" He chuckled to himself. "Beatrice, my dreams are finally coming true! Perhaps I will go to Palestine and fight with the British. Or maybe I will even be assisted to join and fight with the Armenian volunteers. Oh, my beloved Beatrice, if only you could see this!"

The soldier turned around and stopped, looking puzzled.

Souren was singing in Armenian and shouting by now, delirious with joy, it appeared, but the Italian could not understand. Souren shrugged, a little embarrassed, and motioned to the soldier that he should continue.

Upon arriving at the port of Kalymnos, Souren was introduced to *il maresciallo dei carabinieri*, an officer of the military police. He was a man of surprising girth, highly decorated and animated with military zest. He gingerly tried to shake hands with Souren, asking his name and age before then politely escorting a thoroughly surprised Souren to a one-room jail. Two hours later, Souren was taken to the headquarters of the Royal Naval captain and commander of the island. There were five Italian officers present, and an English captain whom he learned later was an intelligence officer, a French lieutenant, and a Greek interpreter. Two carabinieri led Souren to the hall of justice, where he was asked to be seated and make himself at home. Souren suddenly felt less at home than he did anywhere else on Earth.

A Greek dragoman translated into Turkish the first question. But Souren surprised them all by answering the next question in English.

"I prefer not to be questioned in the presence of the Greek interpreter," for he had his suspicions that his previous answer had not been properly translated. He did not know if the interpreter lacked skill or honesty or perhaps both.

The Greek was dismissed. They were pleased to find that Souren could understand English, which one of the officers spoke fluently. They proceeded to ask his name, nationality, and age. A clerk nearby filled in an official document each time Souren answered.

"I am Armenian," Souren said. "I am twenty-two. Before the war, I worked for the British-owned Oriental Railway. I eluded the authorities when Armenians were drafted for the war."

The captain smiled and turned to the English and French officers and said, "Ca me semble un peu etrange."

The Englishman nodded in agreement and said, "Oui, je suis d'accord."

The exchange electrified Souren with horror, but he pretended not to understand the French exchange to the effect that the manner and timing of his arrival were of a questionable nature.

"If you will allow me to send a telegram to my sisters in America, I can prove to you that I am who I say I am. They can vouch for me."

"That may be considered later. For now, just answer my questions," the officer demanded.

Souren saw plainly that these people were indifferent to his situation. Little did they care who he was. Their cause was war and the proceedures thereof, not people.

He explained to his interrogators how he had commandeered a rowboat and made it to the sea.

"Who was with you?" They insisted he had help, for they could not believe he could row such a four-oared boat of that size all alone at such a distance.

"No one was with me. I came alone. I deserted the unit I was with on the coast. You must believe me. German officers are planning to lead raids from the mainland of Turkey. They recruit all kinds of lowlifes to soon wreak havoc on the islanders."

"Go on," the officer said.

"Do you recall the sinking of the British steamer *Ben-my-Chree*?" Souren sought to provide details to prove he was familiar with the sorties launched from the coast. "She was sunk by artillery fire nearly a year and a half ago."

He next recited a long list of attacks on the Aegean Islands with details that only someone close to the situation could provide. "Captains Ittman and Schuler, First Lieutenant Hesselberger, and Major Kolbow are the ones who plan and lead the attacks."

"How long were you on the Bodrum Peninsula?" the officer asked.

"I came to the coast about a year ago. Before that, I served with a general." Souren was careful here. Although he was willing to hand over the names of the officers who led the raids, he was not willing to implicate his beloved commander before the Italians. His sense of loyalty prevented such a betrayal. Instead, he made up a German name.

They continued to cross-examine him step-by-step in minute detail.

Satisfied that Souren had told them all he knew, the officer looked sternly at Souren and announced point-blank that this was war and that Souren was a prisoner.

"Whether what you say is true or not, the Italian government considers you an enemy. It makes no difference whether or not you are an Armenian. Regardless, you are a citizen of the Ottoman Empire. To us, you are a Turk, an ally of Germany and Austria, all three with which we are presently at war. You wear the uniform, which is proof enough."

It was all so matter-of-fact. Souren could hardly believe what he was hearing and mounted a spirited defense. He could feel his face flush with irritation.

"I may be a citizen of the Ottoman Empire, but I am not an enemy, and I am most certainly not a spy. Since the outset of the war, my primary objective has been to escape and to join the Allies. Seventy-five percent of the Armenian population of the country of which you call me a citizen—accurately—have been killed! That's over a million innocent people! Why is it not possible for you to believe that I want to revenge and to help defend my brothers and sisters? I have not come to spy on you. I have been through hell to escape and to enlist in the cause of victory over the Entente Powers. My soul revolts at the mass killings of my people at the hands of the current Turkish revolutionary government now controlled by Talaat Pasha, Enver Pasha, and Djemal Pasha! Why can't you see that I come as an act of friendship, not espionage. I risked my life to escape!"

Souren continued, hoping he could persuade his new captors to release him.

"If I had not come today, who knows but that one of these islands might have been attacked, people killed, and their property destroyed! Now that they know I've escaped, the German commanders will most assuredly have to abandon any imminent plans of attack. They know I will tell you who they are and where they are. I know their equipment, their supply lines, their numbers."

The officer held up his hand and interrupted Souren's impassioned plea.

"You have been ordered to report to the headquarters in Rhodes. Take up your argument with General Mannino, for he wants to talk to you himself."

Souren's heart sank as he realized that, at best, they considered him a common deserter, at worst, possibly a spy. This suspicion was soon confirmed when he was told by another prisoner that the previous week, the Turks had sent an airplane flying low over Kalymnos, which had probably intensified the uneasiness of the Italians and their suspicion toward him.

One morning, a few days after his initial interrogation, and nights spent in a jail cell, a carbiniere conducted Souren on board a torpedo boat. Souren had hoped to arrange to send a telegram before leaving Kalymnos so his family in America would know where he was and could intervene on his behalf. But the opportunity to send the telegram never came. Thus he boarded the torpedo boat to Rhodes, at least glad to have been granted a chance to speak to a general and make his case. He hoped that in Rhodes, he would then be allowed to contact his family.

A charming veteran sea captain broke a few rules to bring Souren up from the cargo hold and invited him to the observation room. This captain had been on the Mediterranean coast most of his life and was anxious to get firsthand news about the Germans and the Turks. With a little French and some Greek, Souren found a true friend and a stout heart in the captain.

In the afternoon, they anchored at Cos, an island so close to the mainland that Souren could hear the braying of donkeys onshore. He was allowed to stroll the docks in the company of a guard. Turkish porters tried to make conversation with the Italian's prisoner, hoping for news about the Old Country. Souren did not want to cause any undue suspicion, so he remained silent, and he and the guard walked back to the boat.

He recovered his spirits at the sight of the island of Rhodes. From the top deck of the torpedo boat, he could see the clean, wide streets. He identified Italian architecture, for the government had erected new buildings on the quay. The colorfully dressed inhabitants moved about with purpose and speed. Despite the heat, even the oxen dragged their carts rapidly. From people to buildings, it was a port city tinctured with a mixture of European and Asiatic life. The sun flooded white marble palaces and ancient city walls, making the port a brilliant spectacle. At its entrance, Souren beheld the ruins of the statue of Helios, called the *Colossus of Rhodes*.

Souren was taken directly to a military court where he was examined and cross-examined by a group of intelligence officers.

After no fewer than four grueling hours, he became exhausted. No matter how many times he explained who he was and how he had come to Rhodes, the interrogators kept asking the same questions over and over again in an effort to make him stumble and thereby contradict himself to prove his guilt. Souren was frustrated and angry. He had thought he could surrender to a member of the Allies, then be exonerated and subsequently allowed to fight within an Armenian volunteer unit. Instead, he was being treated like the enemy. It was not as easy as he had imagined it would be.

He pondered the best way to answer the now-familiar round of questions. *What can I say that I have not said?*

He had offered information about enemy numbers, location, activity, supplies, and topography of the land. In spite of his being forthcoming, his interrogators threatened him. Each time he begged to establish his identity by way of his family in America, they dismissed his claims.

Souren was offered one hundred sterlings if he would take a motorboat and return to the Anatolian coast at night and carry messages to certain people in the interior.

"We will meet you on a specified date at a given location and bring you back."

Souren suspected the trap.

"If I do not accept your offer, you will call me a coward. And if I agree to go, you will brand me as a spy wanting to return to Turkey."

At that point, he refused to answer any more of their questions, resulting in the general calling for a sergeant waiting in the hall. He and members of the military police escorted Souren to a large fortress and then down a worn stone staircase. He was led into a dark dungeon. When his eyes finally adjusted, he found himself in a dingy and damp underground space. He feared for his life when the heavy door slammed shut and he heard an iron bar fall across on the opposite side. He had been through so much and had come so far. Was it to end here in a dungeon at the hands of the Italians?

Souren stared upward twenty feet to see two small barred windows in a wall ten feet thick. He kicked at the little pile of straw on the damp floor that was to be his bedding and saw it was full of vermin. It now fully struck him how dangerous they considered him to be. The ridiculous thought evoked spontaneous laughter.

The next day, after being denied food or human interaction and given only water, Souren was again taken for interrogation. This time, it was the general and an interpreter. The interpreter handed him a pencil and the proper form for sending a telegram.

"The general would like for you to write your family," the interpreter explained.

Souren looked at him, anxious to begin writing. Something inside told him to be wary, but the desire to inform his brothers and sisters of his imprisonment was stronger. He took up the pencil and explained to them his plight.

> With great difficulty, I succeeded in avoiding conscription into the Armenian slave brigades of the Ottoman army by presenting myself as an interpreter to a German commander. After his transfer, I found myself among Turks led by a German lieutenant. There have been actions taken that cannot be described and in which I could not participate. I finally escaped in a rowboat. Authorities in Kalymnos transferred me to Rhodes, where I am now being held prisoner.

Souren paused before deciding to add:

> I am being treated quite well. Free but under constant surveillance. My ardent desire is to come to America and start life over. How much I have prayed for this day and that God Almighty in his providence will lead our people out of their present chaos. Souren

The general picked up the telegram and handed it to the interpreter, who read it to him in Italian. A sharp command produced a clerk, who was given the form and promptly departed, presumably for the telegraph office.

The general had Souren returned to solitary confinement.

That evening an Italian military chaplain came, a priest inviting Souren to confess to him that which he would not disclose to his interrogators.

At first Souren was confused. "I'm not a Catholic," he said.

The chaplain replied that it was not a matter of religion but of repentance and that, before dying, Souren should unburden his soul of all sins so that he might be sure to go to heaven.

The implication that he was withholding information infuriated Souren. The attempt to intimidate him by making him fear execution gave birth to a flood of curses and scornful accusations about the Italian officers' self-interest and inhumanity.

"I told them who I am and what I know. I have no more to say! Now, get the hell out of here and stop pretending you care about my soul!"

The chaplain called the guard to unlock the door. He said he would report straight to the general and tell him all Souren had said.

Souren's spirit sank like a stone. Shattered hopes and unattained ideals haunted his thoughts. He sat for days in near darkness. At certain times of the day, a shaft of light reached through the barred windows and painted a fat stripe of golden sunlight against a wall several feet above him. He longed to feel the sun shine down on his face and warm his cold, tired bones. One of his hands had by now become infected. He squeezed the yellow pustule in one of the wounds until it burst, and drained the infection the best he could. Instead of drinking his daily allotment of water, he used half of it to clean the gashes and sores on his hands.

At night, he listened for voices of people and imagined they were talking to him. He welcomed the screeches of the noisy seabirds. But most of the time, he sat in silence and darkness.

He resided in oblivion.

"No one knows I am here. No one will know if I die," he said outloud.

He thought of his mother, and it filled him with deep anguish. He wished he knew whether the general had actually sent his telegram. One moment he rejoiced at the possibility, the next he descended into despair with the probability that it was only a trick to make him think they were seeking the truth.

One day, Souren had not slept more than a couple of hours when the guard unlocked the door and told him to get up. He found himself again in the office of the general and his interpreter. The general wanted to know about his family.

"Why are your sisters and brothers in America? When did they go?"

"Uh, I-I—my father and mother worried for their safety. During the massacres twenty years ago, thousands of Armenians died. My parents knew that the future for Armenians in Turkey was bleak. They arranged to have each one of their children leave Turkey, but only after receiving an education."

"Why did your parents stay if it was so dangerous?"

"My father was a minister, and my parents ran an orphanage—"

"Ah, you finally tell the truth!" the general sneered. "In fact, your parents' orphanage was in partnership with the Germans, wasn't it?" He barked in Italian and barely waited for his interpreter to finish before continuing his accusations about Souren's parents.

Souren had walked right into the trap. He had as much as admitted his parents worked closely with Germans. He tried to backtrack.

"As I said, my father was a minister, and my mother worked at his side. Together they rescued Armenian orphans, victims of the massacres perpetrated by Sultan Abdul Hamid. They were not spies. They were good people! My father is dead, but my mother continues at great risk!" Souren's face glowed red.

The general sat down and gloated over his small victory. "And how is it then that you found yourself assistant to a German officer?" he asked.

Souren now had his guard up, so that when the Italian general attempted to trick him, now addressing him in German, he squelched the instinct to reply. Instead, he let his eyes do the talking. Souren stared intently and with as much visual anger as he could muster back at the general and sat in silence.

"Have it your way," the general growled in Italian. He bellowed a command, and a sergeant obediently appeared to return Souren to the dungeon.

The general did not call Souren to his office the following day. Nor did he send for Souren the next. The isolation and loneliness were meant to torment him. He steeled himself and tried to remain strong in the face of this cruel torture. Along with water, he was only given bread twice a day.

He once thought about taking his miserable life and even looked around his cell for the means. He realized, though, that if he killed himself, the general would heap insults upon his family and label them as "German sympathizers." That very thought gave Souren the will to fight back.

In his loneliness, he talked to Beatrice. They made love. They danced. She told him stories and urged him to be brave. "It will all work out, Souren. You must believe it will!" He caressed her smooth arms and pressed his face against her warm breasts for comfort. He cried in her arms and slept while she cradled his head in her lap.

"Beatrice," he would say to her, "you are the only reason I am still living."

The intense loneliness led to a friendship with two mice whom he named Kaiser and Sultan. He shared his bread with them, and they promptly came out of their holes whenever he called them by name.

"Kaiser," he would begin, "why did you start this war?"

The nervous little mouse twitched its nose and darted around, waiting for bread.

"And Sultan, why did you let a rabble like the Young Turks take your throne?"

The mouse hunched over its dinner and busily devoured it.

"I predict history will count you both as fools," Souren pronounced. He gently stroked their fur and lectured them on how to run a world where peace prevails, people of different persuasions get along, and where war is abolished.

Early one morning, about the time the welcome shaft of light dispelled the oppressive darkness of another interminable night, Souren was startled awake by the clanging of metal. The cell door opened, and the general himself stepped through it.

"Come!" he ordered.

Souren followed him out of the cell, up the stone stairwell, and into the bright light of day. He could not open his eyes fully and only staggered around trying to find his way. He listened to the general's boots grind on the stone and followed the sound.

The general stopped suddenly. By now, Souren was able to open his eyes and look around. He saw a contingent of soldiers.

"My execution?" Souren's knees gave way, and he fell to the ground.

The soldiers pulled him to his feet and led him out. Without explanation, Souren was taken to a port on the other side of the island and put on a torpedo boat.

"Where am I going?" he asked in Greek.

"Scarpanto," a familiar voice called from the pier.

Souren found himself staring at the Greek interpreter whom he had caused to be dismissed during the first interrogation.

"Scarpanto?" Souren's confusion pleased the exultant dragoman.

"The Italian ambassador to the United States of America sent a telegram. Apparently, your family contacted the secretary of state in Washington, DC, who contacted our government."

"I'm to be freed?" Souren puzzled at this turn of events.

"No," the interpreter said with mock compassion. "You are still a prisoner of war. In accordance with international law, you will be kept until the end of the war and then returned to your country of origin."

He accurately interpreted Souren's startled expression.

"Yes, one day you will get to go back to Turkey!" the Greek laughed. Fully satisfied with this final act of revenge, the reinstated interpreter ran to get back with the general.

—⋙—

The Aegean Sea is home to a multitude of islands. Two of these are Rhodes and Crete, and between them sits Scarpanto, a desolate island that points lengthwise to the coast of Turkey. Scarpanto is shaped like the upturned sole of a shoe, the "heel" at its northern end marked by bare mountains, where sat an old quadrangular building that the Italian army had converted into a prison. At the same time it took Rhodes, Italy occupied Scarpanto and the entire chain called the Dodecanese Islands. They had been easily wrested from the disintegrating Ottoman Empire.

Souren surveyed the wild beauty all around him. The crystal waters and secret coves in the foreground, framed against the sharply rising peaks in the background, would have evoked awe if he were a tourist. But he was a prisoner, and this historic island, about which he had read in ancient literature, impressed him as a very lonely place. A world war raged all around him, yet Souren was being forced to bide his time here until it ended.

The newest prisoner on Scarpanto paced back and forth in the six-by-ten-foot cell. Souren rejoiced that at least his time of isolation in the fortress had ended and that his family had successfully disproved the accusations of spying. He thanked God that he would not have to die in that dungeon on Rhodes. Yet, he certainly did not feel happy. Thwarted plans weighed heavy on his mind and heart.

He cried out in frustration, "Why? Why?"

Anger repeatedly surged through his body. Despair filled his being like an inescapable, relentless heartbeat. Souren was trying to come to grips with the reality that he had to spend the duration of the war idle. He who had longed to join the fight was condemned to march back and forth across his cell, perhaps until the Turks had finally managed to wipe out his people.

For the first few weeks, Souren languished in self-pity. He ignored the kindness of the Italian guards. He did not strike up conversations with other inmates when they shared the brief courtyard exercise periods. But eventually, boredom drove him to more productive activities.

He constructed a crude homemade lamp from a few simple things at hand. He hammered out the edges of a tin can from America labeled "Meat" and filled it with water. He skimmed the oil from his daily ration of boiled rice upon which a spoonful of olive oil had been poured. He tore a small piece of cloth from his shirt and pulled it through a piece of cardboard that he placed on top of the can. Then he held up his lamp and gestured to indicate to the guard that he wanted a match. Souren struck the match against the stone wall and lit the oil-saturated piece of cloth.

The improvised lamp burned brightly, impressing the guard, who smiled and said, "*Ottimamente!*" (Excellent).

"I would like a book," Souren said in Greek and then French. The soldier shrugged apologetically to indicate he could not understand.

Souren put his hands together and then opened them as if he were holding a book.

"Sì, sì," the guard replied. "Domani. Io porterò i libri di domani."

Souren smiled and said, "Thank you."

"*Grazie,*" the soldier instructed him.

"Yes, of course, *grazie,*" Souren repeated.

"*Di niente!*" the guard replied, grinning broadly.

The following day, the soldier surprised Souren with two books: *La Sacra Biblia* and a tattered copy of *Robinson Crusoe*, his favorite novel as a boy, now in the Italian language. Souren laughed to himself at the irony of being an Armenian stranded on the Greek island of Scarpanto and trying to read in Italian about the world's most famous English castaway.

It began, "Io nacqui nel 1632 nella città di York da una buona famiglia che peraltro non era del luogo."

"I was born in the year 1632 in city of York to a good family, though not of that country." Souren read aloud the first line of this novel, which he knew almost by heart.

He looked at his new friend and said, "Grazie."

"Di niente," he answered.

Since the books he had been given were familiar to him and since Italian bore many similarities to French, Souren was able to teach himself to read this new language without too much trouble. He learned the rules of Italian syntax, numerous verb conjugations, and the proper declination of nouns and adjectives. He constantly practiced his vocabulary, trying to add at least five new words daily. His spoken Italian lagged behind the rapid advance he made in reading, but over a couple of months, he became quite comfortable conversing with the guards and fellow Italian prisoners. They admired his ability to learn rapidly and his desire to communicate with them, which motivated him to further improve his command of the language.

Soon, fellow prisoners approached Souren in the courtyard and asked him to write their letters home. Souren felt nothing but compassion for these men, incarcerated mostly for petty nonviolent offenses like failure to salute an officer or selling meager military rations on the black market and pocketing the profits. These Italian foot soldiers came from remote villages. They had farmed their land, not attended an elite school as Souren had. Their humble requests gave Souren a sense of purpose.

Instead of blaming God or berating himself for his depressing circumstances, he read his books and drew strength from his relationships with the other prisoners. From time to time he could hear his father urging the congregation back in Smyrna with, "Blessed are the poor in spirit, for theirs is the kingdom of heaven. Blessed are those who mourn, for they shall be comforted." Souren found comfort in writing letters for men whose homesickness and love for their families matched his own.

One day in June, a group of Italian soldiers secretly released Souren and took him to their barracks. From what he could understand of the shouts and the songs and the general state of prevailing hysteria, the Italian army had won an important battle against the Austrians at Piave River in northeastern Italy, near Mount Peralba in the Carnic Alps and near the Austrian frontier. The men cursed the Austro-Hungarian Empire, and they confidently predicted doom soon for the Germans and Turks, too.

"Armeno! Per tuo solute!" a soldier shouted. (Armenian! To your health!) The others cheered and broke out in song, declaring the greatness of Italy and their pride in being Italian. The celebration continued late into the night. More wine, more song, more toasts. The soldiers were sure the war would soon be over and they would return home. Souren realized they hated being trapped on this island just as much as he did.

"Comme ti piache il gatto?" one of the soldiers asked Souren.

"Il gatto?" Souren repeated.

"Sì!" the soldier laughed.

Not wanting to appear ungrateful, Souren replied in broken Italian that the cat had actually tasted quite good, adding "It was the best meat I have eaten for a long time." It was not true, of course, but it made Allabrezi, the man who had cooked it, very proud.

It happened to be the cat that had hung around the prison and been fed by all of the men, including Souren. He had been a sort of mascot at the jail. Souren had seen it jump into the lap of Allabrezi and purr endlessly.

"I marinated him in wine for twenty-four hours to drive the gaminess out of the meat," Allabrezi explained as if he spoke of some expensive delicacy. "Then, I roasted him for this joyous occasion. I suppose rabbit would have been preferable, but I couldn't get my hands on any."

Chapter Ten

—ɯɯ—

1919

In September 1918, the Allied armies had made advances in Mesopotamia and in the Balkans that drove a wedge between the Austro-Hungarian and Ottoman Empires. Turkey negotiated a separate peace on October 30 in Mudros Harbor on the island of Lemnos, across from the mouth of the Dardanelles. Here, almost three years before, the Allies had retreated in defeat, and the victorious Turks had exuberantly celebrated an unlikely victory over British and French naval and ground forces. However, after four years of a war it was not prepared to fight, the Ottoman Empire was finally routed by the same foes it had repulsed at Gallipoli. As her representatives boarded the *Agamemnon* to discuss terms of surrender with the British, they wondered at the inescapable irony. Surely the British reveled in the symbolism. The ship's name referred to King Agamemnon, who led a confederation of Greek armies against ancient Troy at the opening of the Dardanelles, and this same ship had bombarded Turkish forts during the 1915 Gallipoli Campaign.

The Armistice of Mudros, negotiated by Britain without the knowledge of France, stipulated among other things that the Allies reserved the right to occupy lands to which Armenians could be repatriated should trouble arise. Ports, railroads, and telegraph stations would be controlled by the Allies. The treaty demanded that all German and Austrian naval, military, and civilian personnel be evacuated from Turkey.

The French occupied Constantinople on November 12. The British landed the following day. The famed city, taken from the Christians by the Ottomans nearly five hundred years before, was now in possession of the Allies. The Young Turk government had already collapsed. Talaat, Enver, and Djemal had escaped to Germany, which had concluded its own armistice.

After the deaths of more than thirty-seven million people on three continents, the Allies congratulated each other on victory, and the Great War—later known as World War I—came to an end.

In May 1919, President Woodrow Wilson, British Prime Minister Lloyd George, and French Prime Minister Georges Clemenceau authorized Greece to land an army at Smyrna. This triggered a spontaneous, frenzied celebration followed by several days of parties and parades. Ancestors of the Greek inhabitants of the historic city had settled it long before the Turkish invasions of the eleventh century. Their descendants plastered the city with blue-and-white flags. In a sacred ceremony, the Greek bishop blessed the soldiers when they stepped from their ships onto the wharf. The soldiers were hailed as heroes as they marched through the streets. A general state of hysteria prevailed. The Young Turk regime that had subjected Greek residents to boycotts and deportations had been vanquished and was defunct. Greece, a former dominion of the Ottoman Empire, turned the tables and was now in Turkey as her conqueror.

The last time Souren had sailed into Constantinople, he was aboard a torpedo boat, dreaming of leaving Turkey. Now he gripped the side of the ship with his calloused, scarred hands. Those wounds had mostly healed, but some of the deepest ones still festered. He and the other returning POWs were processed immediately after disembarking. Souren rehearsed a defense of his status as "deserter." He might have assumed the Allied bureaucracy would receive him with open arms when they learned he had escaped the Turks to join them, but his experience with the Italians had taught him to be wary of saying too much. Drawing upon the lesson he had learned, he hatched a story to buy some time.

He feared that the Turkish authorities had marked him for a court-martial. He stood ready to recount a credible defense, when to his surprise, the British officer waved him through. Souren did not know what to make of this, but he was not going to wait around for anyone to change their minds. Later he learned that his mother had bribed an official in order to make his record as uncontroversial as possible. He quickly negotiated the labyrinth of tables, men, officers, military police, and medical personnel checking repatriated prisoners for infectious diseases.

Once done with the red tape of reentry, Souren plotted the fastest means of returning to Smyrna. He needed to get to the train station. Too exhausted to walk the distance, he jumped on a bicycle resting in a doorway. He thought he heard someone shouting after him, but he figured that since this was his first experience as a thief, the voice could have been that of his conscience.

Masses of exiles expectantly crowded the ports, waiting for passage to Europe and the Americas. They mobbed the train stations with their children, meager belongings, and often no money. Food, coal, and electricity shortages made it impossible for Constantinople to handle the masses of people that coursed through its streets and ports. The upheaval was a typical postwar phenomenon. It also resulted from a stipulation of the armistice. The Allies bore the burden of managing the return of people to their lands, but at the same time, they were hammering out a peace agreement in Paris. The tragic confusion of war had given way to the exuberant chaos of newfound peace. The world, millions of refugees included, breathed a sigh of relief for the cessation of the unending madness of killing.

Souren passed by a strange medley in long lines of carriages and mule-drawn wagons loaded with rolls of blankets, bags of food, rugs, and furniture. They creaked slowly forward to the monotonous rhythm of cooking pans and water containers clanging together with each divot and stone in the road. One man held a goose in his left arm while leading a team of oxen with his right. A barefoot woman pushed two infants in a rickety wheelbarrow. A carpenter was painfully pushing a baby carriage loaded with his tools.

At the train station, Souren beheld a sea of humanity even greater than he had seen in other parts of the capital. Entire families camped on the platforms. He could not count all the travelers that day, but history would record more than sixty-five thousand displaced persons waiting in Constantinople to make it back to their homes.

As a former employee of the railroad system, Souren was able to craft a plan to reach his home. He quickly found a train waiting to leave for Smyrna. The state of disorganization was such that no ticket was necessary to board it. He barely managed to squeeze himself into a crowded, noisy, and ill-smelling compartment. The next morning, with a sense of unreality, he found himself standing at the familiar Smyrna station, a short distance from his home.

As if in a daze, he started walking down the crowded thoroughfare. To his left was battered Mount Pagus, which had taken a few hits from British planes. To his right lay the Armenian neighborhood. Souren noticed a number of British soldiers patrolling. He passed familiar stores, a blacksmith, a post office, and a large warehouse where figs were packaged.

"Souren!" a man behind a counter yelled from within his shop.

As a result of the last few years of living under a false name, Souren stiffened when he heard his name being shouted for all to hear. He looked in the direction of the voice and saw the butcher. He was wiping his strong hands on his apron and running, smiling broadly, to shake Souren's hand. Several other merchants stepped into the street to greet him.

Mass slayings had robbed the Armenian community of its young men. Deportations and arrests had stolen the rest. Souren represented a whole generation of disappeared young men who should have been strolling down this same street and welcomed home as heroes.

Anxious to see his mother, after several handshakes and hugs, Souren took leave of his admirers and turned down the street where he had grown up. A flood of memories washed over him as he saw a group of Boy Scouts being herded into a courtyard for a group photograph.

In a matter of minutes, he stood in front of the church where his father had preached powerful sermons that seemed always to leave the congregation wanting more. Across the street, several Armenian girls walked out of the girls' school and in Souren's direction, excited to see a handsome and robust Armenian young man. Souren nodded at them and smiled. He heard their giggles behind him.

Finally, he was standing in front of his home. His heart beat rapidly, and his throat was suddenly very dry. He did not know how he should present himself to his mother. It took all of one or two seconds before he decided he would give her a big surprise.

Before he had left Scarpanto, the Italians returned all personal items to the prisoners of war. Souren gladly received his piccolo. He pulled the instrument out of his bag, assembled it, and sat on the stairs leading up to the front door. He filled the air with the melancholy strains of the beloved "Groong," a nostalgic lament of a lonely traveler far away from home. Neighbors and their children, as if mesmerized by the familiar melody, made their way to Souren and stood respectfully around him. Mr. Terzian stepped out onto his porch across the street and let out a cry of joy when he saw Souren.

Suddenly, the door of Souren's home opened. His mother was standing there, totally stunned to see her son with his piccolo. The crowd stepped back and let mother and son reunite in a long, intense embrace.

Sophia was weeping. Through her tears, she uttered in partial disbelief, "Oh my God! Oh my God! Thank you! Thank you!"

Mr. Terzian squeezed through the clamoring throng and shook Souren's hands. Then, he threw his arms around him and cried.

He kissed Souren on each cheek almost as if Souren were his own son. The women took his hands and kissed them over and over.

"My son is home at last!" Sophia kept repeating. Tears of joy fell in torrents and streamed down her face and along her nose. "He's home!" she called to all the friends who had gathered around her.

The Armenians lovingly mobbed the returning soldier. They smothered him with affection until he had been kissed and hugged enough for an entire battalion. Mr. Terzian thanked the neighbors and deftly escorted Souren and his mother inside the house. It wasn't long before platters of baklava, pots of pilaf, loaves of freshly baked bread, and basketfuls of food arrived at the Tashjian home to help celebrate the miraculous return of Sophia's youngest son.

For the good Armenian denizens of Smyrna, life was beginning to return to something of normalcy. Families were being reunited; shops were active again; children were playing and running outside. The wash was hanging to dry in the sun, bright and clean. Folk were returning to church, and life was again hopeful.

Before war broke out in 1914, Smyrna pulsed with a quarter of a million people. The population of this cosmopolitan city soared after the armistice, as a million Greek and Armenian refugees migrated from the far reaches of the defeated empire to a city secured by the Allies. The steady stream of exiles and refugees strained Smyrna's limited resources.

One group of exiles was made up of Armenian children who were being sent to the liberated city from overcrowded orphanages as far away as Aleppo and Beirut. In response to their needs, Souren and his mother, along with several other Armenians, established a rescue home for boys. Another group oversaw a home for girls. They turned away no child, but with the numbers increasing daily, workers faced a host of urgent problems.

Sophia had nursed orphans through the previous massacres but could not keep up with the demands of so many children. She had never seen anything like it. In a matter of only two months, the numbers at the home went from three hundred to five hundred boys. She could not find enough supplies. The work suffered from insufficient funding and very little organization because almost everyone in Smyrna was a refugee.

In desperation, Sophia sent Souren and other volunteers to canvas the streets of the Armenian quarter for donations. Souren came back with five hundred discarded flour sacks from a kind-hearted merchant. These were used for bedding. The boys slept on bare floors, lying a foot apart and filling every room in the building, even the kitchen. Each boy crawled under his sack at night. The more fortunate had an extra one for a pillow.

It was dawn as Souren walked down the front steps of the rescue home. His night shift had ended. In accordance with his new routine, he would walk home and sleep for a few hours before returning in the afternoon to help with organizing a Boy Scout troop. He and the others in charge tried to keep ahead of the chaos. Feeding hundreds of boys three times a day, keeping them clean, finding clothing for them, and caring for their various medical conditions overwhelmed the entire staff.

Souren drew in a deep breath, and as the crisp morning air filled his lungs, he thanked God again that he was back in his beloved Smyrna—at least for now, while he waited for the arrival of the visa promised by his sister in Seattle so that he could leave for America. His prayer of gratitude gave way to one of supplication on behalf of the hundreds of needy boys who filled the home.

He was one among several young men stationed in the hallways to monitor the boys at night. The orphans regularly awakened from nightmares, shaking and needing comfort. Souren's heart broke for these poor souls who, after years of deprivations, looked only half their age. He treasured the responsibility of protecting and reassuring his little charges. He wanted to do more, but the task was so vast and the numbers so staggering that Souren had to be content with his small contributions of being a night watchman and a Boy Scout leader.

The boys' nights were not filled with peaceful slumber. Sunken eyes and wan faces made the gaunt children appear as corpses once their eyes closed. Frail, emaciated bodies trembled involuntarily from the cold. With only a tunic to wear and a flour sack for cover, they shivered the whole night through. Each had arrived filthy and without proper clothing, without family, and often having been the victims of violence and witnesses to massacre.

Souren noted that most boys never smiled. Their existence for the past few years had been one of terror and survival, eating roots and leaves as they wandered the streets and roads of the towns where they had been left behind, hidden by relatives or sympathetic Turks who acted to save them from the death march to Der Zor. Most no longer spoke Armenian, but Arabic or Turkish. Perhaps they remembered the names of their mothers and fathers, perhaps not. They were either too young to recall or too traumatized to speak.

One of the boys had lived for two years at the Aintoura orphanage in Beirut run by Djemal Pasha and Halide Hanoum. He surprised Souren by talking freely of what he had lived through. He gave chilling accounts of Armenian children dying from cholera and starvation and then being buried in shallow graves that were dug up at night by jackals.

Another orphan repeatedly woke up screaming. He had escaped massacre by hiding in a food cellar in his back garden that was covered with branches. When he emerged, he found his house ransacked. His father was dead in a ditch with dozens of others, his throat cut, and he slept beside him until it was safe to run away.

The stories like this Souren heard were endless…and he knew there were many more who could not and did not speak of the past at all.

Souren had recently promoted one such orphan to the role of his assistant. Vartan demonstrated devotion and selflessness.

At breakfast one morning, Souren told Sophia, "Vartan would do anything humanly possible to help the other boys. Only a mother or father could show more concern for them."

Sophia asked what Souren knew about him. So far, the only information Vartan had supplied was his name, that he came from the province of Erzincan, and that he had lost his entire family in 1915.

"Give him some time. He will tell you," Sophia said. "The older ones recall with such vivid detail. The poor darlings cannot forget what they saw."

Every Sunday afternoon, Souren and Vartan led a troop of twenty Scouts into the hills around Smyrna. As they marched through the Armenian quarter in their khaki-and-yellow uniforms, each holding a staff he had carved himself, the townspeople leaned out their windows or watched from their yards and doorways. They were proud to see the Scouts, all of whom were orphans.

Souren enforced the strictest discipline on his troop because any activity involving a group of twenty orphan boys, who were mischievous by nature and armed with sticks, could quickly degenerate into pandemonium. He kept the boys busy by showing them how to notch measurements on their staffs. From these marks, the boys would practice estimating the height of trees and buildings. Souren demonstrated how the staff could also function as a splint in case someone broke a limb. He had them practice a makeshift stretcher and told them how he had made one to carry home an injured Scout many years ago.

One Sunday, Souren's lesson was cut short by the noise of a mule-drawn cart that stopped in front of the Scouts. It was an old Armenian couple whose cart was laden with fresh figs they had harvested from their orchard. The man and woman pulled out a worn sheet and spread it on the ground. They dumped the load of figs in sight of the orphans, an invitation. The figs were so ripe, they were bursting. The boys looked from Souren to the figs and back again. They wanted the fruit and anxiously awaited their leader's signal.

When Souren gave them permission, the boys, in a single swoop, dove on the figs and stuffed themselves with the luscious, sweet fruit. Figs had been a staple in their homes before the war, and the boys associated them with happy times. They laughed and played as if they had not a care in the world. Souren could not help noticing the sparkle in their eyes. Under the age-old spell of fresh figs, for a brief period, the boys escaped their dreary lives of want.

The troop returned to the orphanage following the rare feast, and Vartan and Souren sat outside discussing plans that were afoot to rescue more orphans. Thousands of Armenian children were still being held captive, and countless young Armenian women remained in bondage in Turkish harems. The Allied commissioners had battleships in the harbor but told the Armenian people they were unable to cope with the situation. Souren and the other troop leaders met and decided they would have to act on their own.

"When do we go?" Vartan asked.

"We will start this week. Each troop has a designated sector, but we want each group to be accompanied by a British soldier to make us look official."

"The tables have finally turned," Vartan said. "No longer are we helpless and defenseless."

Souren looked over at Vartan, alarmed at the tone in his voice. The gentle, nurturing young man whom he had made his assistant now transformed into a frightened boy at the memories of his own hardships. Souren paused.

"Vartan," Souren said softly, "do you want to tell me what happened to you?"

Vartan was ready to talk. "It all began when the Turkish authorities demanded that Armenians turn in their weapons. They arrested the community leaders and tortured them. One of my professors, Mr. Meguerdichian, was paraded through the streets under armed escort. We all crowded around to see what was going on.

"'Here is the enemy!' one of the soldiers yelled.

"He nodded at his henchmen, and they whipped Mr. Meguerdichian's hands. They dragged him to the public oven, where they burned his hands and feet. Mother grabbed me and took me home so I wouldn't see. I heard they killed him by cutting him open alive.

"One of my uncles was arrested soon after. They flogged him until he fainted. Soldiers sprinkled water on his face. When he regained consciousness, they continued to flog him.

"'Where are the weapons?' they demanded of him.

"He didn't have any. What could he tell them but the truth? They continued to beat him, saying, 'We know you have buried your weapons! Tell us where they are!'

"A message was delivered secretly to my father. The messenger told us the details of my uncle's imprisonment, and my uncle told my father to purchase weapons and turn them in to the authorities. In that way, he could save the rest of the family. My father, and many men in our city, went to some friendly Turks and purchased old rifles at inflated prices. Late one night, soldiers pounded on our door. They told my father to hand over his weapons. My father gave them the rifle he had purchased. Instead of appeasing the authorities, they accused him of being a revolutionary. He was led away in his nightshirt.

"I remember my grandmother crying out in anguish, 'Come down, oh God who has created us! Come down!'

"The following day, a group of Armenian prisoners was deported, my father among them. They had begged to see their relatives one last time and were given permission to do so.

"I cried when I saw my father. His lips were swollen; his face was lumpy and discolored. Everyone resorted to crying, for we had been forbidden to speak.

"My father embraced me and kissed me. Then, for all to hear, he said, 'They have tortured us like they did Jesus.'

"A whip snapped against his back, and he dropped to his knees. Mother pulled me away. We watched as my father was led away with the others. I wanted to call out to my father, but I was afraid they would hurt him more if I did.

"The rest of that day and the days following, the streets of town were deserted. The fear of a terrible massacre hung over us.

"After a few days, the town crier announced that everyone was to come out from hiding. We were being taken to Arabia. My mother was among those who preferred leaving. She and my grandmother began preparing for the journey.

"The first to go were those still remaining in prison and the very sick, who could not make the march with my father and the others. These men were loaded into carts. In less than an hour, those carts returned empty. Fear and dread engulfed us.

"One morning, the town crier brought word that all Armenians were leaving in a matter of hours. We would be safely escorted to a temporary destination. As soon as we reached the outskirts of town, they separated the men from the women. My mother suspected danger and had made me wear a dress. When the men and boys were being collected, they passed me over, thinking I was a girl.

"They attacked us with spades, axes, knives, and bayonets. It wasn't just soldiers. We were ambushed by Turks from nearby villages who had been told we were going to pass through. Mother frantically pushed me down and rolled me under a thick bush.

"'Vartan, I love you. Close your eyes, and don't move!'

"She screamed suddenly. I immediately closed my eyes. I heard them drag her away. I lay perfectly still for a few hours. When I finally crawled out, I saw my mother. She was cut to pieces in a pool of blood. All the other women, too, even my grandmother. The bodies of so many children littered the ground. I recognized Hovsep and Boghos, friends from school. Those who were still alive screamed for their mothers, all of them bleeding from their own wounds.

"'Water, water!' I could hear the faint voices of those clinging to life begging for a drink, but I had nothing to give them.

"I crawled back into my hiding place, and I cried myself to sleep. The next morning I heard horses. I thought they had come back to kill those languishing in the field, but I saw the riders were not Turkish soldiers. I watched as they surveyed the dead. I saw them wretch at the sight of the mutilated bodies of women and children. They were searching for the living, so I crawled out and walked toward them.

"I was taken to an American hospital and sent on to an orphanage. After the war, the place was so crowded they sent some of us older boys here."

Vartan looked up at Souren for the first time since beginning his story. "And that's how it happened for me."

Souren felt the sudden impulse to find all the boys with stories like Vartan's. He grabbed his young assistant by the shirt, and with a decisive voice he said, "Tomorrow morning we gather our troop with a British soldier, and we start our search for Armenian children who are still held captive!"

The British commissioner reluctantly agreed to allow one soldier to escort Souren's troop into the Turkish quarter. They quietly marched in four groups of five Scouts each and in different directions. At each corner, a Scout was left to stand guard while the others knocked at every door. Courteously, but with military sternness, they asked for the Armenian captives to be brought out. Then they searched the houses.

Souren and Vartan's campaign to find enslaved children proved successful. Among those brought back to the orphanage was Karnig, a quiet little boy with curly brown hair and big black eyes. He had the dignity and poise of a preacher, which was strange for a boy his age. At meals he led the boys in the chant of the Lord's Prayer. Karnig would sing a line that was then repeated in unison by the rest of the boys.

"Hayr mer, vor hergeens yes," Karnig's tenor voice rang out. (Our Father, who art in heaven.)

"Soorp yegheetsee anoon ko," the light, agile voice reverently chanted. (Hallowed be thy name.)

"Soorp yegheetsee anoon ko," echoed the chorus of orphans.

During the initial months of caring for orphans at the rescue home, volunteers were plagued by many basic logistical problems. Limited funds prevented any progress. The overworked staff kept the doors open, but everyone worried that if the number of orphans continued to rise, they would have to start turning boys away.

Finally, relief workers arrived from America. Mrs. Clara Elizabeth Van Etten, a warm, maternal figure, took charge of the boys' home. Her missionary coworker, Mrs. Headly, oversaw the girls' home. Under Mrs. Van Etten's leadership, the focus shifted from mere survival to establishing some sort of normalcy. She set to work immediately reorganizing the home. The first step was to give it a name that would inspire confidence and provide a sense of permanency and purpose. Thus, the Central Orphanage, as it was now called, transitioned into an efficient institution.

Mrs. Van Etten's next step was to create the role of dormitory mothers whose responsibilities included defusing arguments, breaking up fights, enforcing curfews, making sure the sick boys received the attention they required, and checking to see that chores were done and done well. These surrogate mothers filled an empty place in the boys' lives and helped smooth the running of a burgeoning orphanage.

The American director of the Central Orphanage cultivated familial ties among fellow orphans by assigning older boys to act as big brothers to small groups of younger ones. She procured additional food, clothing, and medicine from the Red Cross. She couldn't bear to see the boys on bare floors with no more than flour sacks for a cover. It took a couple of months, but she petitioned for and received over a thousand blankets. Mrs. Van Etten spoke only English, so she relied on Souren and a couple of other Armenians who had attended the American missionary school to act as her interpreters.

Souren's devotion to the orphaned boys was total. It was also necessary. Whenever he was not busy, his mind wandered to Beatrice. He had searched every street corner and every store. He looked inside every shop he passed, hoping to catch of glimpse of her somehow, somewhere. If he caught sight of any gypsies performing, he would stop and ask them if they knew of a beautiful dancer with brown hair and blue-green eyes.

"She dances like an angel on a cloud," he would tell them.

Inevitably they shook their heads, pitying the obviously lovelorn young man.

One day, two gypsies stood outside the train station advertising the afternoon performance on top of Mount Pagus. Souren instinctively made his way up the hill. He scanned the stage and benches for any sign of Beatrice. He did not see her, but he did recognize a rich Turk in a European suit. He was Husenedin Bey, the man who had kidnapped Beatrice and brought her with him to Ephesus. He was arrogantly flashing his gold rings inlaid with emeralds, stroking his beard, and twisting the ends of his mustache. His chin was pulled in, and his shifty eyes went back and forth, scanning the environs. After a time, satisfied that those around him acknowledged and envied his station in life, he contentedly rested his thick hands on his big belly.

Souren had heard that this former Turkish officer was raking in huge profits by illicitly collecting and selling surplus arms and ammunition. The disgruntled Turks who opposed the Greek occupation of Smyrna were reliable customers. It was said that Husenedin urged revolt during transactions, though he was no patriot. In fact, if a Greek offered a better price, everyone knew he would sell to him instead. As long as people were shooting each other, he could make a killing.

There can be only one reason he is here, Souren thought. *He is after what he sees as his "property."*

Nimbly, he wove his way through the maze of castle ruins until he spied the gypsy encampment and recognized three ramshackle wagons, even more dilapidated than the last time he had seen them. His heart throbbing, he stood hidden and watched the steps at the back of each of the wagons. He heard a commotion. A curtain opened on the wagon nearest him. Three children scrambled hurriedly down the steps and toward the stage. Souren could barely keep himself from charging the wagons and yelling for Beatrice. But he suppressed the urge and waited.

Finally, one of the boys climbed up the second wagon, stuck his head inside, and called out, "Hurry up! It's your turn!"

"Okay," a truly familiar voice replied.

The boy jumped off the back of the wagon and ran off.

Souren immediately left his hiding place.

His breath caught when Beatrice appeared. She looked startled to see him. She lifted her long skirt and descended the steps. They stood just two feet apart. Neither moved. Their eyes locked in wonderment. Neither could speak.

Beatrice reached out and touched Souren's arm.

He took her by the hand and said gently, "Husenedin Bey is here. Grab what you need. We must leave quickly."

Beatrice's eyes widened, but she remained calm. "My bag is packed," she assured him. "All I have to do is get it. You wait here."

Souren nervously looked around. He worried that her delayed entrance would alert their enemy, but it was only a moment before Beatrice tossed her bag to Souren and leapt from the wagon. Without looking back, the pair ran away hand in hand. Husenedin waited exultantly for the dancer to take the stage.

Souren took Beatrice to the girls' home. Mrs. Headly, the American in charge, listened sympathetically to Souren as he related to her the danger Beatrice faced, by Turkish custom, if not given protection. Mrs. Headly readily accepted Beatrice into the home without delay. Souren translated the good news for Beatrice.

"Please thank her for me," Beatrice said with tears of relief and gratitude.

Their culture forbade the couple from staying together, so they arranged secret rendezvous behind a certain row of shops once a week for half an hour. Souren always arrived first. He sat on an abandoned wicker trunk, but if Beatrice were the slightest bit late, he would jump up and pace until she arrived.

At their first meeting, he said to her, "That day you left me standing in the dark near the cove, I went back to my cot and lay awake, imagining what I wanted to say to you. But when I came back in the morning, you were gone."

"I'm so sorry I behaved that way, Souren."

"No, it was the right thing to do. It was motivation and gave me to courage to act."

Souren went on to tell her how he had escaped in a rowboat and wound up a prisoner of the Italians. The agony of separation and his heartache melted away in the presence of this beautiful young woman who leaned over and kissed his cheek and whispered in his ear, "You are remarkable, my dear. And very brave."

After they had revisited the past and caught up on one another's lives, their weekly conversations turned to the future. They were in love and hoped to marry. However, obstacles prevented them for doing so in present circumstances. Souren had no profession, and according to Armenian custom, this was a major obstacle to his eligibility. Also, as he had always dreamed, he planned to go to America as soon as his visa came. He explained to Beatrice that his brother-in-law and sister were sponsoring him and that, with their connections, he should be able finally to go to medical school.

Beatrice's situation remained tenuous. She had an uncle whose last address she had was in Boston. Mrs. Headly was trying to locate him but so far had been unable to establish contact. Beatrice would not be able to immigrate unless she had a relative willing to sponsor her.

In all likelihood, Souren would leave first. As soon as possible, he would go to medical school. When Beatrice did come, she would be able to find him by contacting his sister in Seattle, Washington. They anticipated as many problems as their young minds could conjure up, but then found solutions that would bring them together again.

It was after one of these clandestine meetings that Mrs. Van Etten called Souren into her office. She held a letter from the American consulate about Souren's visa.

"First, you are to pick up your visa. Then you will go and purchase your ticket to sail to America." Mrs. Van Etten beamed with pride and shook with excitement. Each time she could help one of her boys—orphans or volunteers—to get out of Turkey and on a ship to her country, she rejoiced. She found opportunities in America for as many Armenians as she could. In the case of Souren, it was just a matter of a letter to the consulate.

"Thank you so much," Souren said with tears in his eyes, "for everything you've done for me."

"Souren, I have not a doubt that you will seize this opportunity." Her fondness for him was reflected in her smile and cheery voice. "I will be short one translator, but the world will be blessed with one wonderful doctor."

Her faith in his abilities humbled Souren.

The next few evenings as he walked the halls of the orphanage, Souren's mind raced. For years he had dreamed of going to America, of being a doctor, of living in a land where he would be free. But he had not anticipated the waves of sadness that now inundated him. Souren felt pangs of homesickness at the thought of leaving the boys he had grown to love. He already missed singing the Lord's Prayer with Karnig. He did not want to leave Vartan.

Even though he and Beatrice spent time planning their future, he worried about leaving her in Smyrna. What if her uncle did not sponsor her? What if Husenedin Bey finally found her?

His increasingly frail mother needed him now more than ever. Souren and his brothers and sisters in America all urged her to come to America with Souren, but she would not hear of it.

"How can I leave now?" she had insisted. "I am too old to start over. I want to stay here where there is so much work to be done."

Souren knew she could not bring herself to abandon her work at the orphanage and that her mind would not be changed, but how could he bear to leave her alone?

Souren also still worried greatly for the Armenians in general. Yes, the war was over, and the Allies now assured that the Christian Armenians and Greeks were beginning to rebuild their lives and even reengaging with Turkish families and businesses. Greek troops were now in control of the city, and British battleships were in the harbor, but what would happen if and when the Allies left? The situation was certainly not stable. Souren knew that while the Ottoman Empire was now at an end with the military defeat, and that the "Three Pashas" had all fled to Germany, the Young Turks were still very much a powerful and increasingly resentful force in Turkey. Rumors were that in central and eastern Anatolia, there was a burgeoning and spreading independence movement being led by a Turkish military officer, Mustafa Kemal Ataturk. Where was this headed?

The questions kept him awake when he tried to sleep. When he saw Beatrice again, she noticed immediately that his eyes were ringed with dark circles.

"My dear, how are you?" Beatrice cooed.

When she heard Souren had secured his visa and passage to the New World, she threw her arms around his neck and gave him a light peck on the mouth. Her unbounded joy led to several minutes of intimate caressing.

Souren pulled away.

"Beatrice, I can't leave you. I can't! I waited so long to find you again." He sought her neck and pressed his lips against her silky skin.

Beatrice kissed Souren tenderly and then instructed him firmly, "You must. You will go to America. You cannot just drop a dream you have held for years. A wonderful dream. I will join you as soon as I can. Mrs. Headly finally heard from my uncle! He has moved and now lives in another city. You see, it will all work out, my love."

Encouraged by her news and resolve, Souren embraced the delicate but strong frame seated beside him. He ached for her even though he had her in his arms. They would meet only a few more times before he set sail for his new life in America. He could not bear the thought of saying good-bye, even if it was not forever.

The day of their last rendezvous came. Souren arrived early as usual. This time, he could not sit down on the wicker trunk. He paced back and forth. Part of him did not want to see Beatrice because they were going to say good-bye. Another part of him felt he would literally die if he did not hold her close one more time before he left.

"Where is she?" he fretted out loud. The thought of her not coming at all worried him deeply.

Beatrice arrived nearly ten minutes late.

"Where have you been?" Souren asked.

She had no time to answer because he swept her into his arms and began kissing her with more passion than he ever had before. Beatrice sensed his desperation and held Souren close.

"I can't stay long," she said apologetically. "Mrs. Headly sent me out for a prescription. One of the girls is sick."

Souren noticed that she looked tired and like she'd been crying. He knew she was trying to be strong for him.

They pledged again their love. He gave her a piece of paper with his sister's address in Seattle. She promised over and over again to find him when she got to America.

All too quickly, the time came to part. As her hand slipped from his grasp, Souren held on to her fingertips. He could not let her go. They hugged once more and then turned away resolutely, not knowing when or where they'd see each other again.

On the afternoon of his voyage, hundreds of people crowded the quay. Women in long dresses and wide-brimmed hats, supported by the strong arms of debonair husbands, boarded the ship followed by their young children, whose eyes were ablaze with the excitement of travel. Relatives and friends shouted their well-wishes. The scene was altogether joyous.

Souren stood heavyhearted in front of his mother. He held a large brown leather briefcase with shiny copper latches. He wore a suit that was too tight, with sleeves that were too short. His pant legs fell two inches above his shoes so that his white socks were showing. His mother fixed his tie and straightened the wrinkles on his white dress shirt. She even adjusted his straw hat. Souren was sweating profusely under the bright midday sun. He silently vowed to take off his suit jacket as soon as his mother was out of sight.

Sophia extended her arms. "Let me look at you again, Souren. Perhaps for the last time in my life."

The day before, he had said good-bye to everyone at the orphanage. A short program of songs and recitations by his Boy Scout troop had brought the staff and five hundred boys to their feet. Vartan had cried when Souren hugged him. The ceremony of saying good-bye was long and filled with emotion.

First Beatrice, then the boys at the orphanage. Now, Souren had to endure one more painful farewell.

A long, uninterrupted blaring horn signaled the final call for boarding. Souren hugged his mother. He knew she was a deeply religious woman, but she astounded him by removing his hat and reaching up and laying her hands on his head. She committed him to the safe hands of God. She prayed that he would be faithful to his calling and to serve his people wherever he might go. Then she held his face, looked into his eyes, and commanded him to fulfill his dream of becoming a doctor.

Souren scaled the ramp and was swallowed up in a throng of passengers standing along the side of the ship, excitedly waving good-bye to their loved ones.

—⟶⟵—

When Souren arrived in Seattle, his sister Armenouhie was there to meet the train from New York. They had not seen each other for nearly fifteen years. She ran out onto the platform to greet him as soon as she saw him disembark. He dropped his briefcase, and they hugged a long time. For the most part, tears replaced words! Then, clasping hands, they hurried back to the station door where her husband, Dr. Otis Lamson, a tall and vigorous man with sparkling blue eyes, was waiting with a broad smile. The two men, one already a leading surgeon and the other dreaming to be, shook hands firmly and looked into each other's eyes. The respect was mutual and instant.

Almost as soon as Souren arrived in Seattle, his sister took him to a tailor and had him fitted properly for his new station in life as her little brother. Armenouhie had become a popular socialite in Seattle and also was active in a number of humanitarian causes. She filled her schedule with banquets and meetings and wrote letters to American politicians and to heads of state around the globe about the necessity for Armenian justice. She made sure that Souren looked like he belonged where he was.

She arranged a number of speaking engagements for him. His English, although heavily accented, was quite good and his suit the finest quality. Audiences sat in rapt attention as they heard this handsome and dignified foreigner recount his miraculous escape and impart firsthand accounts of the savage killings, desert death marches, traumatized orphans, Armenian girls despoiled and held captive in harems, and how the revolutionary Turkish government had sponsored all of it. He always ended with the hope his people placed in the United States to help them get back up and build their future.

Souren never failed to thank his American listeners for their concern and their donations that fed the "starving Armenians." He only hoped, he told them, that America's leaders would guarantee that the newly formed Armenian republic remained free and that her historic lands would be returned to her. The people sat in fervent attention and vigoruously applauded. They gathered around Souren as if he were a celebrity. They asked him to speak at their churches and clubs, so moved were they by his accounts.

Although he was immersed in his new life, Souren anxiously followed the news, reading reports and newspapers for information about the latest developments in situations he had left behind. One week an article announced: "American Relief in Smyrna Discontinued! Near East Relief reports American relief activities have been discontinued in Smyrna, headquarters of the Greek force in Turkey." Souren read that the orphanages had now been turned over to the Armenian community thanks to the improvement of political conditions and to the competency of a well-trained staff.

A few days later, Armenouhie handed Souren the morning paper after she had finished reading it. "Here's another article about Smyrna," she said, then dashed out the door to a fundraiser.

Souren unfolded the newspaper and saw Mrs. Van Etten's picture on the front page. Mrs. C. E. Van Etten, Armenian Relief Worker, Relates Sad Scenes Witnessed, the headline read. Beside the photograph of her was another picture. Mrs. Van Etten, who had received a gold medal for her work, was flanked by two rows of Armenian Boy Scouts. Souren imagined the festivities as they might have unfolded: Mrs. Van Etten receiving a large bouquet, a choir singing to her as a procession of influential Armenians approached with great ceremony to pin a medal to her dress.

As he read the article, ensconced in the leather armchair behind an imposing desk, Souren found himself pausing after each sentence and recollecting.

"Because of the high cost of fuel, the poor boys suffered immensely until we were able to have enough blankets and shoes shipped to them," Mrs. Van Etten had told the paper. "The food was of necessity very limited."

Souren recalled Karnig's crystal-clear voice leading the boys in prayer in the dinner hall. There was little to be thankful for in terms of the actual meal, yet the boys were grateful to eat even if it was only thin soup and coarse bread.

Souren could not hold back tears as he read on.

"Under these conditions I made an appeal to the Near East Relief for an extra supply of blankets and some cases of condensed milk. I asked them to be furnished as soon as possible. At night I gathered the little folks about me in the office and gave them each a cup of hot water with a little milk and sugar in it, so they would have enough warmth in their starved little bodies to be able to sleep for the night."

Souren looked up from the paper. He sighed heavily, and unconsciously shrugged his shoulders as if to get rid of a burden. What he read next made him smile.

"I found the children naturally intelligent, industrious, ambitious, proud, exceptionally talented, and willing to make any sacrifice for an education. They were rapidly being exterminated through the ruthlessness of the Turkish policies, but if we can hold the remnant of the nation through the storm and stress of the coming year, until the world regains a saner outlook and some definite policy is adopted regarding Turkish atrocities, we will save a people well worth saving."

Souren studied the photograph of the Scouts. He recognized several faces and longed to be there with them, leading his troop up to Mount Pagus or marching them through the Armenian neighborhoods where they received cheers and adulation.

In a letter from his mother two weeks before, Souren learned that Beatrice had obtained a visa. Plans were under way for her to sail from Turkey to the United States as soon as possible.

Souren leaned back against the soft leather. He could not dispel the feeling that leaving Smyrna had been a mistake, even though both his mother and Beatrice had insisted that he go. His brother-in-law was a prominent and influential Seattle physician and had just recently helped him gain acceptance to the University of Virginia medical school. He was to move to Virginia in a few weeks. But as much as he was gratified that his long-held dream was within reach and he tried to look forward, his mind wandered back to Smyrna, to the orphans, to his mother, the Armenians still there devoting themselves to rebuilding. The lines of a poem he had recently received from a guest at one of his speaking engagements haunted him:

> *If I were a poet,*
> *I would weave the lily and the rose into garlands*
> *Of glory for Armenia's brave daughters.*
> *I would touch the heart of humanity*
> *With a mournful threnody of wrongs against Armenia.*
> *The land of martyrs and suffering, the cradle of sorrow,*

The nursery of liberty.
Tortured in dungeons, murdered on scaffolds,
Plundered by the ignoble Turk
And driven—driven by the avarice of heartless Power
Like Autumn before the bitter winds of winter and now,
Armenia's sons and daughters are homeless
In the land of their fathers, and the land of their birth.

Chapter Eleven

—⁓—

1922

The situation in Smyrna had deteriorated since Souren left for the United States. The Greek forces that had occupied the city in 1919 with the support of the WWI Allies, particularly the British, turned out to be spearhead troops for Greece's visions of territorial expansion, to be implemented by the military occupation of Smyrna and several other cities in Anatolia. At the same time, the Young Turk revolutionaries, under the leadership of Mustafa Kemal Ataturk, were increasing in power, very successfully regaining momentum, expanding their forces in central and eastern Anatolia. Their vision was the recapture of the Turkish government in Constantinople, throwing out the Allies, and creating a new Turkish state.

A new war was essentially inevitable. The Greek advances were stopped by the Turkish forces at the Battle of Sakarya on the coast of the Black Sea in 1921, and a well-planned Turkish counterattack resulted in the collapse of the Greek front and the retreat of Greek forces from the regions they had temporarily controlled. Tensions once again were rising rapidly in Smyrna.

—⁓—

In Charlottesville, Virginia, Souren sat at a small desk in his cramped two-bedroom apartment provided by the University of Virginia medical school and pondered what to write to his mother. He worried for her safety and missed her dearly. Led by his sister Armenouhie, he and his siblings had consistently urged her to leave, but she still steadfastly refused. Burdened with his stiff academic load and volunteer work, Souren had not replied to her last letter several weeks ago.

He sat thinking, while absentmindedly adjusting the bandage on his hand. It was a new invention called a "Band-Aid," and this was the first time he had used one. A few days before, he and two other students were volunteering among the destitute in the Irish ghetto when he cut his hand lifting an ailing child from his rickety metal cot. The laceration was not deep, but it was painful. Worse than the small, annoying wound was the low-grade fever he couldn't seem to shake.

With his elbow on the desk, he held his forehead. The words came slowly. He stopped. Started. Stopped again. He had so much to tell, but strangely, Souren could not find his habitual ease with the flow of sentences.

My dear Sophia mayrig,

First, I want to tell you how much I miss you even though I have neither the time nor the leisure to write to you often. I hope you get my letters. As you could tell on the Smyrna quay when we said good-bye, departing to a far country with the uncertainty of ever seeing you again was a wrenching experience for me. The long boat trips—from Smyrna to Marseille and on to New York—did not make things better. I arrived to this country like a fearful child. As well as I know English, I have still found myself having trouble understanding Americans. They talk so quickly, and they use words I've never heard. Medical school has been a big adjustment as well. But I am doing well and am proud that I am at the university created by Thomas Jefferson, the philosophical father of America.

Do not worry about me, dear mayrig. I have quickly discovered that the way you raised me—hardworking, honest, and resolute—and the hardships I experienced in the Turkish military and escaping have had the effect of preparing me well to meet the challenges that I have faced in this strange but welcoming country since my arrival. America is very different from what I had imagined. It seems I'm always uncovering another feature to life that surprises me.

Souren closed his eyes. His back ached for no particular reason. He attributed the discomfort to his fever. He reached up and felt his forehead, and it felt hot. But he picked up his pen and continued to write.

I have learned that, according to the newspapers I read here, the Treaty of Sèvres has no chance of succeeding. Of course, if it fails, this would mean a big step backward for all Armenians. That treaty is our only means of reestablishing our claim to our historic lands. I hope that Mustafa Kemal's nationalist army will be stopped. But try to tell that to the average American on the street! The prevailing atmosphere here is one of what they call "isolationism." After American losses suffered during the war, they don't want to be caught up again in the world's problems.

Most people here want to live and let live, a saying I have heard over and over. Since they are living on a separate continent, most citizens here believe they are in a position to forget about the rest of the world's problems.

At that moment, Souren's roommate burst in with a few friends in tow.

"Souren, we're going to the dance. Are you coming?"

"He's busy reading news," one of the guys said, poking fun at Souren, who had a reputation for devouring newspapers.

"Hey, you don't look well. Are you sick?" one of the young men asked.

"Just a low-grade fever. It's nothing," Souren replied. "I'm going to stay in tonight and write some letters."

His American friends filed out noisily. He heard them talking about a speakeasy with plenty of whiskey, music, and women.

Souren took up his pen again.

Mayrig, one of the most interesting things is that the American unmarried young women and men go out together freely together on what they call "dates." It is the same word for the dried fruit I enjoy so much! On these "dates," there are no chaperones. Some go in groups, but most are in pairs. And even stranger is that now some of the girls are asking me to go on one of these dates to go dancing!

City life is certainly different here. The women—even girls—cut their hair short, and their dresses, too! However, in the countryside where I've done some volunteer work, the habits are different. There, they don't go to movies or speakeasies. They wear their hair and their dresses long. Grandmothers wring their hands and worry that the city life is going to ruin America. I find that even though I grew up in the bustling, cosmopolitan city of Smyrna, I relate more easily to the country people here than to the city folk.

Recently, an outbreak of meningitis took me to an Irish ghetto for volunteer work. I discovered a level of poverty in America that quite surprised me.

Surrounded by so much that is unfamiliar, my thoughts often go back to how life used to be in Smyrna before the war. And as you can suspect, I still have deep feelings for that Armenian gypsy girl Beatrice that you met when I brought her to the orphanage. I am totally without news about her, and I wonder if she's still in Smyrna or whether she came to America as she was planning to do. If you can find out anything, Mayrig, please write and let me know.

Souren wiped the sweat from his forehead. Now he realized that he was burning up with fever. He left his desk and crawled into bed and shivered spasmodically. It was a hot August night, but he could not get warm.

—⚊—

Souren's fever grew worse, and he was soon committed to the hospital of the University of Virginia medical school, hovering between life and death. Though only semiconscious, he discerned the usual hum of a busy hospital floor. Suddenly, a voice emerged, one that sounded familiar to him. He thought he heard a woman with a thick accent discussing his condition with a doctor. Souren was on the verge of identifying the voice, but his mind was not clear enough to bring the name to recollection.

He heard someone tell the woman, "Of course, you are welcome to assist him," just as he sank back into his tormented world of fitful nights, long episodes of shaking uncontrollably, cold sweats, and terrifying nightmares.

The small, seemingly superficial cut on his scarred hand had led to a life-threatening case of sepsis. The infection had traveled through his blood stream. Blood poisoning developed. For a long time, Souren lay unconscious and was delirious. The doctors held little hope. As a last resort, they decided to try blood transfusions. Although blood transfusions were a relatively new medical procedure, it had been accepted as an in extremis treatment for patients with certain illnesses. A bulletin had gone out requesting volunteers to donate blood:

> Volunteer medical student needs blood transfusions for blood poisoning. This medical student, an Armenian immigrant from Turkey, contracted an infection while helping an ailing child during the recent epidemic. He who escaped the horrors of massacre is lying sick in a hospital because of his unselfish dedication. If you are able, please apply to help this young man by donating blood to save his life.

The bulletin succeeded, and so did the treatment. After a series of transfusions, the day finally came when Souren woke up. Still quite groggy, he sensed a presence by his side. After making an effort to turn his head, he discovered a person standing there.

Thinking he was seeing a vision, he whispered, "Beatrice? Beatrice?"

A woman reached out and squeezed his hand.

"How did you find me?" Souren said.

"I saw the bulletin sent out by the doctors, and you know the Armenian community. Word gets around, Souren. Our people never seem at a loss for gossip."

It was indeed Beatrice's bright face smiling down at him!

Souren noticed she wore lipstick and thought it very becoming on her. Her long tresses that twirled when she danced were gone, cut off in the fashion of American women. She wore a white nurse's uniform.

"What are you looking at?" Beatrice teased.

"I think I am looking at an angel," Souren replied.

Beatrice shook her head, rolled her eyes, and proudly stated, "I have been to nursing school."

Souren rattled off several questions, but Beatrice urged him to rest, promising, "We will talk about all of that when you are stronger."

The next day, after she had removed his breakfast tray, Beatrice reached into her pocket and held out a telegram. She also bent down and picked up a stack of newspapers.

"Ah! You have saved me, Beatrice." He smiled weakly.

But Beatrice did not smile back. Although he had not seen her in more than two years, and although he was not yet fully alert, Souren could read the distress in her expression.

"What is it, Beatrice?"

She opened up a copy of the *New York Times*.

Souren scanned the very top. It was dated September 26, 1922.

"It's September?" Souren exclaimed, shocked at now realizing he had been unconscious or semiconscious in the hospital for several weeks.

Beatrice sighed and pointed to a headline near the bottom of the front page: Smyrna Burning! 14 Americans Missing. 1,000 Massacred as Turks Burn City. Kemal Threatens March on City.

"Mother?" Souren's eyes pleaded for hopeful news.

Beatrice read the telegram she had received from Souren's sister. "Mother not found. Multitudes destitute. Males deported. Making supreme effort to find Mother. Tell Souren we are doing all we can.

"I contacted your sister Armenouhie in Seattle. She sent me the telegram."

"Can you read me the rest of the headlines?" Souren requested of Beatrice.

She sifted through the newspapers and several other gloomy headlines: 340,000 Herded in Smyrna. 60,000 Are Left Homeless. Hundreds of Corpses in Streets. Many Slain in the Night. Greek Archbishop Brutally Slain. Hundreds Caught in Flames.

Beatrice stopped. "I can't read any more right now, Souren," she said, beginning to cry. "I'll come back tomorrow." She squeezed his hand and left.

Souren watched her walk away. He didn't want her to go, but he could tell she was deeply troubled. He himself was in near panic about his mother.

For the next several days, Beatrice arrived at Souren's bedside, usually to feed him his breakfast and to oversee his care until the afternoon, when another nurse took over. Each morning, she carried with her a number of newspapers that she and Souren read together. Sharing the anguish made the burden a little lighter for both of them.

Under Beatrice's care, Souren recovered steadily. "You saved me," he would say to her before she left his side after each shift.

"Blood transfusions, medicines, excellent doctors, and the grace of God saved your life," she would reply.

In a matter of days, he was sitting up in bed and able to feed himself. He wanted to ask Beatrice important personal questions, but she seemed to be preoccupied by the news coming out of Turkey. He decided to enjoy the attention she provided and to wait for a good time to talk to her about the future they had envisioned during their many secret rendezvous back home.

Each day he saw her, he would ask for news of his mother. But the dismaying answer was always the same.

"There's still no word, Souren. Your family is in touch with the American missionaries, but even they cannot account for all of their workers. We must be patient, and we have to remain hopeful about your mother."

"I could not endure the agony if you were not here with me," he said. "Every day I kick myself for leaving her there alone back in Smyrna. But everything seemed to be developing well when I left, and she insisted over and over again that I go."

"We all thought Smyrna was safe, Souren. Don't be so hard on yourself. It was also your mother's dream, not just your own, that you be here. We must have faith, and we must be patient," Beatrice instructed him. "Don't give up hope." She kissed his cheek.

The next day, a nurse brought Souren his breakfast. Beatrice arrived as usual with several newspapers. Together, she and Souren scoured them for news of home and read this summary of the devastation at Smyrna.

"The loss caused by the destruction of tobacco in Smyrna is enormous. Foreign trade has sustained enormous losses, especially the branches or agencies of the big American tobacco houses."

Souren tossed a paper aside in disgust. He glanced at the nurse who was collecting his breakfast dishes and moaned, "The price of cigarettes is going up while the value of human life is plummeting."

"I don't smoke," she replied.

He looked with raised eyebrows at Beatrice, reminding himself just how much he valued his stimulating conversations with her.

There was more upsetting news. Kemal had set a deadline for all Christians to be evacuated from Smyrna, except for boys and men ages fifteen to fifty-five, who once again were being conscripted for hard labor. Souren's mind raced. He worried for the orphans he had left. Some of them would be fifteen by now and perhaps prisoners of the Turks. The thought nearly drove him mad, but there was nothing he could do. He clenched his teeth and let out a loud sigh of frustration. They sat silently, blankly staring out the window for several minutes.

When the nurse left with the breakfast tray, finally their conversation turned to the personal matters that had been on both their minds but repressed by their daily concern about what was happening in Turkey. They looked into each other's eyes, immediately broke into smiles, and embraced. Beatrice sat on the edge of the bed. Souren was anxious to know how she had come to America and, of all miracles, ended up in Charlottesville, Virginia.

Beatrice said that her uncle, who had immigrated previously and had been living near Charlottesville for several years, had arranged her visa and sent the steamship ticket for her travel. But once she arrived in America, her uncle had become insistent that she marry a man that he repeatedly emphasized was "a prominent Armenian physician." He was a man who seemed nice but to whom she had been introduced only after she arrived. It did not matter because among the traditional Armenian families, a young woman needed to marry, her husband-to-be needed to be a man of professional means, and it was common that he be selected by a father, or in this case uncle, and she had virtually no say in such matters.

Shaking her head and nervously toying with a couple of strands of hair, Beatrice recounted to Souren how difficult it was to resist her uncle's insistence. Several times their arguments had actually led to yelling matches and had changed their relationship. They had not spoken much to each other recently.

Souren felt his heart begin to race, but he remained outwardly calm and looked at her with admiring eyes. *Not lost her strength of character,* he thought to himself. *Strong and determined as ever.* Nevertheless, Souren well understood the power of Armenian tradition.

He squeezed her hand. "Don't worry, Beatrice. This is America. Just give it some time. One day your uncle will understand this new contemporary world, and I am sure you will win back his good favor."

He winked at her, adding with a smile, "Thanks to you and the medical center here, I am alive again, and within a couple of years, I, too, will be a prominent Armenian physician!"

She giggled at his subtle sarcasm. They held hands and again looked into each other's eyes. They agreed that there was no choice but to take things one day at a time with their relationship, particularly with Souren still being in medical school and while she gradually made amends with her uncle and hopefully was able to change his mind.

Beatrice's recounting of the confrontation with her uncle reminded Souren of something he had been working on before he became ill. He asked Beatrice to fetch his old leather briefcase from across the room.

"I want to share something with you," he said. Sitting more upright in bed, he pulled out a lined pad and read to her from his handwritten notes.

Our conscience is guided more or less by custom and tradition. No doubt climatic influences, environment, and education mold our actions. As a man without a country, I ardently hope, with other thousands like me, while enjoying such boundless hospitality under the protection of "Old Glory," that conditions will improve in the future; that our devastated country, and all heterogeneous nations, will unite with one common purpose and that they will not struggle to be masters of each other. Let justice be their god, and mercy will not be needed.

Let us have a fixed faith in this destiny. Let us feel an unbending happiness in that faith. Let us remember the fact that the trail of the past, though sorrowful, is short compared with the road we and our descendants must travel in the future.

The wise fatalist understands that what has happened was unavoidable, but that in what is to happen, he may have a part.

Nothing is gained by mourning too long over the past, but a great deal may be gained by considering and preparing for the future welfare of all. In this way it is possible for mankind to carve its own destiny.

Beatrice's head was bent, her eyes staring at the floor as she listened intently to what Souren read. She remained silent for a few moments, then looked up at him with tears in her eyes. She got up, went over to him, and held his face in her hands. She kissed him on the forehead.

"This is why I love you so much, Souren. Your unyielding faith in the innate goodness of mankind, your consistent optimism as to its future, and your courage—remarkable courage—to work to make it happen." As she left the room, she turned, smiled, and blew him a kiss.

—⁂—

A few days later, Souren received a letter from his sister Armenouhie. In it, she explained that their mother at last had been found, had been rescued from the Smyrna fire, and that she was in Athens. Arrangements were under way for her also to come to America.

Souren jumped from his bed, hospital gown flapping, and yelled for all to hear, "My mother is alive! She's in Greece!" Spontaneous cheers and applause erupted out in the hall.

Souren sat back down on the edge of his bed and reread the letter three more times. Softly he laid it on the blankets. He hung his head. His shoulders shook as he softly wept. These were tears of joy. He had, against incredible odds, survived—first from the terrorists of a brutal war and now from a terrible illness. By the most fortunate of circumstances, so had Beatrice, and somehow, unbelievably, they had found one another again. And now his mother was alive, well, and safe—finally to rejoin her adult children and their families in America. For the Tashjian family, the long and tortuous nightmare was finally over. And he, Souren Barkev, was about to live his dream.

Epilogue

—⟋⟍—

June 1970

Souren relit his pipe and turned to look out the window. The bus ride from Seattle to Spokane was four hours, and now the bus was passing Cle Elum on the east slope of the Cascade Mountains, about an hour and a half from Seattle. I was seated in the window seat next to him. He nodded toward the pacing scenery and told me that the landscape and mountainous background reminded him of his boyhood in Anatolia.

Souren was a member of his North Seattle Democratic district delegation, and we were on our way to the 1970 Washington State Democratic Convention. For a man in his midseventies, he was healthy and vigorous, and a successful physician in Seattle. He had been happily married for many years. Beatrice's uncle and Armenian tradition had ultimately prevailed, and she indeed had been given in marriage to the man her uncle had selected for her. After completing medical school and spending a year at the Mayo Clinic in Rochester, Minnesota, Souren had returned to Seattle and there fallen in love with a pretty and remarkable young woman from Yakima who shared deeply his philosophy of life and passion for justice. They had an adored son, now several years graduated from high school and with a deepening interest in horticulture.

I admired Souren for his courage and heroic escape but even more so for his passion and dedication to peace and justice. In character and personality, my great-uncle seemed to me the personification of the character Zorba played by Anthony Quinn in the 1964 movie *Zorba the Greek*. He had become an inspiring force in my life—physically strongly built, street smart, real-world insightful, politically astute, a bit irreverent, and with an energetic love of life.

As we together looked out the bus window, he told me he felt like some of the Greek music he enjoyed—a little happy and also sad at the same time. The sadness he felt arose from the fact that worldwide violence, needlessly pitting people of different cultures, religions, and political or economic philosophies against one another, seemed never to end. At the moment it was the Vietnam War that troubled him. He had treated several young men who were maimed in the conflict. He could clearly sense their psychological pain as well and was sympathetic to their troubled psyches because he knew personally what they felt. He had been so traumatized by his own war experience that it had taken over a decade before he healed enough to even begin writing it down, and then four more decades to piece together memoirs.

I had just turned twenty-eight. I was also a delegate to the Democratic Convention, a first-timer. I had recently returned to Seattle from Washington, DC, where I had been a defense economist at the Institute for Defense Analyses (IDA). With a top-secret security clearance, I knew much about what was actually happening in Vietnam at the time. I shared Souren's view.

Souren shifted in his seat and exhaled a rather angry puff of pipe smoke. "I was just thinking again how sad it is to spend a beautiful weekend like this to yet again try to halt a war in a poor, underdeveloped country where women and children seem to pay a higher price than the troops themselves." He sighed. "It is a winless war, propping up a corrupt government and tearing apart the lives of millions of innocents. Reading newspapers about whole villages destroyed, often just burned to the ground, and soldiers shooting villagers reminds me far too much of what I witnessed in Turkey during the war, and what my mother experienced in barely escaping the burning of Smyrna 1922. How do you young people say—it all just pees me off?"

I nodded agreement. "It pisses me off too, Souren. But at least this time we may end it before most of the population is wiped out. The Democratic Convention could be a significant step if the troop-withdrawal initiative passes."

The twinkle returned to his eye. He opened his old, greatly worn leather case and pulled out the proposed 1970 Washington State Democratic Platform pamphlet.

Slapping it on his knee, he chuckled. "I've had three meetings with Senator Henry Jackson about this. He doesn't exactly welcome me, but he is courteous. I sit in his outer Senate office all day, until his assistant gets tired of chatting with me and the coffee I fetch for her has turned sour. Then she finally gets me in to see him. Senator Jackson is a nice man. He is always pleasant, but he is such an advocate of the war. He finds me a major annoyance, I'm sure. The party in his own state being one of the first to formally call for US troop withdrawal would definitely not make him happy!" His pipe needed to be refilled and relit.

We spent the rest of the bus trip analyzing the upcoming 1970 campaign. The bus driver made a couple of wrong turns and got lost for a while, but ultimately pulled up in front of the Spokane Convention Center. The scene was a circus of Senator Jackson's pro-war delegates and aides intermixing peacefully, but warily, and at times argumentatively, with antiwar delegates and activists. There were to be two very different official dinners this evening before the convention. One was hosted by the supporters of Senator Jackson, and the other by the supporters of Carl Maxey, the powerful black Spokane attorney and civil-rights leader, now an anti–Vietnam War activist who had declared his candidacy as Jackson's opponent in the Democratic primary.

Souren and I worked our way through the crowd and presented our credentials at the delegate's check-in tables. We received seat assignments for our respective delegations. Souren's delegation was to be seated in the balcony and mine on the convention floor. After checking in to the budget motel where we shared a room, we attended the Maxey dinner, sharing conversations and predictions about the next day's events with the other delegates.

There was still half an hour until the opening session when we arrived the next morning at the convention center and took seats with our respective delegations. The stage was manned by the convention chairman and supporting staff. More than a few clearly confident aides to Senator Henry Jackson were being overly friendly, backslapping and joking with the convention officials. I interpreted this as part of their strategy to control the convention discussion and voting process. I turned in my seat and looked up to the balcony to see if I could locate Souren. I finally found him, seemingly relaxed, pipe in hand, and chatting with the two women delegates seated next to him.

The convention was gaveled open by the chairman and began with the Pledge of Allegiance. The first order of new business was the Washington State Democratic Platform. The introductory section, laying out the vision for the nation and political philosophy of the party, was general and noncontroversial. A few amendments were passed virtually unanimously with little fanfare. Several platform "planks"—written statements stating the party's position on specific matters—concerning the party's view of the national economy, the environment, civil rights, international trade, and agriculture were also passed with little controversy. But every attendee to the convention knew that the big one—national defense and the Vietnam War plank—was where things would heat up and the action would be divisive. An undercurrent of anxiety grew in each delegation as the time grew near. After the last of the less controversial planks was passed, the convention chairman called a recess.

Finally the time had arrived! Knowing the controversy about to emerge, the convention chair rather sternly established the rules for the debate. It would be conducted by alternating an equal number of brief speeches by delegates in favor of and delegates opposing the plank. Against a backdrop of murmuring by the various delegations, he read the proposed language. He finished and summarized again that voting *for* the plank meant supporting the position calling for the removal of US troops from Vietnam.

Microphones were located in the aisles throughout the floor and the balcony of the convention hall. Senator Jackson's aides immediately left the stage, where they had been sitting during the proceedings to this point. They spread out among the various delegations, alternatively greeting and smiling with supporters and staring sternly at delegates they knew were going to support the plank.

Short speeches by delegates began, alternating for and against the troop-withdrawal platform plank, just as the chairman had instructed. The plank's opponents stressed repeatedly the military might of the United States and urged even more aerial attacks and troop action to eliminate the so-called domino threat—the spread of Communism throughout the world if South Vietnam failed to win the war. The pro-plank speeches, on the other hand, focused on widespread news articles and photos of the consequences the war—the deaths of women, children, and elderly in the villages of South Vietnam, and the lasting environmental consequences from the defoliation chemical Agent Orange. The increasingly documented corruption of the leaders of South Vietnamese government also received attention.

I knew that all this caused Souren to reflect back on the tortures and deaths of the Armenian women and children during the Genocide in Turkey—suffering that he had personally witnessed and miraculously escaped. I was sure he was thinking of the parallel of the Turkish government's official rationale for the elimination of Armenians: such terror of innocents was justified because these Christians, if not eliminated, would pose an everlasting—domino—threat to undermining the foundation of a Turkish Islamic nationalist state.

Glancing toward the balcony, it was plain to see that Souren had had enough of it all. He stood and worked his way to one of the microphones in the aisle nearest him. He got in the short queue.

Shortly he found himself first in line at the microphone. It was the turn for an anti-plank speaker, and the convention chairman asked Souren if he was to speak in this capacity.

I could tell Souren was by now energized by the nature of the debate. He lied. "Yes," he responded.

He began speaking in his heavily accented English. "I know personally of the unimaginable horrors of war and the unjustified cleansing of innocent people as a consequence. I am Armenian, and my mother and I barely survived the Genocide launched by the Turkish government against my people during World War One. Over a million Armenians perished, maybe a million and a half, since many just disappeared without any accounting. Deaths occurred in some of the most terrible, tortuous ways imaginable. Women raped and dismembered, babies butchered in front of their mothers, old people starved to death in desert marches, able men and boys arrested and sent to slave-labor battalions and worked until exhausted—then gathered together and mowed down with machine guns.

"I myself was arrested several times, each time barely escaping, the last time thanks only to the sympathy of one commanding German general. But after my final escape, rowing my way to the Greek islands, the Italian military authorities in command there thought that I was lying about being Armenian. They thought I was a Turkish spy. So I know the hell of solitary confinement in dark, dank prison cells. To this day I suffer from nightmares, and my hands were so badly scarred and stressed that I could not become the surgeon I had dreamed of becoming since a young man.

"I know only too well the horrors of a chaotic and undisciplined war. And unless you have personally experienced such terror, you can only somewhat understand how the indelible stain of innocent blood acts like a cancer to the emotional and mental state of the survivors."

He raised a fist in the air and continued, "Man's butchery of man in the name of some ridiculous claim is nothing other than group insanity. It cannot be justified—not then and not now. In Vietnam, it must stop!"

The entire room had become quiet and seemed transfixed on Souren—this old, heavily accented Armenian speaker, so passionate, yet also dignified in sharing his experience and demanding an end to the war.

At this point the chairman banged his gavel on the podium. "Sir—you are supposed to be speaking against the troop-withdrawal proposition, against the plank. You are out of line. Please step back and let someone who is so motivated take the microphone."

Souren began to continue, "Death by—"

But the chairman interrupted again, banged his gavel loudly, and shouted at him, "Sir, I said, step back from the microphone and sit down."

At this point, amid the boos and catcalls aimed at Souren by the delegates against the troop-withdrawal plank, most of the pro-plank delegates in the room rose to their feet and began yelling, "No-o-o-o. Let him speak! Let him speak!" And then they chanted in unison: "No more war! No more war! No more war!"

The chairman banged his gavel repeatedly, shouting, "Order, order!" until finally the convention hall quieted somewhat. "All right. I will let the gentleman continue—your time is almost up, sir. But following him, I will recognize two speakers in succession to speak against the troop-withdrawal plank."

Souren continued, "Death of innocent people by terribly in-human means, simply because they stand in the way of irrational obsessions of a corrupt government and its machinery of war, is a crime against God. It is wrong, and I, for one, cannot yield to such insanity. So, as a physician, I offer here that any young man who faces being drafted for this war against his will may come to me to receive a medical deferment. He will not be forced to participate in the butchery!"

The entire convention erupted at once. Delegates supporting the troop-withdrawal plank jumped to their feet. They clapped, shouted, whistled, raised their arms with fists or victory signs, and even danced. Several had tears running down their cheeks. At the same time, those who supported the war effort and were against the troop-withdrawal plank hooted, screamed "Traitor! Commie!" and worse at Souren, and shook hands thumbs down in opposition.

It was a political circus, and it went on quite some time. When things finally quieted down enough, the convention chairman did as he promised and recognized two speakers consecutively to pres-ent against the platform plank. But by now the entire convention was energized. Each speaker was greeted by a conflicting chorus of supporting and opposing clamor.

Finally the chairman announced an end to the debate and called for the vote. Each district delegation was to poll its members and report the results to the appointed party officials on the stage, who would calculate and report the final tally of votes.

By a slim majority, the vote to include in the 1970 Washington State Democratic Party Platform a plank seeking the withdrawal of American troops from Vietnam carried. When the results were announced, new bedlam erupted. The convention center filled with competing cheers and jeers, hugs and tears of joy, victory signs, fists shaking in anger, broad smiles, and heads bowed in defeat. The scene around me was both amazing and inspiring. I was stunned. While there had been signs of growing support, few had expected the plank to actually carry. It seemed the tide had been turned by the impact of one incredibly powerful soul.

On the bus ride home, we again sat next to each other. He quietly puffed on his ever-present classic big-bowl pipe. I interrupted him and told him how much I was moved by his speech and how amazing it was that he had likely been the difference maker in the passage of the troop- withdrawal initiative.

He looked at me for a few seconds, and I noticed the sparkle in his eye. "You know what was the best part?" he said.

He had my full attention. I anticipated profound insight as to a part of his speech or the way the convention delegates had responded to it.

"Twenty-three women came up to me afterward and kissed me on the cheek," he said.

I laughed hard, especially at the fact that he had actually counted! He chuckled as he patted his cheek where his awards had been planted and then went back to stuffing fresh tobacco into the bowl of his pipe.

In spite of the seriousness of the current situation, the difficult journey of terror he had managed to navigate, and the horrific events he had witnessed, Souren had never lost his sense of humor. It was this beautiful balance—this combination of courage, strength of purpose, power of personality, and the love of life—that impacted me again as I studied him for a few moments. Our bus rumbled on. I felt most fortunate to know so well this extraordinary man.

—w—

Souren Barkev Tashjian lived his remaining years continuing the good fight whenever the opportunity presented itself. He had a peaceful passing after a short illness in the fall of 1979. My wife, Elizabeth, and I visited him just a couple of days before his passing. Propped up in the hospital bed that had been delivered to their home, Souren still could get a gleam in his eye.

"Just once more before I go," he said, "I would like to enjoy again the taste of Greek olives."

Elizabeth went to the nearby grocery-deli and purchased several. He ate two, smiled, and squeezed her hand. That was our last visit. His funeral filled the Congregational Church in North Seattle to overflowing.

One of the insights Souren shared with me shortly before he died, and that I shared with the congregation at his funeral, is this: Human beings do not all of a sudden and on a whim decide to collect themselves into groups for the purpose of committing terrible acts of violence against one another simply because they do not share the view of another culture or another religion. These tragedies occur repeatedly because ambitious politicians and soulless religious organizers engage in egoistic battles for power. They find that inciting ethnic and sectarian violence is too often easy. It can be aroused simply by dishonestly manipulating fearful instincts and thus creating a convenient tool to further their own self-seeking agendas.

This was certainly the case with the revolutionary leaders of Turkey during World War I. It is tragic that, yet today, the current Turkish government continues to try to deny its well documented past and to pressure other governments, often under threat of severing relations, not to mention its history. Even more unfortunately, officially sponsored hatred and terror continues in many regions of the world today, particularly once again in the Middle East, where most likely the Armenian Genocide set the awful template.

Author's Note

—‌⟋‌⟍‌—

I have written this book not only in honor of Souren Tashjian but also as a mark of sympathy and respect for the millions of Armenians who met their untimely deaths or suffered other terrible consequences in Turkey during World War I and its aftermath. I am also motivated by the possibility that the sharing of tales such as this may have an impact. In some small way, perhaps, they help move us closer to the day when enough citizens of the world so abhor government or religion instigated violence that they simultaneously stand forward to press these institutions to fundamentally alter course. I continue to believe, as my great-uncle did, that that day will someday arrive

The book is the result of a two-year undertaking that simply would not have been possible without the efforts and support of many people.

Of course, the story itself would not exist but for the strength of character and dedication of Souren Tashjian to actually write down his experience. This was not an easy thing for him to do. English was not his first language, and it took over four decades of persistent, piecemeal, and at times painful effort because of the traumas he had to relive in committing his experience to paper. In our discussions, at times tears would fill his eyes, and periodically there were long silent pauses. I regret only that he is not alive to see what his effort and our many wonderful times together have come to.

The writing of a book, particularly one such as this, is one of those wonderful teamwork endeavors that requires people of many different persuasions and talents to participate together in a common effort. In that spirit, I want to express my deep appreciation to all of you who helped along the way.

First and foremost among those is devoted historical researcher, partnering storyteller, and, as a result of our work together, my friend, Rosemary Russell. Her long-standing interest and dedicated research concerning the Armenian Genocide is remarkable in itself, and Rosemary's professionalism, talent, thoroughness, creativity, and mastery of the English language are second to none. Her untold hours of effort truly have been irreplaceable. Together we decided that Souren's story was best presented in the third person. Together we determined when and where to take literary license. References to actual historical events and figures that Souren did not mention directly in his manuscript, but which had significant influence upon his experience, were included with Rosemary's guidance. In short, this book would not exist but for Rosemary's interest, expertise, and dedication in working with me.

My colleague and coauthor for a previous book, Glenn Pascall, is next on the list of key collaborators. A seasoned student of history and accomplished writer, Glenn voluntarily took the considerable time necessary to read the original manuscript and make recommendations for significant improvement, as well as make some edits directly himself. In a similar vein, Jenna Land Free of Girl Friday Productions is also to be credited for upgrading the presentation. Her substantial edits, and recommendations for paring and rearranging some portions of the text, have improved the flow of the narrative and helped bring clarification to several events described. My friend and colleague George Masters took on the difficult challenge and detail work of creating the maps necessary to show where various parts of the action took place. Because many of the names of places in the story have changed with time, this has been a particularly difficult task. The dedicated efforts on the part of the talented professionals at CreateSpace resulted in the cover design and helped transform all this into the finished book.

Among those whose contributions helped support necessary research and publishing expense, I especially want to express my deep gratitude to Armene Lamson-Miliken, June Lamson, Barbara Schmidt, Charles and Alberta Lamson, Porter Hovey, Hugh and Linda Straley, Doug and Judy McBroom, and Graham and Ginny Dorland. Too numerous to list here also are the family, friends, and colleagues who discussed certain aspects of the tale with me or read and commented on various portions of the manuscript along the way, offering valuable feedback. You know who you are, and I thank each of you.

One of the nicest aspects about writing a book like this is that the experience cannot help but bring a deeper appreciation for the life I have been so fortunate to live and for the family I am privileged to be part of. In particular, I am both proud and grateful for the interest and consistent encouragement of my lovely daughters, Melissa and Kristy, and my five wonderful grandchildren, as

I have worked and shared portions of this book. For them I hope the completed story may be of some inspirational consequence. My gratitude for the love of my life and wife of more than fifty years, Liz Lamson, is difficult to express in just words. She also knew Souren Tashjian very well. Our frequent discussions about him and his life, and her reading portions of the manuscript and offering feedback from her memories and perspective, have been invaluable. Her consistent encouragement, advice, and insistence that I take breaks and get up from the desk and walk around periodically—to keep my legs from cramping—has made the process of writing this tale a truly fulfilling and enjoyable one.

To each and all of you, once again I thank you!

Souren Barkev Tashjian in military uniform with piccolo
(circa 1915)

Souren Barkev Tashjian at medical school
(circa 1924)

Souren Barkev Tashjian, Seattle physician
(circa 1975)

Author's Bio

—ᄳ—

R obert Lamson is an author and senior business counselor. A former defense economist, he holds a BA in economics from Yale University and a PhD in economics from the University of Washington. He has been co-founder and senior executive of several successful technology companies, and most recently is founder of Historical Accounts Repository Partners (HARP), a 501(c)(3) educational foundation. HARP is focused on bringing to light stirring true personal stories such as in this book. His previous publication is a nonfiction work on military spending and the economy, Beyond Guns and Butter, co-authored with Glenn Pascall.

Married for fifty years, Lamson has two daughters and five grandchildren and lives in Seattle, Washington.